COACHING

AT WORK

COACHING

AT WORK

Powering your Team with Awareness, Responsibility and Trust

Matt Somers

BICENTENNIAL

1807

WILEY

2007

BICENTENNIAL

JOSSEY-BASS
A Wiley Imprint
www.josseybass.com

Other Wiley Editorial Offices

Wiley have other editiorial offices in the USA, Germany, Australia, Singapore and
Canada.

Wiley also publishes its books in a variety of electronic formats. Some content that appears
in print may not be available in electronic books.

Library of Congress Cataloging-in-Publication Data

Somers, Matt.
    Coaching at work: powering your team with awareness, responsibility, and trust/
Matt Somers.
        p.   cm.
    Includes bibliographical references and index.
    ISBN-13: 978-0-470-01711-1 (cloth: alk. paper)
    ISBN-10: 0-470-01711-2 (cloth: alk. paper)
        1. Employees—Coaching of   2. Teams in the workplace—Management.
    3. Employee empowerment.   I. Title.
    HF5549.5.C53S66 2007
    658.3′124—dc22

                                                                        2006016581

British Library Cataloguing in Publication Data
A catalogue record for this book is available from the British Library

ISBN13 978-0-470-01711-1 (HB)
ISBN10 0-470-01711-2 (HB)

Typeset in 11.5/15pt Bembo and Univers by SNP Best-set Typesetter Ltd., Hong Kong
Printed and bound in Great Britain by TJ International Ltd, Padstow, Cornwall, UK

This book is printed on acid-free paper responsibly manufactured from sustainable forestry
in which at least two trees are planted for each one used for paper production.

CONTENTS

FOREWORD   vii

PREFACE   ix

ACKNOWLEDGEMENTS   xiii

INTRODUCTION   1

PART 1   HOW TO COACH

1   Peak Coaching Model Pt 1 – Potential &
    Interference   9
2   Peak Coaching Model Pt 2 – Performance,
    Learning & Enjoyment   33
3   Peak Coaching Model Pt 3 – Coaching &
    Communication   57
4   Peak Coaching Model Pt 4 – The Coaching
    ARROW   85
5   The Model In Practice   115

PART 2   HOW TO APPLY COACHING

Introduction   135
6   Sales   137
7   Presentations   157
8   Personal Organisation   177
9   Performance Review   199
10 Career Development   219

PART 3   HOW TO IMPLEMENT COACHING

Introduction   241
11 Towards a Coaching Culture   243
12 Implementing a Coaching Programme   259
13 Evaluating the Programme   279
14 Making the Business Case for Coaching   297

EPILOGUE   315

REFERENCES   317

INDEX   319

FOREWORD

At the basic level coaching is a technique, with practice it becomes a skill and with dedication it can become an art form, always different, always an opportunity for learning. I first met Matt many years ago when he attended a 'Coaching for Managers' course at a big bank for which he worked. Every so often someone unexpectedly finds the course more important than the corporation. So it was with Matt. He really took to coaching. To prove it, this is now his second excellent book on the subject.

Imagine my surprise then to find I was becoming more and more frustrated as I continued to read. Suddenly I realise why. I was looking for faults, for its weakness so I could give Matt wise council before it was set in print. I became irked because I could not find anything to correct or complain about. I laughed at my folly and thoroughly enjoyed the rest of my read.

Often authors try to be clever to demonstrate they are superior to the reader. Matt does not fall into that ego trap. *Coaching At Work* is a very sound, logical, practical guide to the many applications of coaching in business, written with the passion that Matt has for the subject. Of course you can read it cover to cover as I did, but the alternative that Matt suggests is to read it in segments.

This is my opinion and would be best for the user. Matt thoroughly covers many business applications with their subtle differences. I recommend that if your focus is in sales for example, that you read part one on how to coach then read the section on sales in part two. Other such sections reside in part two on the most common applications of coaching at work, presentations, personal organisation, performance review, and personal development. Part three deals with implementation, and building a coaching culture in an organisation. This something that is in my opinion so much more worthwhile and productive than providing executive or specialist outside coaching to organisations. It can really make a difference and its impact can be evaluated as Matt also shows in this section.

As a long standing professional coach I am very selective about my coaches. As a result I have been coached by a few excellent coaches. I have never been coached by Matt but in his case I would not hesitate to accept.

John Whitmore
Author of *Coaching for Performance*

PREFACE

I am obsessed with work.

I realise in making this claim that I risk alienating those readers who have worked long and hard to bring a little balance into their own working lives and those of their colleagues, so let me qualify the statement.

I am not obsessed with *working*. I believe that for the most part people spend too many of their waking hours in factories, shops and offices and that many of these hours are not really productive. There is a difference between business and busyness. Throughout Europe and perhaps the UK in particular, this is further exacerbated by appending the start and end of each working day with as much as two hours travel in either direction. The promise of home working has also yet to materialise in my experience.

No, my obsession is with work itself. The way that places of work are organised and structured, the way that business is run and won, the increasing importance of work in people's lives and most crucially the business of deploying and developing staff.

This preoccupation started early for me. I left school at aged 16 with the four 'O' Levels I needed to secure my job with a high street bank. Almost from the first day I was more interested in what was happening on the office side of the business than anything the customers might be getting up to. I was particularly puzzled by the way that one group of people apparently called *management*, would talk to another group of people apparently called *staff*. These interactions were usually terse, unfriendly affairs consisting of managers more or less ordering staff to do certain tasks which the staff then carried out to whatever minimum standard was necessary to get by. Looking back it all seemed quite adversarial with little sense of mutual success.

In my naivety I thought that people were people and that if you expected people to work hard and achieve results then you ought to treat them well; 'Do unto others . . .' and all that. This being the early 1980s however, high street banking was characterised by complacency, knowing that customers would continue to come and profits continue to flow however the business was run, and however its people were treated.

The de-regulation of the industry and the consequent increased competition in the 1990s changed all this. Now there was a need for staff to provide superior service lest the customers take their business elsewhere. People working in banks needed to become sales people and actively promote the bank's products and services. Jobs which had been thought of as secure for a lifetime were now the subject of continual uncertainty.

The whole backdrop to the business changed irreversibly, but the management style did not. Those who struggled to make the change from bank clerk to sales person were told to shape up and get with the times. They were sent on sales training courses and if that didn't work they were sent on them again. The pressure was on to perform; crude targets and incentives were introduced. Managers were hauled before directors and told to try harder, Staff were hauled before managers and told to try harder, or else.

Yours truly watched all this unfold with a sort of morbid fascination.

Of course banking as an industry was not alone in experiencing change of this kind or on this scale. Globalisation, the march of technology, downsizing and so on were all transforming the whole landscape of work and organisational life.

By now I was working in Personnel and had been introduced to the world of training and development. I'd had some exposure to management and team leader type roles and was seen to have an ability to get people on side and achieving results. As a management trainer I was similarly able to press the right buttons and to help people access their ability. I guess I was *coaching* them although I had no idea at the time that there even was such a thing, certainly not in the world of work.

In 1995 I was given the opportunity to attend a Performance Coaching course run by Sir John Whitmore and his firm Performance Consultants. As I learnt about coaching principles and practices I came to realise that coaching was simply a way of describing an approach to people at work that I had always believed in but had never been able to articulate. It offered an explanation as to why certain of my managers had been able to get the best from me and why others had left me exhausted and scanning the job advertisements. Coaching described a management style that I could see was essential for the turbulent times that were coming.

From that point forward coaching became the lynchpin of all my training and development work. I left banking and established my own consultancy practice where I found myself extolling the virtues of coaching and high performance even when I'd essentially been hired to teach Time Management or Presentation Skills. Eventually I decided to grasp the nettle and focus my practice on teaching managers how to coach.

Over the years we have taken coaching and applied it across the widest variety of organisations; public and private, small and large, in virtually every sector. All of this work has informed the ideas that I will present in this book.

This book is intended for anyone who must achieve results through others irrespective of age, gender, job-title, seniority, qualifications or experience. Indeed our training courses often attract people with no line management responsibility at all but whose work as business advisors or career counsellors for example suggests that coaching principles can apply to the external client as well as the internal team member.

That being said, I have written the book with the Human Resources (HR) Professional closest in mind as it seems that HR is often given the role of being both coach and implementer of coaching at the same time. This does not seem unreasonable and I think that HR is well-placed to act as champion of coaching. However, I hope that any of the increasing number of students of coaching be they formal or casual, will find a wealth of ideas here to help achieve coaching's ultimate goal:

To see people fulfil their potential.

Matt Somers
March 2006

ACKNOWLEDGEMENTS

I sometimes think my life is just one big role-play exercise with my family, friends, and colleagues having been briefed to make sure I learn some important lessons. So, in no particular order . . .

Thanks to Timothy Gallwey and Sir John Whitmore for making me think, 'that's interesting. . . .'

Carol. Thank you for teaching me about resilience and never giving up.

Kenny. Thank you for teaching me that learning is easier than being taught.

Ian, thanks for the concept of useful thinking. Never stop looking for the cart wheelers my friend.

Thanks to Samantha, Francesca, Jo, Darren and Dan at John Wiley and Sons Ltd for helping me turn this vague aim into a detailed way forward.

Thanks to my Mum, Dad and sister for giving me the values of fairness, hard-work and honesty.

Thanks to my extended family for showing me that those values are widely held.

Thanks to my wonderful wife Lesley for teaching me about doing instead of thinking and thanks to my beautiful daughter Evie for teaching me that life is for living and that it really doesn't matter if it's raining.

You are all wonderful coaches.

INTRODUCTION

COACHING IS AN IDEA WHOSE TIME HAS COME

The challenges have never been greater for anyone who must achieve results through people. Ferocious change, flatter structures and new technologies have all conspired to render old style leadership by command totally irrelevant. If we continue to attempt to solve 21st century problems with 19th century solutions, the chances of failure are high.

Organisations are finding that the tired old rhetoric of 'people are our greatest asset' really is true. Install a new piece of equipment or IT system and your rivals can have the same in place by the following month. Secure some capital and you'll find that the competition had their money secured several weeks earlier. In the age of the knowledge worker competitive advantage surely lies in the capacity to have employees performing happily at their best over the long term.

Furthermore it is no longer possible to develop people only by passing on other's wisdom. This is the orthodox approach to training and development but it is flawed. It assumes that the reason for less than peak performance must be due to a lack of certain knowledge or skills. However it ignores the crucial role that attitude or state of mind plays in performing any task. Most of us can call to mind several examples of people with seemingly all the knowledge and skills they could ever need but who for some reason seem unable or unwilling to translate this into high performance.

What is needed then is a method for *realising* potential, for enabling people to perform at their very best. As traditional structures have disappeared, people now want and need to be empowered to find their own way and to access their creativity and flair. These are crucial qualities but they cannot be *taught*. They have to be *nurtured*.

I believe that coaching is fast becoming the key to business success in the 21st century, and will be a vital leadership skill for decades.

When leaders understand and apply coaching, astonishing things can happen: People relish change and move things forward at pace. Apathy disappears and is replaced by energy and enthusiasm. People consistently perform at their peak and achieve amazing results and their organisations waste fewer resources and generate more income.

BUT DO WE REALLY NEED ANOTHER BOOK ON COACHING?

At the time of writing if I type coaching into the search engine on Amazon UK, the on-line book seller, I get over 3,000 hits. This is not surprising given the amount of interest in the topic and the number of people keen to find out more. However a more refined search would suggest that a book which concentrates more on coaching applied in day to day work situations is lacking at the moment. There are coaching books with a strong emphasis on the links with sport and others which concentrate on executive level, external coaching. Then there are those that draw links between coaching and psychological approaches such as Neuro Linguistic programming and Transactional Analysis.

Many of these books can and do draw parallels with work but still leave you to make many of the connections for yourself. I wanted to write a book about coaching grounded in the ordinary, mundane, frustrating, yet wonderful world of organisational life.

I see this book as being both a 'how to' and a 'why to' as far as coaching is concerned. Its focus is very much on corporate life as this is the world I best know and understand. I will not deal much with the world of the independent Life or Executive Coach except where such professionals are hired by organisations.

HOW THIS BOOK IS ORGANISED

I have used the word *coach* to describe the person who will deliver the coaching. This will typically be a line-manager, leader, supervisor, charge hand, foreman, officer or any of those terms organisations use to describe people whose job it is to achieve results through others.

I will similarly use the word *coachee* to describe the other party or parties to the coaching process. It is an inelegant word which, I realise, will jar with many, but it aptly captures the variety of people and roles who may be coached and I prefer it to student, pupil, client or customer which for me do not reflect the nature of coaching within a work situation.

As a profession and an area of academic interest coaching is a relatively new field. The coaching industry is encompassing practitioners from a wide and diverse pool of prior experience. Everyone from psychotherapists to sporting champions can contribute models and ideas and I believe that all are potentially useful and should be welcomed and absorbed.

My own coaching paradigm is rooted in the *inner game* approach pioneered by Timothy Gallwey [4], [5]. In 1971 whilst on sabbatical from a career in higher education Gallwey worked as a tennis professional. He noticed that the instructions he gave to his tennis students seemed to cause more harm than good and create more confusion than focus. He decided to research the conditions that are really necessary to promote high performance and this work culminated in the publication of *The Inner Game of Tennis* in 1975 [4].

The ground-breaking ideas Gallwey presented quickly caught the interest of the corporate world and he began working with the likes of AT&T and IBM on applying inner game concepts to working life. The outcomes of these experiences were published as the *Inner Game of Work* in 2000.

> There is always an inner game being played in your mind no matter what outer game you are playing. How aware you are of this game can make the difference between success and failure in the outer game.

Tim Gallwey

We can see that there are any number of inner games being played at work. There is an inner game of sales, with members of the sales team needing to address self-doubt and cope with rejection. Conquering the inner game of time management is likely to have a far more enduring effect than constant training in the outer game.

The concept of the inner game has profound implications for organisational coaches as we too are there to help performers access their own ability to learn and not to solve problems for them. Experience suggests that in the end *people get in their own way* and that coaching on the inner game presents the greatest opportunities for success.

In writing *Coaching At Work* my intention is to present an up to date synthesis of many disparate ideas on coaching at work albeit with the inner game at its core.

I have split the book into three parts. Part 1 – How to Coach will give you the principles and tools to undertake coaching on a formal or informal basis.

In Part 2 – How to Apply Coaching, I have picked a number of key areas which my experience suggests are the typical issues for which people will seek coaching. A series of inner games if you like.

Part 3 – How to Implement Coaching examines how to move beyond coaching as a stand alone skill towards coaching as an overall management approach.

A book is a book and can only develop your ability so far. You could no more become a proficient coach just by reading than you could become an expert golfer. Ultimately you learn to coach by coaching and I would invite you to try out the ideas here in a spirit of experimentation and discovery and see how you can develop them for yourself.

You may choose to read the whole thing in sequence or use each part separately. To this end I have tried to make each part work on a stand alone basis and thus some ideas may appear more than once.

If in time you want to develop a career as an independent coach you will need extensive, specialist training, but meanwhile use the basic tools presented in this book to help people find their focus and be the best they can be. Nobody loses in this scenario.

PART 1

HOW TO COACH

CHAPTER 1

PEAK COACHING MODEL PT 1 – POTENTIAL & INTERFERENCE

WHAT IS COACHING?

This first part of the book is about describing in depth a coaching model that I have developed gradually in my firm Peak over the last 10 years. It is possible to coach others with a few simple tools and techniques that could be gleaned from a book a fraction of this size. However, these behaviours tend not to endure in the face of pressure to achieve results and so it appears my challenge is to bring about a change in your *thinking* so that you can internalise these coaching principles and eventually use them without thinking about it. For this reason I intend to go into some detail.

To begin with let me be clear about exactly what I mean when I talk about coaching. Coaching is a relatively new field and as such it is often confused with other methods such as training and counselling. Some managers are using coaching as a new label for behaviours they've used for years such as telling people off and dictating the precise ways things must be done. We must be careful that coaching is not seen as 'old wine in new bottles'.

On our training programmes we often ask participants to list and discuss exactly what coaching is and what it isn't. The following points would be typical:

Coaching is . . .

- About drawing out, not putting in
- Helping others to learn as opposed to teaching them things
- Motivational and enjoyable
- Performance focused but people centred
- About releasing potential
- Helping people move out of their comfort zones

Coaching is not . . .

- Telling people what to do and how to do it
- The same as instructing, training or counselling
- Offering uninvited feedback
- Rescuing people and having all the answers
- Only for poor performers
- A disciplinary measure

Coaching is fundamentally about helping people fulfil their *potential* by allowing them to recognise the things that hold them back and by helping them discover ways around them. It is at the level of potential then that our detailed examination must start.

POTENTIAL

What percentage of people's potential do you see at work?

I have asked this question dozens of times at seminars and training courses and have yet to get an answer of 100% or even close. Most responses come in the 30%–60% range suggesting that there's a lot of ability out there that remains untapped. That's a pretty strong business case for having effective coaching at work I would suggest. After all, you pay for 100% potential, but how much do you actually get?

But how do people even form a view? On what do we base our estimates? Asked to justify their answer people will point to a variety of explanations. I remember one lady telling me about a member of her team who was difficult and unpopular at work yet who achieved great results as a youth volunteer in his spare time. On another occasion somebody highlighted the many working mums tucked out of sight in mundane roles despite being able to run a household, raise children and run the family finances at the same time. What if work was organised in such a way as to give people a chance to let these hidden talents shine through?

Often the answer is 'I've absolutely no idea what percentage of people's potential we see at work!'. We can fairly easily see the *results* or outcomes of using potential by way of the amount or quality of a person's work; their performance in other words. But judging how much of their potential was used to bring this about is difficult, time consuming and arguably unnecessary. Unless we want performance and results to improve of course, in which case it's vital to understand how much capacity for improvement there might be.

I believe there is a compelling case for organisations to spend more time considering potential. Businesses obsess over performance and results and rightly so as this is how we determine how well we're doing, but in terms of making changes and improving things we need to start thinking in terms of potential; what we *could do* just as much as what we *have done.*

Unfortunately the world of work is not organised this way. It is hard to make a case for retaining an employee who is under performing but who we sense could go on to great things. Employers understandably hedge their bets and seek to buy proven potential directly from the labour market. Top jobs are to be filled only by those on the graduate development programme. External candidates must have the 'right' MBA and so on. But just as with the Stock Market, past performance is no guarantee of future results. What people have done is not necessarily linked to what they could do. Nevertheless, we can't employ people based on a leap of faith or retain poor performers on the basis of benefit of the doubt, but we do need to manage them in such a way as to give them every chance to let their potential come out.

Potential is by definition latent – i.e. hidden or under-developed – and so we cannot ask prospective employees to bring a sort of 'certificate of potential' with them to the recruitment or promotion interview. We have, instead, to take a view on how much potential a person may have and this view is likely to be informed by our own beliefs and values and by our own experience at work.

THEORY X AND THEORY Y

Perhaps the most popular and accessible piece of management research on this point was presented by Douglas McGregor [17] with his Theory X and Theory Y suppositions about management behaviour.

According to McGregor, Theory X Managers take the view that people:

- essentially dislike work and will avoid it all together if possible
- are motivated only by money or fear
- need discipline and constant supervision
- can't be trusted
- avoid responsibility
- lack loyalty and commitment
- lack creativity – except in finding ways to avoid work!

Let's just stop for a moment and consider how a manager would treat people if she held this view. I think it's likely she would:

- put tight controls in place to ensure people are working when they should be
- exercise firm control over all activities and have rigorous reporting procedures in place
- Define work to a fine level of detail and prescribe precisely how tasks should be carried out
- remind people often that the organisation pays their wages and how easily they can be replaced

Let's now think about how people are most likely to react if this is how they are treated. I would assume that they would:

- do what they need to do to get the job done, but no more
- resist change
- refuse to take on extra responsibility without more pay
- resist at all costs requests to work more flexibly

I can't imagine that creativity and innovation would flourish in such an atmosphere.

Theory Y managers, on the other hand, take the view that people:

- have psychological as well as economic reasons for working
- are motivated by achievement, recognition, praise, etc
- work to their own standards – often higher than the boss's
- are totally trustworthy
- seek responsibility
- are keen to be loyal and committed
- are a great source of ideas

How would a manager treat her staff if she believed Theory Y to be true? Perhaps she would:

- offer praise and encouragement, thanking people publicly for their efforts
- look for contributions from team members in terms of what needs doing and how it should be done
- set objectives for the team and then leave them alone to carry them out

Treated this way, I think it's reasonable to expect that her team would:

- justify the faith she has shown by getting results
- put in the extra effort when required
- take on extra responsibility
- be loyal in difficult times

Neither of these views is right or wrong and each is clearly quite extreme. Most managers are probably a blend of parts of each and their views will probably change depending on how things are going when you ask them.

The question therefore becomes if neither view is right, wrong or permanent, which view is more *useful* to us as managers who coach?

Theory Y would seem to offer the greatest scope for achieving improved results because of a concept known as the self-fulfilling prophecy. As we saw above, if we treat people as if Theory X were true they will tend to behave in a way which reinforces that belief. The same is true for Theory Y.

SELF-FULFILLING PROPHECIES

Researchers refer to three kinds of self-fulfilling prophecy, one of which creates a negative result.

The Galatea effect refers to self-belief, the idea that if you believe you can succeed you will. High-performers in any field are blessed with strong self-belief. They trust themselves to succeed, take an optimistic view of most situations and see 'failures' as learning opportunities.

When coaching someone over the long term you'll almost certainly want to help people access this state of mind, but it may take some time and patience if they're carrying a lot of negative baggage. In which case the second kind of self-fulfilling prophecy may be useful.

The Pygmalion effect describes the notion of believing in others' ability to such an extent that they begin to believe in it themselves. In George Bernard Shaw's play, *Pygmalion*, Professor Henry Higgins is able to pass off flower girl Eliza Doolittle as a duchess through a combination of appropriate training and, more importantly an unwavering belief that she could succeed.

In his book *The New Alchemists* [6] Charles Handy examined the key attributes of successful business and social entrepreneurs. Many of the entrepreneurs interviewed spoke of having someone in their background who believed in them no matter what. Handy refers to such people as sewing golden seeds but I think coaching is as good a term as any for describing what they do.

Finally, we need to be wary of the Golem effect, which like Theory X suggests that if we expect people to do badly they won't disappoint.

Some years back whilst I was still working at the bank, a memo arrived explaining that due to the Data Protection Act coming into force we could have a look at our staff files if we wanted to. Previously these had been kept under lock and key and were considered none of our business. I thought it would be great to find out what had been written about me at appraisal interviews and so on down the years, so I responded to the memo and arranged to look at the file. Most of the content was boring stuff but there at the bottom of the file were my original interview notes completed at the time of my application as a 15 year old schoolboy. Most of this sheet was taken up with administrative detail but the interviewer's comments caught my attention. The final line on the page read: 'Mr Somers is worth taking on as a low-achiever'.

Now, the point of this anecdote is not to suggest that the interviewer was completely wrong and that in fact I went on to set the world of banking on fire because I didn't. What's more to the point is to think about the impression such a comment created in the minds of my first managers. It's likely that I would have been given the most menial tasks, being a low-achiever and that any mistakes I made would confirm the view that I was a low achiever. Thank goodness it was more than 10 years before I realised that such a comment had been made or I'd have ended up believing it too!

In short, as coaches we need to take a positive view of people. We need to believe they can before we decide that they can't. Yes there's a chance that people might not succeed and we might be disappointed but the alternative is to keep people small.

This is a good time to introduce the first in a series of 'The Laws of Coaching' which will crop up throughout the book.

1ST LAW OF COACHING

If you treat people as small, small is where they'll stay.

PERFORMANCE

Our job as coaches then is to convert as much potential as possible into performance, but of course performance means different things to different people. An actor will have a different view to an athlete and a team leader may have a different view to a team member when it comes to defining performance.

In the world of work it seems that performance usually amounts to being about one of five things:

- Increasing revenue – sales or other income streams
- Providing an excellent service
- Reducing cost
- Increasing or maintaining quality
- Reducing time, e.g. in production lines or in bringing a new product to market

Each of these areas of performance can improve as a result of effective coaching, and often coaching is sought because things aren't going well in some of these areas. But these very broad areas of work performance are really *outcomes*, i.e. the results and consequences of people's ability to perform in a host of other areas, increasing personal productivity, increasing team productivity, generating leads and opportunities, making presentations, managing others' performance, and so the list goes on.

As coaches we need to be sure we have an agreed understanding with our coachees of what performance actually means in their role and how we would know if it had been improved. We'll also see later on that if we want to establish a strong business case for coaching and measure its success then having a clearly defined and shared interpretation of performance is absolutely vital.

Living in the real world, one thing is certain: there will always be a gap between potential and performance (life wouldn't be much fun if there wasn't) and we need to look at ways of closing the gap so that more potential is converted into high performance.

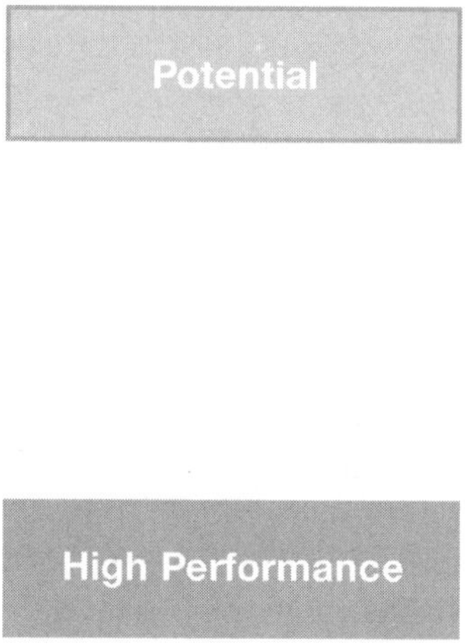

Figure 1.1   The gap between potential and high performance.

In the same way that we need to think carefully about judging potential and defining high performance, we need also to recognise that the gap between the two could exist for a variety of reasons and there could be different ways of closing the gap.

Suppose you have a member of your team whose job it is to produce the monthly sales figures. This they do by using the table function in a word processing programme. Unfortunately, this programme does not have the flexibility to produce the ratios and percentages that you need to really understand whether sales are going well or not.

In terms of high performance you need a detailed analysis and in terms of potential we can assume that as your team member can find their way around the word processing package they'd have the potential to use other similar programmes.

The performance gap here is to do with knowledge. If they knew how to use a spreadsheet programme they'd be able to produce a more useful set of monthly sales figures.

Such a performance gap is straightforward to fill. Find a course or a CD package that teaches how to use the spreadsheet programme and away you go. Simple.

Now suppose you have a team member whose job it is to handle customer complaints. This they do in accordance with your organisation's policy and procedures but always with a slightly abrasive edge. They have had all the necessary training and up until recently were one of your best performers on complaint handling. Lately though there seems to have been an increase in escalated complaints and other team members are getting tired of having to sweep up.

Here the performance gap is much less obvious and unlikely to be closed by sending your team member on refresher training. In fact, that would just make things worse. The gap here is a subtle one concerning attitude or state of mind and needs a similarly subtle response.

In these situations we need to recognise that the gap between potential and high performance doesn't need filling it needs *shrinking*. In other words we need to remove the things that interfere with potential being converted into high performance.

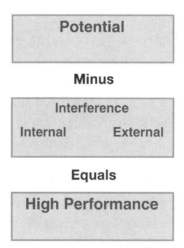

Figure 1.2   potential less interference equals high performance

EXTERNAL INTERFERENCE

Let's talk firstly about what I call external interference. By this I mean the things that go on around us at work which may make it difficult for us to work near to our potential. Once again we'll refer firstly to a typical list of such things produced by the many people I have asked to consider them:

- Management
- Restrictive policies and procedures
- Blame culture
- Ideas not accepted
- Lack of opportunity

Let's deal with each of these in turn.

Management

Now how's that for irony. We, the very people who are supposed to mobilise the abilities of people at work are seen as actually getting in the way. This seems to be due to the prevalence of Theory X thinking amongst the management ranks. This style of thinking and subsequent behaviour is perpetuated by a lack of alternative role models. I remember once attending a meeting to discuss the possibilities of implementing a coaching programme for a prospective client. After the usual small talk his opening line was 'Well I've brought you here because I used to get them working by shouting at them, but apparently you can't do that anymore'. Well, shout at people all you want but is this really how we're going to tap into their discretionary effort?

Restrictive policies and procedures

Obviously places of work need rules and systems and to establish acceptable practices. Without them there would be anarchy. But in these times when competitive pressures are increasing the need for people to work with their imagination and to think creatively such rules can be overdone. This is not restricted to obviously creative endeavours like marketing or advertising. From the factory floor to the retail sales floor we need people to be able to take action and make things happen particularly if directly involved with customers. So many practices from signing-in sheets to six-page expenses claim forms seem to be there because of a lack of trust in the workforce. Why would any organisation employ people they can't trust?

Blame culture

What happens in your organisation when things go wrong? Is judicious risk taking extolled in the business plan and then utterly condemned in practice? Against this background is it any wonder that people keep themselves small, safely tucked up in their comfort zones and keeping their ideas to themselves?

Ideas not accepted

On a similar note, what happens in your organisation when some-body has a good idea? Is there a means to capture ideas, to nurture them and let them grow, or are they left to wither on the vine choked by an endless stream of position papers, inception reports or suggestion scheme submissions?

Cartoon 1.1 Blame culture

This factor is exacerbated the greater the distance on the hierarchy between those who generate ideas and those who can chose to act upon them. It is once again ironic that in most structures it is the former who are closest to the customers and the latter who are many steps removed.

Lack of opportunity

This can come in many guises. Perhaps you've got great potential but because you weren't hired on a graduate intake stream you are barred from applying for the top jobs. Perhaps your circumstances make it difficult to attend the training programmes you'd need to progress. Perhaps you're too young or too old, too black or too white, under qualified, overqualified, inexperienced or over experienced, a female in a male dominated set-up or vice versa. Even today there are so many discriminations that still prevail, despite the efforts of many to eliminate them. The simple truth is that it is clearly nonsense for any organisation to deny itself access to talent wherever it may lie.

These are but examples of common sources of external interference and I realise many of you reading this will have limited ability to influence them in your own organisations, Nevertheless, I would encourage you to grasp any opportunity to examine these areas to see whether they encourage or discourage high performance and make changes where you can.

We must accept that some of the issues we've spoken about in this section are a necessary part of the fabric of working life. In many ways people's reaction to them is more crucial and this is what we'll consider next.

INTERNAL INTERFERENCE

A typical list of sources of internal interference would likely include the following:

- Previous negative experience
- Negative expectations
- Negative self-talk
- Fear of failure

Previous negative experience

My first assignment as an independent consultant was a disaster. I was asked to facilitate some sales training for a group of sales managers from a major airline. I misjudged the ability of the group and was ill-prepared to answer their questions. I got my timings all wrong and my sessions overran leaving my co-facilitator some serious remedial work to rescue the project.

Some months later I found myself assigned to a similar project. Reflecting on the first experience I was beginning to worry that the same thing would happen again which, given what I now know about self-fulfilling prophecies, it probably would have done. Luckily my coach at the time was able to help me make rational sense of my first experience, to put it into some perspective and, most importantly, take action in terms of preparation to avoid repeating the same mistakes.

Negative expectations

> You'll like this, not a lot, but you'll like it.
>
> **Paul Daniels**

Some people see the glass as half empty and for others it's half full. Some people expect the best to happen while others assume the worst. Critics of the coaching approach often accuse coaches of insisting every situation be viewed with breathless, naive optimism, but really the point is this: We tend to attract the situations we think about the most and so expecting the worst to happen increases the chances that it will. Coaching helps people shine a light on their expectations and check whether they are accurate or based on false assumptions.

Negative self-talk

Many people are in constant conversation with themselves, but the nature of this internal dialogue can have a profound effect on how well they might perform. 'You're gonna blow it you fool', 'Who do you think you are?', 'Why on earth would anyone buy from me?' and 'I'm so tired' are just some of the ways in which we get in our own way and make things more difficult than they need be.

Fear of failure

This is a classic but is based on an entirely false premise. Failure is an abstract concept; there is actually no such thing as failure. There are only results. We take action and results ensue. These are either results we want or do not want. They are either expected or unexpected but they have no absolute link with success or failure. This exists only in our own minds. In my experience it's the consequences of 'failure' that people really fear in an organisational setting. They fear that they'll be told-off or embarrassed or that they'll miss out on promotion or whatever. There's a clear link with the blame culture phenomenon we looked at before. How do you want people in your organisation to feel when something has gone wrong? Do you want them to go and hide in a corner or pick themselves up, learn from it and move on?

You cannot fail at anything until you give up.

Richard Denny

I stress again that these are only examples and this list is far from exhaustive. They differ from external sources of interference in that they are *felt* rather than observed. They can have a huge effect on reaching one's potential but it also follows that coaching can pay huge dividends in dealing with them.

At the core of each of these symptoms runs a central theme which we'll call Limiting Beliefs. In many ways the factors we've discussed serve to militate against my potential *only* if I believe them to be true. Let's examine this in more detail.

LIMITING BELIEFS

There's much talk in self-help and business improvement literature about beliefs. There's also much talk about vision and values, culture and ethos and much blurring at the edges of them all. So let me firstly be clear about what I mean when I talk about beliefs. It's those things you hold to be 'true'. For example, 'the purpose of business is to make money'.

I attended a seminar recently and the first speaker clearly held this particular belief. At one point he said that he defied anybody to claim that they were in business for any reason other than making money. A hand went up and a young man explained that no, for him business was about providing opportunities for people and building something from scratch. This was particularly galling and embarrassing for the first speaker as the young man was due to speak next and was clearly not 'on message'.

Limiting beliefs are therefore those that interfere with our potential being released. They are the things which we hold to be true that prevent us taking action or doing things differently. Here are some I've come across on many occasions:

- I will be in trouble if I get this wrong
- Senior management will never support this idea
- I'm the manager, I'm supposed to have all the answers
- I have to win at all costs
- I am working, I am not here to enjoy myself

Some of you might believe some of these statements to be 'true' for you, and you might be right. Beliefs can never be proved as 'right' or 'wrong' or they'd be facts and not beliefs.

Our role as coaches is not to agree or disagree with such statements of belief; rather it is our job to encourage deeper thought and challenge the assumptions on which such beliefs are often formed.

Let's imagine we're coaching someone who wants to implement a new shift rota because they feel it will be fairer and more efficient but who also articulates the belief that *I will be in trouble if I get this wrong*. Some might say, 'don't be silly' or 'of course you won't' or 'to hell with them, do it anyway', but this is unlikely to prove helpful as none of these responses challenge the basis of the limiting belief. Instead we could ask, 'How do you know you'll be in trouble?', 'what sort of trouble will you be in?', 'have you been in this situation before?', 'do you know other people who've handled this situation?', 'What can you do now to ensure it won't go wrong?'.

We can see that these questions would encourage our coachee to think in greater detail about why they believe they would be in trouble and to consider whether to risk it. None of our questions are judgemental and so we are unlikely to get into an argument over who's right and who's wrong.

Simply inviting the people we coach to re-consider the basis of their limiting beliefs is often enough to leave them feeling mobilised to do something in spite of them. Other times, when the belief is deep rooted, it may be necessary to explore further and to consider how such beliefs come to be formed.

LIMITING BELIEFS ARE BASED ON EVIDENCE

Jo and Sam both work on the Organisation Development (OD) section of a large local authority and their work involves submitting proposals for OD projects to the Senior Management Team for approval.

Jo believes that *Senior Management do not support new ideas.* She backs this up by explaining that her budget submission for this year was turned down flat and that this particularly upset her given that her previous year's budget had been approved. She goes on to point out that in the last six months 6 out of 10 project inception reports had been declined. She feels that senior management are just too conservative and tend to reject anything new.

Sam believes that *Senior Management are supportive of new ideas.* To illustrate this he points out that although his budget for this year was turned down, last year's submission, which was far more radical, was approved. He says that four out of every 10 project inception reports are approved and that many of those rejected should never have been submitted in the first place. In Sam's view the Senior Management Team are very conservative and so need a compelling case to support a new idea.

Same roles, same circumstances, same Management Team, but utterly polarised beliefs about them.

Believing the Senior Management Team to be unsupportive Jo is likely to work on her budgets without any real enthusiasm and to do only what is necessary on her reports knowing they'll probably be rejected anyway.

Believing the Senior Management Team to be supportive, Sam is likely to produce a highly detailed budget submission and to make sure his reports show a strong supporting case for his suggestions.

Jo is likely to be turned down, Sam is likely to be supported, adding further supporting evidence to each of their beliefs.

The reinforcement of beliefs is further strengthened by an area of our brain known as the Reticular Activating System (RAS). Our RAS is a filtering system that prevents us being overloaded by the huge amount of stimuli that assail our senses every day. Have you ever noticed that if you see a car with an unusual colour that you suddenly seem to see them everywhere? This is your RAS at work. Cars of that colour were always there but your RAS has now been alerted to notice them.

In our story above, Jo's RAS will provide lots of supporting evidence to reinforce her belief about the senior team. Her brain will filter out anything that runs contrary. Sam's, on the other hand, will do the opposite, providing proof that the team are supportive and confirming his beliefs.

The message for coaches is a simple one. If you uncover a limiting belief, challenge the evidence. Offer an alternative point of view and encourage your coachees to widen their perspective and to consider other points of view. You may not take away limiting beliefs overnight, but you can certainly loosen their hold.

SUMMARY

The fundamental role of the coach is to minimise interference so that more potential can be turned into performance.

Even today work seems to be organised in such a way as to make it difficult for people to reach their potential, but there is increasing pressure to get the people side of business right. Already some big corporations are including reports on their 'human capital' in their annual report and accounts. It can surely not be long until shareholders begin to hold boards to account and demand proof that their Human Resource Management is as strong as their Financial or Commercial Management.

The potential is all there to begin with. We need to take the view that the staff in any organisation are a resourceful group of people with the ability to help the business achieve its aims. Such a strong philosophical standpoint will reap dividends as the phenomenon of the self-fulfilling prophecy takes hold. In the short-term there may be people who take advantage, who are lazy, disloyal and intent on high-jacking progress, but we cannot structure the whole organisation to try to prevent this. As a high performance culture takes shape such people become increasingly marginalised and can no longer muster support for their subversive behaviour. We need to give every opportunity for people to perform, but respect people's choice to reject these opportunities. In these cases we must provide a dignified means of exit so that people may move on with their self-belief intact.

Potential is suppressed by a host of external and internal sources of interference. Key amongst the external factors is the management style of the organisation. People will deduce the prevailing management style based on a number of indicators but probably the most compelling is the behaviour of the most senior team. People these days demand that the leadership team 'walk the talk'. Post Enron and other scandals there is a growing feeling that business ethics must once again come to the fore. Organisations are responding by articulating statements of Corporate and Social Responsibility but these initiatives must be seen as genuine by employees or they'll be dismissed as just another management fad.

A greater challenge is to identify sources of internal interference. There are few people working in 'the zone', most are dogged by low confidence, fear of failure and subsequent reprisal, doubts about their future and a fundamental limiting belief that they are somehow not good enough.

Coaching is the means by which leaders and managers can deal with these and other challenges. Coaching is *performer centred* which means it's an approach that sees the individual as hard-wired with all they need to achieve results. Coaches do not rescue or save people, rather they facilitate learning and liberate talent.

Coaching at work needs also to be *performance focused*. It's about getting people to be bigger and better at what they do. It's difficult to see that such a move could produce anything other than a positive result.

Of course the challenges of working life mean that it is not enough to produce high performance on an occasional basis, we need to keep it there.

CHAPTER 2

PEAK COACHING MODEL PT 2 – PERFORMANCE, LEARNING AND ENJOYMENT

GETTING READY FOR COACHING

In Chapter 1 we saw that in order to turn more potential into high performance we needed to minimise the sources of interference which work against that happening.

But this presupposes that people come to us *wanting* to produce high performance, and this isn't necessarily so.

If you've been asked or employed to provide some one-to-one coaching to a member of the executive team you can probably assume that they will be motivated to undertake some coaching with you. It follows that they are likely to give honest answers to your questions, to listen to your ideas and suggestions and to take action on the things you've discussed between meetings and phone calls.

But in trying to bring coaching into general play; to position it as a management approach rather than a discrete intervention, you might find conditions less favourable. In some ways coaching has become a term cheapened by misuse and because of this you may encounter a certain amount of resistance. This can range from the mildly apathetic to the downright hostile. It all seems bizarre, given that we're simply trying to help people so let's look at the common reasons for this resistance:

- Management is up to something
- Coaching is for poor performers
- I'm okay where I am

Management is up to something

Okay, it's a cynical view but is hardly surprising given the way some management teams behave. People have had change in- itiatives thrown at them for years now and most of them have amounted to very little. If this has been people's experience then it's small wonder that coaching is greeted with little enthusiasm. People can tell when you've been away on a course and been 'got at'. They also know that if they keep their heads down then after a few days you'll probably go back to 'normal'.

Coaching is for poor performers

Nobody likes to be thought of as needing special lessons, but all too often coaching is presented this way. A strong desire to improve performance in the organisation gets mutated into 'I'm being coached, so I must be doing something wrong' in the mind of the individual.

In my experience this particular worry is most easily countered by pointing to the worlds of entertainment and sport where coach- ing is a vital ingredient whatever the level of current performance,

Great sportspeople and entertainers welcome regular and intensive coaching even though their level of performance is already astonishing by most standards.

Be mindful though that sporting analogies and so on can seem a little facetious for some.

I'm okay where I am

An over zealous approach to coaching can make it seem as if we want everybody to be Superman. Some people resist coaching because they're quite content where they are and do not want to actively pursue a promotion or a change of role. Great! That's fine but let's make sure that people realise that coaching isn't just about climbing the greasy pole. We can coach to help people feel less threatened by change. We can coach to help people get back to the parts of their job they really used to enjoy. We can coach to help people find a work-life balance. Coaching is a way of taking the next step and as such it has applications throughout working life and, I think, should be made available to all. However, let's also respect people's right not to be coached if that is what they would prefer. To do so goes a long way to establishing the credibility of coaching and building the trusting relationships so vital to its success. In time even the most reluctant of people will try coaching when they have something in mind they'd like to achieve.

In the rest of this chapter we'll consider some of these issues in more detail and explore the factors that influence people to want to improve performance.

MOTIVATION

On our courses we often ask groups to produce a list of things that, in their experience are motivators at work. The following would be typical:

££££!, Incentives, Status, Fear, The cause, Holidays, Bonuses, A worthwhile job, Self-esteem, Pride, Self-actualisation, Achievement, Fun, Getting better, Self-development, Socialising, Praise, Career prospects, Carrot & Stick, Recognition, Belonging, Safety, Security

Do you notice anything about this list?

What about now?

A worthwhile job, Self-esteem, Pride, Self-actualisation, Achievement, Fun, Getting better, Self-development,

££££!, Incentives, Status, Fear, The cause, Holidays, Bonuses, Socialising, Praise, Career prospects, Carrot & Stick, Recognition, Belonging, Safety, Security

Everything on the list – and I'm sure there are more besides – has the power to motivate, other things being equal, but there are two distinct types of motivator featured here. They are called Intrinsic and Extrinsic motivators.

The bottom set, Extrinsic, whilst definitely being motivators need to be *provided* by somebody. They also have a fairly short shelf-life before people get used to those levels and want more.

The top set, Intrinsic, however are *self generated* and as such tend to motivate over the longer term. They boil down to being about performance, learning or enjoyment.

When things are going poorly in organisations and management take the view that motivation needs to improve it is invariably the Extrinsic set which gets attention. Incentive schemes and bonus payments are all employed to try and 'buy' performance since these are all money related directly or indirectly. Academics and other commentators have written vast amounts about the power of money to motivate and it would be inappropriate to try to capture all of that thinking here so let me give you my simple interpretation:

It's not money that motivates it's the prospect of getting more.

Matt Somers

Let me explain what I mean. I contend that your current salary does not motivate you. It does not get you out of bed with a spring in your step and keen to perform at your peak. The prospect of a 20% increase might though. In pursuing it you'd probably pull out all the stops and perform wonders. But how long after getting that increase would it still motivate? How long before you'd grown used to it, spent it or allocated it towards paying bills? How long before you wanted more?

The problem with money as a motivator is that it needs to be increased regularly if it is to continue having a motivational effect.

It's also worth noting that the Extrinsic set costs a lot to supply whereas the Intrinsic set can often be promoted with little, if any, extra cost, especially where coaching is the predominant management approach.

So Intrinsic motivation can be readily accessed, involves little added cost and is seen by most people as being more enduring. Extrinsic motivation fades with time, is expensive to cultivate yet enjoys the bulk of management attention when it comes to considering motivation.

Perhaps this is an over-simplistic argument. In truth organisations need a combination of all of these motivators. But the blend must be carefully considered and we need to separate what will motivate truly exceptional performance from what simply keeps people on the payroll.

I used to live next door to a young lady who worked for the health service. Sometimes we would leave for work at the same time each morning. She would usually make some cynical comment about only being motivated by the money, but I would have struggled to have found anybody less motivated. What she really meant was 'I hate my job, but I put up with it because I get paid and I can go and spend the money on having a good time to forget that I hate my job!' A life coach would have a field day and from an organisational point of view how can we hope to get anything like high performance from a person who feels so low?

There are dozens of theories that attempt to explain the nature of work motivation and many of their suggestions conflict. All of them seem at least partially true for most people and can help explain why people behave in the way that they do. It seems unlikely that there will ever be a single motivation theory that explains everything although the search for such a tool goes on. Nevertheless *any* tool which can help in understanding motivation must be useful and so we'll examine here the three theories I think all coaches must know. These are the classic models developed by Maslow and Herzberg and the Path-Goal theory of House and Dessler.

MASLOW

Abraham Maslow was one of the first people to be associated with the humanistic approach to management. In sharp contrast to Frederick Taylor who believed that effective deployment of people was a question of scientifically defining tasks, Maslow recognised that work was always going to be carried out by living, breathing human beings and that as such there would always be an emotional content to work and management. As a psychologist Maslow was also unusual in being more concerned with studying success than with studying problems, an idea which still prevails within the field of Human Resource Development (HRD). Proponents of Nero-Linguistic programming, for example, encourage modelling excellence and success rather than analysing failure.

He is best known for his hierarchy of needs theory which first appeared in *US Psychological Review* in 1943 and then again in *Motivation and Personality* in 1954 [16].

The central tenet of the theory is that each human being is motivated by the desire to satisfy needs. These needs are grouped and presented as a hierarchy suggesting that we move up to higher level needs as the preceding group is satisfied. The hierarchy is often depicted as a pyramid although this was not the case originally. From the most basic needs upwards they appear as follows:

Physiological needs

These are our most basic needs – air, food, water, sleep, etc. If these are not satisfied we will feel sickness, irritation, pain or discomfort. Only when satisfied will we think about other needs. It will hopefully be rare that people at work will have needs at this level.

Safety needs

Psychological in nature these needs are mainly to do with the security that comes from a home and family, etc and again one would like to think that feeling safe is a given at work. However, an employee who is being bullied, for example – and there are too many of them – cannot begin to even think about the needs that are satisfied by work performance if they are constantly concerned for their safety.

Belonging needs

These come from our basic human desire to want to belong to a group, be that a work group, religion, football club or gang. We want to feel wanted, accepted and appreciated by others. In short we need to be needed.

Esteem needs

These can be satisfied in part by the sense of satisfaction that comes from performing a task well and in part by the admiration and respect that comes from others.

The need for self-actualisation

According to Maslow to self-actualise is to 'become everything that one is capable of becoming' At this level people are driven by a need to maximise their potential or to seek peace or self-fulfilment.

There is a temptation to look at Maslow's hierarchy in quite rigid terms but this was never the intent. The order of the hierarchy is not fixed, for example a gifted web-designer may be more concerned with self-actualisation than with belongingness. Similarly, one need does not have to be fully satisfied before moving on. Most people are partially satisfied and unsatisfied at the same time.

There are several aspects of this theory of which coaches need to be mindful:

As soon as one need becomes satisfied it ceases to become a motivator. Constantly reminding people that 'this job pays your bills' doesn't really work after a while.

In the affluent West, it's as if those in work have moved wholesale from safety needs to belonging and esteem needs. People can be confident that even if they were to be out of work, their physiological and safety needs will be met. This means that the satisfiers of those more basic needs, our Extrinsic set are proving much less effective at generating real motivation and that we need to look towards the Intrinsic set as being more useful in trying to satisfy the higher level needs.

The key message is to treat people as individuals and to use a coaching approach to discover where on the hierarchy an individual may sit, what needs they are seeking to satisfy and whether the organisation can help to satisfy them.

HERZBERG [7]

According to the Two Factor Theory of Frederick Herzberg, levels of motivation are influenced by two factors. Satisfaction and high performance are the result of Motivation Factors whereas dissatisfaction and poor performance are the result of Hygiene Factors. The diagram at Figure 2.1 shows the elements within each of these factors.

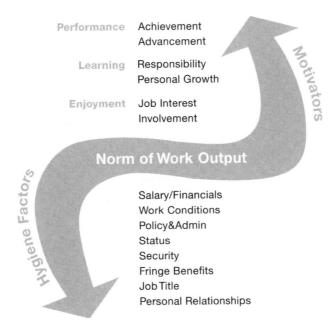

Figure 2.1 Herzberg

Herzberg conducted his initial research on around 200 accountants and engineers in the USA. He was interested in finding out the effect of the two factors on levels of productivity. As we've already seen, all of the items in each of Herzberg's factors can have an impact on motivation, other things being equal. The nature of the impact though is quite different.

The Hygiene Factors are necessary for basic motivation and to produce a normal or typical level of performance, what Herzberg referred to as the 'Norm of Work Output'. Real motivation and enduring high performance though only resulted from the presence of the Motivation Factors in the employee's situation. The conclusion being that whilst the Hygiene Factors are necessary for overall performance they actually have much more power to demotivate if they are ill-conceived or meddled with by organisations. In other words even when we get the Hygiene Factors right, the best we can hope for is perhaps 'not demotivated', but for real high performance we need rather more than this. For real high performance we need to appeal to the elements within the Motivation Factors.

A couple of examples may help. When I joined the bank back in the early 1980s it was usual for each employee to expect to receive a profit sharing payout around May time each year. Although this was a non-contractual, discretionary bonus, dependant on the bank's financial performance, people became quite used to it. Many of the bank's staff factored their profit sharing into their yearly plans and looked upon it to pay for a holiday; others would save it towards the deposit on a car, for example. Then, in the late 1980s we had a recession and the bank made a loss not a profit. The Chairman wrote in the report and accounts that there would be no profit sharing. Pandemonium followed; there was talk of industrial action, threats to leave and all sorts of weeping and wailing and gnashing of teeth! Profit sharing had been introduced to motivate the staff and it probably had, but this was nothing compared to the damage caused to morale and motivation by taking it away.

At the time of writing the Royal Mail – the UK's postal service – has just introduced a scheme of rewarding employees who do not take time off sick. I gather that absence rates have improved as a result but what will happen to the absence figures if this scheme is ever revoked?

The Hygiene Factors act only as a kind of launch pad to sustainable high performance. When damaged or undermined there is no platform to launch from, but in themselves they do not motivate.

I also think it's interesting to consider the permutations of combining the two factors. We can get:

- High Hygiene & High Motivation producing a great scenario of highly motivated employees with few complaints
- High Hygiene & Low Motivation which results in the 'I only do it for the money' scenario
- Low Hygiene & High Motivation which is often the case in vocational type careers like teaching and nursing
- Low Hygiene & Low Motivation which is a situation even the best of coaches would struggle to improve

You might not be able to change policy, procedure, salary levels or any of the other Hygiene Factors in your organisation, but you can have a positive effect on the Motivation Factors through a coaching approach.

PATH GOAL THEORY

This theory developed by House and Dessler and presented in *The Path Goal Theory of Leadership* [8] states that all human activity is goal oriented. In other words we don't do anything without a reason, nor do we pursue pointless activity. In this way activity becomes merely a pathway to achieving a goal.

Path goal theory also suggests that 'Achieving a goal may satisfy more than one need'. There is therefore a strong link between this theory and Maslow's Hierarchy of Needs presented earlier in that they both take the view that motivation is the drive to satisfy a need.

Imagine a Deputy Head at a Secondary School who has performed successfully at that role for some years, but who feels constrained and frustrated by the policies of the Head Master. We might expect our Deputy Head to pursue a complex series of activities which include creating a CV, scanning the job adverts in The Guardian on Wednesdays, submitting application forms and attending interviews.

The goal at which this complex activity is aimed is a new job, hopefully with a job title of 'Head Mistress' Attaining this goal may increase needs satisfaction on a number of different levels on Maslow's hierarchy.

The freedom to run her own school and make her own choices without the constraining practices of a Head Master will lead directly to a sense of self-actualisation.

Our Head Mistress can now afford membership of her local gym and health club instead of using the public facility and enjoys the self-esteem that this confers. Her need for self-esteem may also be fulfilled through something as simple as a new job title.

It is likely as well that the lower order need of safety will be additionally satisfied by the higher salary and improved contract terms of her new role. The higher salary may also mean more money is available to entertain friends, satisfying belonging needs.

Notice here as well that we're talking mainly about the needs satisfied in *getting* the job. Lower order needs in Maslow terms or Hygiene factors in Herzberg terms. Later on, high performance in the role will mean appealing to the Intrinsic motivators outlined above.

So, when people do things repeatedly and we notice regular patterns of behaviour, it is because in some way these patterns are helping them to achieve a goal. Probably a goal that will satisfy more than one need and thus create strong motivation.

Now consider what happens when a manager tries to introduce some kind of change at work. The change is likely to be seen as a blockage to the individual achieving a goal and may be seen as a threat to satisfying certain needs. No surprise then that resistance occurs.

This implies an obvious tactic for achieving willing change at work. Before suggesting new methods or introducing change pro-grammes managers would be wise to find out what goals people are trying to achieve and what needs would therefore be satisfied. If the proposed change can then be positioned as increasing the chances of goal attainment and needs satisfaction, the change is much more likely to be accepted.

This insight, impossible with a command and control approach, but virtually guaranteed with coaching, is vital if resistance to change is to be avoided or minimised. It is also a pre-requisite if high motivation is to be achieved and maintained.

THE PLE TRIANGLE

In studying the Hierarchy of Needs, the Two Factor Theory and Path Goal theory, we have but scratched the surface of the vast amount of research that has gone into the subject of motivation at work. In the end your own experience will prove most insightful since nobody is closer to your people than you. Nevertheless, these theories present important lessons of which all coaches need to be aware:

- Motivation is the desire to satisfy a need, and therefore a satis-fied need no longer motivates

- Some factors have a greater potency to be demotivating if organisations get them wrong than they do to be motivating when organisations get them right
- People are active in pursuit of a goal. It may not be a goal we can readily identify or be one with which we would agree, but it will be there nonetheless

With these lessons learned let's return to our more simple grouping of motivators as Intrinsic or Extrinsic that we looked at earlier. The Extrinsic set are strongly linked to that marvellous 20th century management technique of Carrot and Stick. The carrot being money and promotion and the stick being fear of getting fired. These are useful tactics for appealing to lower order needs or hygiene factors, but the world has moved on at pace and this approach is not going to produce anything like high performance.

Why then do organisations persist with this approach? I think it's because organisations don't know how to tap into intrinsic motivation, or worse don't even bother trying because 'we're doing ok anyway'. This mediocre approach may have sufficed a decade or two ago, but seems unlikely to be good enough in our times of globalisation and relentless change.

Let's turn our sights then on the Intrinsic set. There are many elements to this as our listing showed, but I think they boil down to being about one of three things:

Performance   being more productive and the satisfaction that comes from doing the job well

Learning   satisfying curiosity, learning from mistakes and experiencing a sense of growth in individuals and teams

Enjoyment   The idea that work should be pleasant and that we are each entitled to a quality of life at work

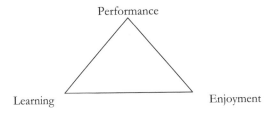

Figure 2.2   PLE Triangle

I like to show these as a triangle, like the one in Figure 2.2.

I use a triangle because it is one of the strongest structures known to man. It also implies balance which is crucial when considering how to use these elements to promote performance. So crucial in fact that I will capture it as our next law of coaching.

2ND LAW OF COACHING

We need Performance, Learning and Enjoyment, but we must keep them balanced.

We'll look at this in more detail in the sections that follow but for now let's add PLE to the Peak Coaching Model. The first part of the model showed how we can reduce interference to bring about high performance, which we now understand to be one of the three key intrinsic motivators. Adding in Learning and Enjoyment gives us a real chance of achieving that overarching objective of Human Resource Development: Sustainable High Performance. This is shown diagrammatically at Figure 2.3.

PROMOTING PERFORMANCE

When asked to describe the constituent parts of the Intrinsic motivator of performance people will normally suggest: satisfaction,

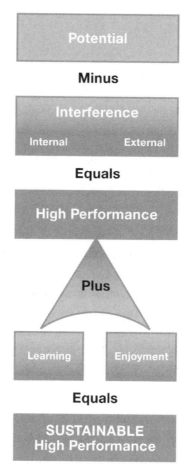

Figure 2.3   Coaching Model Part 2

pride, sense of achievement, beating the competition, hitting standards, etc. All by-products of doing a good job.

It makes sense then for us as coaches to promote high levels of performance and to encourage people to relish the warm feelings that it generates. But as we've said unless this is balanced with an equal amount of learning and enjoyment in the work situation it is likely to be counter productive.

To give a simple example, imagine a lecturer who had painstakingly learnt, practiced and delivered a demanding lecture over a number of years. At the outset her PLE triangle will have a healthy balance. Firstly, she will be learning as she researches the details of the topic and experiments with different explanations, visual aides and so on. Assuming she has an interest in the subject matter we can expect that she finds the time she is spending on research hugely enjoyable and finally she will get satisfaction and pride from delivering the lecture well to an appreciative audience.

But what if she were never required to learn another lecture? What if her boss just implored her to deliver that one lecture as well as she could week after week after week? There would be no learning going on and not much fun to be had. It is very likely that she would soon become bored and tired. She would then lose focus and start making mistakes and so not even get the motivation that comes from performing well. Her boss would likely become angry and start putting her under pressure to perform like she could, but our lecturer, not really understanding what was going on, might be mystified as to why she was making mistakes, feel under stress and start making more mistakes. A very unhelpful cycle has been created.

Let's take another example. Imagine a machine operator who has to load materials in at one end of a machine, monitor that everything is working as it should be, and check for the quality of output at the end. In the early days we might once again expect a healthy PLE to begin with. Learning about the machine and the procedures, having fun being in a new and different situation and getting a sense of performance from seeing high quality finished product emerge from his machine at the required standard.

But what if our man is still stuck there months or years later? No learning going on because he knows the machine backwards. No enjoyment because the whole thing has become tedious and dull. There might still be some motivation to be had from performing the function well, but the lack of learning and enjoyment is likely to cause the same loss of focus and so on that happened to the lecturer with a similar effect on performance and the creation of another vicious circle.

This is a well known phenomenon and has been solved over the years with things like job rotation and job enrichment. But of course it's not always possible to swap duties or take on new tasks and so we're left with unhappy people doing work they don't like. Not a recipe for sustainable high performance.

Another solution is to introduce a distraction. A radio perhaps on the shop floor or allowing a healthy banter amongst the teams. This makes some sense but can be taken too far. If people become too distracted or it's too difficult to concentrate mistakes or accidents can occur.

What if instead we encouraged people to re-discover that sense of performance? What if instead of saying 'The wastage figures are hopeless, sort it out!' we asked 'how could you improve the wastage figures by 2%?'?

How different would the sense of pride and satisfaction be in the worker who discovered the answer for themselves rather than the one who achieved it through blood, sweat and tears to get the boss off their back?

What if we genuinely celebrated high performance, and sincerely thanked people for their efforts? What if we threw praise, appreciation and encouragement around without restriction?

Barking at people to perform – with the possible exception of certain military leaders and colourful sports managers – no longer works – and I'm not sure it ever really did. Providing an environment in which people really can perform, are encouraged to try and receive recognition when they do is a strong and enduring motivational force.

PROMOTING LEARNING

If we were not hard-wired from birth to be naturally motivated to learn, then none of us would be able to walk, speak or eat solid food. I would like to point out that you were never really taught to do those things. It is more accurate to realise that you found your own way to walk, speak and eat in an atmosphere of support and encouragement involving people who were utterly determined to see you succeed.

I believe that we never really lose this natural urge to learn, but that it becomes submerged beneath a great weight of internal interference instilled – irony of ironies – from our experience of formal education. And that this gets carried forward into our working lives.

Our third coaching law captures this apparent paradox brilliantly:

3RD LAW OF COACHING

Learning is easier than being taught

We'll see later on that we can use coaching to help people rediscover their natural, enduring sense of learning and that skills learnt in this way will be far more deep rooted and flexible than those taught in a formal way. First let's consider the problems of an ill balanced PLE triangle with an over emphasis on learning.

One of my first assignments when I became an independent trainer was to deliver some induction training for new recruits at a contact centre. New starters spent their first three weeks in a classroom environment learning about the organisation's products, systems, and modes of behaviour. The set-up was fantastic; state of the art e-learning systems, multi-media audio visual equipment, brilliant learning materials with the highest production values and a crack team of world class facilitators. And me.

To begin with the new starters sucked this up and loved it. They felt highly valued and could not possibly have failed to appreciate the level of investment that was going into their learning, but three weeks later they were utterly drained and giving serious thought to whether they had made the right decision. Many decided that they hadn't and left before the training had even finished.

Of course there could be a host of reasons for this, but in my view the biggest reason was that there was too much learning and not enough performance and enjoyment. The learning was great but people wanted a chance to put their new found knowledge and skills into practice. Many of them were straining at the leash to get out onto the live floor and start taking calls. Enjoyment was there to begin with, but the other facilitators and I found it waned over the three week period.

Looking back what should have happened was to intersperse the training with shadowing on the live floor to include taking calls. I think the new recruits should also have had more opportunities to meet with existing staff to find out where the possibilities for enjoyment in this type of work were to be found.

It's not even as if learning this intently is actually efficient. Kolb's learning cycle [13] suggests that for learning to occur effectively we need to plan an experience, have the experience, review the experience and draw conclusions from the experience. My contact centre staff were spending the thick end of three weeks planning an experience!

Once again we see the importance of keeping PLE in balance.

PROMOTING ENJOYMENT

Before we go further I must stress that by promoting enjoyment at work I do not mean trips to the pub, dress down Fridays, five-a-side football tournaments or team away days. All these things have their place and I've been known to enjoy them all as much as the next person, but they're external, outside of normal activity and often introduced because the actual day to day work seems to have lost its enjoyment for most people.

Similarly, prescriptive approaches to enjoyment at work are hazardous. Humour, for example, is extremely subjective and what one group of employees find hilarious, others could find very offensive. Exhortations to loosen up and attend the team night out can put pressure on those with other commitments. The best advice would seem to be to allow individuals within teams a high degree of choice in choosing their extra curricular activities.

I consider it more important that work itself be enjoyable. I base this on the simple notion that unhappy people are unlikely to produce sustainable high performance. My next door neighbour who worked in the health service could have been the most gifted employee they ever had, but was too miserable to ever utilise those gifts.

It's essentially a matter of quality of life in the workplace, where people can wake up in the morning expecting a pleasant day. My experience suggests that this is usually a question of making people feel valued, involved and fulfilled.

Of course not everyone can be involved in entertaining work or jobs which make a great social contribution, but everyone is making a difference in some way or there would be no need for their role at all. Many of you will be familiar with the story of the cleaner at NASA who, when asked about his role, explained that he was there to help get man into space.

Again enjoyment at work can be over played. Too relaxed an environment can leave people feeling confused. Enjoying the banter and having a good time, but going home with that uneasy feeling that they didn't really earn their money that day. In other words plenty of enjoyment but no performance or learning.

Most people I talk to recognise that there is a blend of Performance, Learning and Enjoyment in their work but not usually the balance. Unless things are going exceptionally well it seems that performance is always being stressed to the exclusion of the other two. Learning and Enjoyment it seems are luxuries to be had only when orders have been won, projects implemented, targets achieved or whatever the performance metric may be. But how can we hope to win the orders or hit the targets with a group of unhappy people who are not really learning and developing? This is captured in our fourth coaching law.

4TH LAW OF COACHING

The higher the need for performance, the higher the need for learning and enjoyment

It's as if the PLE triangle is hooked onto external measures of success. If these measures move the whole of the triangle must move to keep up not just the performance element.

SUMMARY

This chapter has been about understanding how we can access the motivation required to bring about sustainable high performance.

There is a solid theoretical background to much of the thinking that has gone into producing motivation at work and as a manager who coaches you would be wise to consider the main lessons.

Maslow has shown that we are motivated to satisfy a need, but once satisfied, that need ceases to motivate. If we link this to the PLE triangle though I think it's fair to say that our basic human drive to perform, learn and enjoy is too enduring to ever be thought of as finally satisfied and offers great prospects for lasting motivation.

Herzberg has taught us that not all motivators work the same way. Hygiene factors like salary and work conditions will produce a minimum level of performance but will not be enough for people to deploy their discretionary effort and produce real results. However, if we get the hygiene factors right and then move on to work on getting a balanced PLE triangle the chances of success greatly improve.

House and Dessler's path goal theory suggests that people are always moving towards a goal, which is intended to satisfy a need. Understanding individual goals and needs offers powerful ways to get the blend of motivators right.

In any event you probably have little scope to change Extrinsic motivation and are better advised to work on promoting people's sense of Intrinsic motivation and that means getting the PLE triangle in balance.

In adding this thinking to our model which appeared at Figure 2.3 we can see that coaching is about removing or reducing interference and achieving a balance between performance, learning and enjoyment. The problem with models though is that they present the world in over simplistic terms. I am not suggesting that if you reduce interference on Monday and promote PLE on Tuesday that all your people issues will be solved by Wednesday! Nevertheless the model does give insight into the conditions necessary to achieve lasting performance:

Belief

People perform when they believe they can. For this to be the case we need to make sure that they have been trained in the knowledge and skills they need to undertake their roles and that more importantly they are not being held back by negative internal interference. Coaching will reveal gaps in knowledge and skill and identify the sources of internal interference. It will also enable people to find their own way of dealing with issues in these areas.

Desire

People perform *well* when they *want* to. People may be *compelled* by fear or inducement to perform at a minimum level but to tap into really high performance we need to heed the lessons in motivation outlined in the chapter.

Willingness

Finding a way to perform well in some ways requires people to take a risk; it's moving them outside their comfort zone. As coaches we need to support this move and encourage them to give it a go; to take a calculated risk without fear of recrimination.

Time now to get practical and see how coaching, as a particular communication tool, can enable us to bring these conditions about.

CHAPTER 3

PEAK COACHING MODEL PT 3 – COACHING AND COMMUNICATION

COACHING *IS* COMMUNICATION

Let's start with our next coaching law:

5TH LAW Of COACHING

Your team view you as their coach, whether you like it or not

I realise that this is a bold assertion, so let me explain what I mean.

At any time your work requires you to achieve results through others, you are a leader, i.e. people will take their lead from you. You may have a formal position as a director, manager or team leader and have a line management relationship with a permanent team. Alternatively, you may be a project manager, consultant, HR Business Partner or any role which requires an influence over people. The situation is irrelevant, any time your work requires you to achieve results through others, you are a leader.

Now, there has been more written on the nature of leadership than I could possibly summarise here, but few hard and fast facts have ever really emerged. Debates still rage about whether leaders are made or born and the similarities and differences between management and leadership. To me, however, one thing seems certain. Leadership is asserted through our ability to communicate. This is in part to do with winning hearts and minds and outlining a compelling vision or strategy. It is also to do with an ability to relate to people, to understand them and to help them realise their potential. This of course is also the nature of coaching and it is this that makes the law hold true. Your people, whoever they may be, are looking to you to help them perform, however that performance be defined or measured. To be a leader is to be a coach, they are interchangeable. You have always been your people's coach although neither of you may have used that term. This is not surprising as we have had coaching for years but it has only recently been given a label. It follows that if leadership is all about communication then so is coaching.

To begin with let's look at some of the different ways we go about communicating at work. The following diagram, Figure 3.1, is based on the well-known model by Tammenbaum and Schmidt [20].

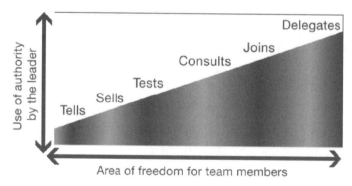

Figure 3.1   Leadership Communication

The diagram suggests that there are two variables at play in communicating at work, the use of authority by the leader and the area of freedom for their subordinates. At the far left we have *Tells*, maximum use of authority by the leader with little, if any, scope for team members to exercise any discretion. By the time we get to the far right, *Delegates*, we have basically swapped things round with a large area of freedom from team members and little use of authority by the team leader.

There is no absolute right or wrong, or good or bad inherent in any of these styles, they each have their strengths and weaknesses as summarised in Table 3.1.

Whenever I ask my coaching students to tell me which style is best, their answer, of course, is always 'it depends'. It does indeed depend on a mix of three factors:

The situation

In an emergency, we need clear authoritative leadership. There's five minutes to go before the team are due to deliver a presentation as part of a tender response for a potential new client and someone's left the laptop on the train. No time for sitting around discussing options or debating tactics. This is what we'll tell the client. This is how we can adapt our presentation. This is how we can use what we do have with us, and so on.

Note that contrary to popular belief not every day at work is an emergency, but working in this way can be habit forming!

The needs of the person

A new person on the team will need lots of information and guidance to begin with while they learn the requirements of the job. However, as they develop their capabilities, we need perhaps to

Table 3.1

	Advantages	Disadvantages
Tells Sometimes referred to as 'command and control' or being autocratic	Quick Clear Precise Unambiguous Total control	The team are not involved and thus unlikely to feel committed The leader has no access to ideas within the team There is little opportunity for learning
Sells A style largely based on persuasion with the leader seeking to convince the team of their ideas	Quick, if there is buy-in High degree of control Seeks to acknowledge the team's need for a reason behind a decision	No real team involvement Team may feel a little patronized Very little learning
Tests Where the team leader, tries out certain suggestions and ideas to gauge the team's view	Quick, if there is buy-in Reasonable degree of control Gives a feel for the level of commitment the team are likely to show	What do we do if the team do not like the idea? We're probably faced with having to resort to *Tell* and this may make them feel unclear about our leadership style

Consults
A style based on the idea of reaching decisions by consensus and seeking involvement

Involving
Leader gains access to the creativity of staff
A chance to uncover any real issues

Time consuming
Can raise false expectations if people's contribution cannot be taken forward

Joins
Where the leader position themselves as merely part of the team

Respectful
Encourages contribution from team members

Can be seen as weak
Quality of decision making may be poor

Delegates
A style based on giving team members some direction around what needs to be done, but allows them considerable scope in deciding how

Developmental for the person to whom responsibilities are delegated
Builds capability in the team
Accelerates learning

Need to have skilled people to whom to delegate
Accountability still resides with the leader
Requires a certain tolerance for mistakes as people learn

move across the diagram giving them more freedom to take action and use their discretion.

If you feel they're not up to it or can't be trusted you have a recruitment and selection problem.

The leader's preference

In truth, some people are just naturally more at ease towards the left and others are more naturally inclined towards the right of the diagram. The best advice is always to act with integrity and at least try to have people clear about the sort of communicator you are. We can get into real trouble when we falsely adopt a 'softer' style as we will probably revert to type when things get difficult and this just leaves people feeling confused.

We now know more about our communication options, their relative strengths and weaknesses and the factors which will influence our choice. We can now turn our sights on where coaching fits.

STYLE OR PHILOSOPHY?

In truth, none of the communication options outlined above is wholly satisfactory because each denies either the leader or the team member the vital element of control. Leaders and managers want control to know that tasks will be handled correctly and effectively. Team members want control over how they complete tasks and how they might use their initiative.

At the far left of our scale, *Tells*, the manager has total control but the team member has none. This is likely to result in a manager exercising a tight grip over a team who will produce the minimum necessary to get by. A degree of performance, but not one that any of you reading this is likely to find satisfying. At the far right of the scale, *Delegates*, we have team members exercising a great deal of control and probably feeling highly responsible, but a manager feeling somewhat uneasy that they do not have a tight grip on everything. Unless results are absolutely outstanding and sustained it is likely that the manager will come under great pressure from their own boss to get back in control and the team members – having experienced a taste of freedom – may become resentful about this.

A coaching approach irons this out. In coaching, both manager and team member (coach and coachee) are in control. When I coach my Business Development Manager she gives me her views on our current challenges and outlines ways in which she feels we could deal with them. She is in full control. Nevertheless, it is with me she is having this conversation so I am absolutely aware of whatever action she intends taking. In this way, I too am in control.

But what if I don't agree with her plans? Well, provided I have established a relationship of trust – of which more later – there is no reason why I should not be able to point out why I am unable to support her ideas. Coaching someone is not the same as giving them permission to do whatever they want.

What I'm really suggesting is that coaching does not compare with the communication styles outlined above. It is not a style, it is more of a communication philosophy. (Figure 3.2) I've described coaching as being performer centred and performance focused and this intent can sit behind any of the communication styles from *Tells* to *Delegates*.

I was once coaching a team leader in a contact centre who was under pressure to drive up the number of sales leads generated by her team. At their morning meeting her instruction was generally the same 'Come on guys get those leads up today' or words to that effect. After some coaching she decided to change that to something along the lines of 'We all know we need to increase the number of leads we generate, today I'd like each of you to identify

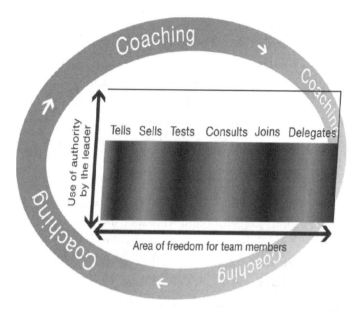

Figure 3.2   Coaching & Communication

three blockages to doing so'. Same objective, but a very different communication approach.

Making a link to something we looked at earlier, her first instruction is a plea to perform, her second recognises the need to also incorporate learning and enjoyment.

COMMUNICATING FOR DEVELOPMENT

Let's imagine you're an HR Manager and that once a month you have to make a presentation to the executive team. This presentation includes statistics on recruitment, retention, sickness absence, etc. The executive team are most vexed by your firm's high staff turnover as it's costing a lot of money and proving very damaging to morale. They tend to get very upset each month when this figure comes up for discussion and can even get quite angry with you. They see it as a HR issue.

You're about to be seconded to a special project that will mean you cannot give the presentation for the next six months. Instead you need to develop your HR Officer to do it for you. You would seem to have four options:

- Tell her how to do it
- Show her how to do it
- Leave her alone to get on with it
- Coach her

Tell her how to do it

Whilst it will be relatively easy to explain to your HR Officer how to pull the statistics from the computer, how do you *tell* her how to cope with an angry senior team? You have probably developed your own way of dealing with this over time, but do you know exactly how you manage their responses? Could you define the intricate step by step process that your HR Officer would need to follow to be able to do this? Probably not.

Show her how to do it

Instead you could explain to your HR Officer how to access the statistics and suggest she shadows you on your final time in front of the executive team. In this way you're demonstrating an appropriate level of assertiveness that she can then try to emulate. But again, does it really reveal how exactly she could achieve similar results? Probably not.

Leave her alone to get on with it

Sometimes known as the 'sink or swim' school of management development and whilst it has been known to work to a degree, I would question the quality of learning that results from this sort of experience. If it goes wrong your HR Officer could have her confidence shattered.

Coach her

What if instead of all this we sat down with her in advance of her presenting to the executive team and asked her what she would like to achieve, how she envisages the experience going, what difficulties she perceives and how she might handle any difficult questions. You could then agree how much of a first presentation she felt able to handle and you could deal with the rest. You could do some follow up coaching just afterwards to understand what she'd noticed (probably a lot of internal interference if it went badly or a lot of PLE if it went well). You could agree on the key qualities it would be necessary for her to use on the next occasion and suggest she focus on those areas next time.

Tell is still the predominant management style at work because it's the one we've been taught and still see most of but as a means of developing performance it's deeply flawed. To develop another by telling requires that you firstly know how you get results yourself and if you're naturally good at something you probably don't. It then requires that you can find words and language to convey that to someone else in a way that they can understand. We all form our own model of the world based on our unique experiences and it's very difficult to convey precise meanings that any two people can accurately share.

Okay, so perhaps we should *demonstrate* instead, but again this requires that we can do the task in question. Managers can no longer be the source of all wisdom in the team. The world is changing too fast to keep up.

Even if you can overcome the difficulties presented by telling or demonstrating you're still only going to end up at best with somebody who does it like you. Not much creativity or innovation is going to come from this approach.

The final problem is recall. People simply don't remember what they've only ever been told about or shown. For lasting learning to take place people need to *experience* completing a task.

A coaching approach enables people to not only have an experience but to gain maximum learning from it. As a piece of communication it is founded largely on the notion of asking insightful questions, but we can look at this in more detail later.

For now it is vital that, before we move on, we examine the key principles of coaching – the fundamental reasons for communicating through coaching at all.

AWARENESS

Trying fails, awareness cures

Fritz Perls

This section on Awareness and the two which follow on Responsibility and Trust are the three most valuable parts of this book. These are the three key principles of coaching at work and without an understanding of them all you've read so far and everything that follows is useless. Conversely a coach who understands the need to raise awareness, generate responsibility and build trust will almost certainly be a successful coach.

Let's deal with awareness first. I define awareness as 'the raising of high quality focus and attention without judgement'. Let me give you an example. Suppose I have been asked by Tom, a newly qualified teacher, to observe a lesson and give some coaching afterwards as he is concerned about disruptive behaviour.

Here's how I would likely have handled this before I appreciated the value of raising awareness:

Matt	That went well Tom, well done.
Tom	Thanks. It felt ok
Matt	Obviously you could have been stronger when Michael was playing up, but I realise it's difficult
Tom	Stronger?
Matt	Yes. You should have taken the ruler away from him and made him return to his seat. You see when I was teaching, I quickly realised that you need to stand up to the kids and show them who's boss
Tom	Well that's not really my style and besides I think that's just what he wanted and would have been playing straight into his hands
Matt	Well that's your opinion, but at this school we really need to be firm. How could you be more firm?
Tom	Erm, I suppose I could have raised my voice with Michael
Matt	That's not what I mean. Don't you think it would be better if you used a more subtle approach?
Tom	Er, maybe
Matt	Good so we're agreed that you need to work up a more firm but subtle method. Let's think about ways you could do this

Now contrast this with an awareness raising approach:

Matt	That went well Tom, well done.
Tom	Thanks. It felt ok
Matt	What did you most notice about that lesson?
Tom	Well . . . I noticed that I felt uneasy when Michael began to misbehave
Matt	How uneasy did you feel?
Tom	It was quite bad actually. I couldn't decide whether to intervene or just ignore him
Matt	(nothing at this point just quiet attention on Tom)

Tom	I think I should probably have stopped him, but I just let it go
Matt	What did you notice then?
Tom	I found myself thinking of ways I could justify not taking action if you asked me about it! What I really want is to be able to develop the ability to intervene when it's appropriate

The underlying situation is the same in both cases, but in the second example my coaching has enabled Tom to consider his experience without fear of judgement and get closer to what was really happening. In the first example, my attempts at awareness raising were confined to making Tom aware of what *I'd* noticed and what *I* thought he needed to do. I was effectively telling him what to do.

I stress again that telling is not fundamentally wrong. Sometimes it's what the situation demands and that's fine, but let's not call it coaching. Coaching involves awareness raising. It is analogous with making ourselves presentable by looking in the mirror. We get insight but not input from the mirror. In raising awareness through coaching we are also trying to promote insight so that people better understand what's happening to them and can make better choices about how to respond.

Let's have a closer look at how the process of raising awareness would actually help Tom the newly qualified teacher develop an ability to deal with disruptive behaviour.

The following model – whose origins remain unclear – helps illustrate this point (Table 3.2).

To begin with before he becomes a teacher or perhaps just after qualifying Tom is in blissful ignorance that he can't handle disruptive behaviour, but it doesn't matter because he doesn't need to.

Tom gets qualified and starts work. He becomes conscious of the fact that he can't deal with disruptive behaviour. However, he

Table 3.2

	Unconscious	Conscious
Incompetence	1 Tom can't do it but feels ok because he doesn't realise he can't do it	2 Tom tries to handle disruptive behaviour but discovers it is difficult
Competence	4 Tom handles disruptive behaviour without really thinking about it	3 Tom develops some ways of handling disruptive behaviour but it takes a conscious effort

does need to come to this realisation before he can do anything about it.

Aware now of what's happening Tom begins to consciously try new things. He'll find that some things don't work and discard them and others that do work which he'll refine and adapt.

After a while Tom will internalise what he's learned and developed and do it without thinking.

The awareness raising principle of coaching puts people in the conscious layer of this model as it is only at this level that they can affect change. Awareness helps me move from *Unconscious Incompetence* to *Conscious Incompetence*. This may be an uncomfortable feeling, but a necessary one in order to move on.

Being aware is also what will then move me into *Conscious Competence* as I try things out and notice what happens.

Eventually, in any given endeavour, I will probably become unconsciously incompetent again as I develop bad habits. Once again if someone coaches me well and I become aware of these things I will be able to correct them and refine my skills.

Very often in coaching at work all we need do is raise awareness and let performance improvement take care of itself.

In concluding my session with Tom I might suggest that in his next lesson he just notices how at ease he feels in handling disruptive behaviour (since this is the positive opposite of the uneasy feeling he described to begin with). This sounds too simple to be true and in a way it is but just think about what Tom would be focusing on as he tried this out next time. He'll become highly aware of what makes him feel at ease and what makes him feel uneasy. He'll naturally and automatically begin to do more of the former and less of the latter. Furthermore, he can do this without any further input from me.

RESPONSIBILITY

The way this word sounds gives us the biggest clue as to its value as our second key coaching principle. Response ability – the ability to respond. The word responsibility has developed negative connotations in the world of work. What's your first reaction when told your boss wants you to take on responsibility for something? If you're anything like me it will be to run for cover knowing that your workload is about to increase. Taking on responsibility has become synonymous with being given more work. However, being asked to accept new responsibilities sounds better than being asked to do a load of new work. We know from looking at motivation earlier that taking on new responsibilities is often a motivator and so managers have used this to appeal to our better judgement. In truth taking on more responsibility should mean *different* work not *more* work.

In a work situation a responsible person is a person who chooses to own a task and see it through. The key words here being chooses to. Once again we can see that forcing or telling people to accept responsibility will only go so far. It may produce an acceptable level of performance but it is unlikely to tap into people's discretionary effort.

As a trainer, I have often included role-playing exercises in the various courses I have designed. For a long time, I would take total responsibility for setting these up. I would painstakingly explain the reason for doing role-plays, persuade the participants that they would learn a lot and do everything in my power to make them a learning experience rather than a trial. I only ever had limited success.

These days, I explain that we need to do a role-play because it is the best way to learn a particular skill. I then ask the participants how I could best set up the session so that they experience the minimum nerves and maximum learning. Normally, I'm told that they want to work in small groups, to not have to perform in front of the whole group, to be able to call 'stop' if they get stuck and so on. This invariably produces a great session.

Ironically, I would have suggested these things anyway, but that's exactly the point. Because they would have been *my* suggestions there was no choice, no responsibility. By involving the participants in deciding how the session should run, they feel responsible and therefore take ownership for their own learning.

I think there is a valuable lesson here in a host of work situations. I realise that we cannot always give people choice around *what* they do at work but there is usually a lot of scope around *how* they do it.

This lends itself to a coaching law:

6TH LAW OF COACHING

There is no responsibility without choice, there is no choice without ownership, there is no ownership without involvement.

So now we have some clarity around our first two key principles, Awareness and Responsibility. Take a moment to consider high performers you have worked with in your time. Were they not highly aware? Sensitive to what was happening, what they felt about what was happening and how it affected others around them? Were they not highly responsible? Able to take the initiative, to make decisions and to work with integrity? Take a moment to consider your own performance history as well. When you've been at your best were you not highly aware and highly responsible? Furthermore, were you not encouraged to be this way by your bosses and others around you?

TRUST

Awareness and Responsibility are always key components in high performance in any field. For coaching at work to be able to cultivate the benefits we need to add in a third key principle and that is Trust.

Where an external coach is appointed trust is a given in the relationship. Or, more accurately, an appropriate level of trust is established before the coaching relationship begins. Nobody would appoint a coach who they didn't believe they could trust.

Coaching at work, within the line management relationship, is more complex. Being at work throws people together who might otherwise not choose to be together. We may not always like the people we coach and they may not always like us, but this does not mean we cannot establish a relationship of trust. There are three aspects to trust in a coaching relationship that we need to consider:

- Trust in oneself
- Trust in the coach
- Trust in the process

Trust in oneself

To trust oneself to perform requires a high degree of self-belief. We saw earlier how an absence of self-belief can be a pervading source of internal interference. Coaches often have to spend time, particularly at the start of a relationship, encouraging people to give something a go and displaying a lot of belief in their abilities. We know that if we do this there is a strong chance of success. This is the Pygmalion effect; the self-fulfilling prophecy we looked at earlier.

Trust in the coach

In order that your people will trust you as their coach you need to be a trustworthy person and to do trustworthy things. This means that what gets said in a coaching session remains confidential, all things being equal. It also means that performance difficulties are explored in a supportive environment and not used as a 'weapon' to deny progress or suppress a performance bonus.

I often get asked whether it is better to keep coaching within the line management relationship or to bring in an external coach, e.g. a HR Manager or independent consultant. There is no easy answer to this and much depends on the circumstances, although I definitely do not believe that coaching is incompatible with a line management relationship. Yes sometimes we may have to discipline or restrict as a manager, but we have always had to. The advent of coaching has not changed this. The job of management is to produce results from resources and we need to do what the occasion demands. The key is to act with consistency and integrity. Act on your values and do what you believe is right. Treat people with dignity and respect whether congratulating or condemning and you'll not go far wrong.

In fact I believe that trust is strengthened when managers take a strong stance on performance issues.

Trust in the process

There are a lot of misconceptions out there about coaching and these can mean that people are uneasy about being coached and somewhat mistrustful of it.

Common amongst these misconceptions is that coaching is only for poor performers and we, as managers who coach, need to challenge this view. Yes, coaching can work well as a means of addressing poor performance but only if there is a genuine desire on both parts to consider sincerely what the issues might be. Furthermore, why limit coaching to addressing poor performance? A sideways glance at the worlds of entertainment or sport shows that those under the greatest pressure to perform value coaching even when performing at the height of their powers.

There is also the question of whether to 'announce' that people are being coached or whether to just get on with it. Once again your own judgement is best and you need to consider the circumstances in your organisation at the time. Where people are feeling a bit jaded or suffering from 'change fatigue' you're best advised to just get on with the business of coaching and worry less about giving it a label. To launch a 'coaching initiative' may be seen as just one more change. Your people will keep their heads down and hope that you'll go back to normal in a few days. This attitude will mean that you will only get superficial responses to your coaching questions and may spoil the outcome. I don't think it's dishonest to coach covertly as long as your intention is to raise awareness, generate responsibility and to build trust. How could anyone be annoyed with us for doing that?

We once trained a group of senior managers and then their own teams about six months later. I remember one participant in the latter programme saying suddenly 'so that's what my boss has been doing these last few months, I thought it was a bit odd!'.

On the other hand if there is an appetite for change and for learning and development in particular, then let's talk about coaching, explain what's involved and outline the benefits. When people understand what coaching is all about they tend to get more thoroughly involved in the coaching conversations.

I believe that much organisational coaching fails because inadequate attention is paid to the matter of trust. I like to express this as a coaching law.

7TH LAW OF COACHING

The success of your coaching is proportional to the level of trust you can establish.

We've now looked at Awareness, Responsibility and Trust. Let's look at how these principles connect to our coaching model.

Awareness enables me to gather high quality information about any job of work before, during or after I perform it. I will therefore become aware of the internal interference I experience or the external interference I notice. I will similarly become aware of whether my performance, learning and enjoyment are in balance or whether something is missing.

Responsibility enables me to feel mobile. I can exercise choices and act on my own accord. I can choose to fall victim to my internal interference or I can do something about it. I can choose to feel frustrated with a working life that is all performance and no learning and enjoyment or I can do something about that too.

Finally, trust enables me to take action but to feel safe. I'll be confident that I'm doing the right things for the right reasons and, more importantly, that I have the support of my coach.

Let's now consider the sorts of performance issues that coaching with these principles addresses so well.

KNOWLEDGE, SKILLS AND STATE OF MIND

Imagine your local temporary staff agency have supplied two people to run your organisation's reception desk while the permanent member of staff recovers from a long term illness. You need two people because you want to experiment with organising the role on a job share basis.

They each arrive with similar backgrounds in terms of education and experience and they have done this sort of work before.

During the morning, the first person makes an effort with your clients, occupies herself between visitors by learning the IT system, and offers to help your sales team make any outbound calls.

In the afternoon, the second person does nothing other than sign visitors in and answer incoming calls.

Both of these employees have broadly similar knowledge and skills, but it is their attitude or state of mind that makes the difference. More and more these days we're realising that this is the case. If I lack the requisite knowledge and skills, with a positive state of mind I'll go and find them. Without a positive state of mind I'll just shrug and do my best to get by.

We need to consider exactly the state of mind most conducive to performing at our best. It is the state of being aware, responsible and trusting. It is best described as being focused.

FOCUS

To be able to achieve focus is the primary skill in producing high performance in any endeavour. Focus at work refers to that feeling of relaxed concentration we can sometimes achieve. When we're focused things get done, issues are clearer and decisions easier to make. When we've been focused we can go home from work feeling as if we've made real progress but not necessarily exhausted by our efforts.

Contrary to popular belief, focus is not a happy accident, it is a faculty that we each have, but most of us have allowed to decline. Coaching restores a level of focus that generally gets submerged beneath layers of internal and external interference.

Every coachee I have ever worked with has reinforced my belief that regaining focus is the major key to unlocking higher performance, but I have also learnt three important lessons that must always be borne in mind:

Focus is not the same as 'trying really hard'

It is of course possible to achieve results at work by 'trying really hard'. This usually equates to taking on more work than is sensible and then arriving early, skipping lunch, and leaving late. In the short term this might be a necessary step and we've all done it.

The problem is that this working pattern – certainly in Western cultures – is becoming the norm rather than the exception. The unfortunate consequence of being able to achieve results only by 'trying really hard' all the time is stress, burnout, resentment, fatigue and poor concentration. This is likely to lead to shoddy work and/or missed opportunities and so we have to work even harder to catch up.

Focus is different to this. Achieving results when focused feels *effortless* not *effortful*. It is the difference between the fast food waiter who takes a genuine interest in the customer and lines up the order smoothly and the one who adopts a false smile, intones 'have a nice day' through gritted teeth and flies around the kitchen like a maniac.

This concept, whilst being easy to understand, is hard to apply. We live in a society that sets great store by effort and trying. How many promotions still go to those people who've 'put the hours in' or 'always given it a go'?

When I first tried my hand at delivering training I found it natural and comfortable. I felt a little nervous to begin with but found I was always able to focus on the needs of the audience and get good results. My achievements though were often dismissed out of hand. 'It's easy for you, you're a natural', or 'yes, but you've got the gift of the gab' were often offered as explanations for my success. The real plaudits went to the trainers who were physically sick before the session and who'd stayed up all night preparing their notes.

Now there's nothing wrong with making great efforts and trying hard, but they are not constituent parts of consistent high performance.

Focus needs to be single and appropriate

I remember working in a team with seven top priorities. This is of course nonsense as, by definition, there can only be one *top* priority. If I ever found there was more to do than time in which to do it and asked my boss what to focus on he'd invariably end up listing all seven!

In truth, we can really only do one thing *well* at a time. Of course it's possible to do many things at once, but any of those tasks is likely to be done better if it is the sole focus of our attention. In business this equates to teams developing a shared sense of what's really important, being able to operate in the here and now and trying, as far as is possible, to do one thing at a time. Single focus is the best focus of all.

Similarly, we need to focus on the right things. Focusing on 'staying calm' is better than focusing on 'not getting angry'. Focusing on producing a 'clear and concise report' is more useful than focusing on 'trying to get that report in on time'.

Focus follows interest

If you're imploring me to focus on spotting a sales lead in a telephone conversation, but I'm more interested in customer care, I'll either be focused on customer care or not focused at all because I'm trying to act on what you want me to do rather than what my instinct tells me. That focus follows interest is hugely frustrating to a lot of coaches at work because so often people don't seem to be interested in the same things that the organisation wants or needs them to be interested in. The solution is the same as the problem – focus follows interest. If you need me to focus on driving up sales leads you need to get me interested in this. Why is this important? What's in it for me? How can I do this? Who else does this well? How can I develop my skills in this area and so on? Until I'm interested I won't focus properly. I'll probably try to focus, but this is unlikely to produce great results. Granted this can be seen as being a little Utopian, but remember coaching is not a panacea or a replacement for good old fashioned performance management. Sometimes you will have to insist that people focus on say, sales lead generation and that's fine providing you realise their results are unlikely to be as good as if they'd come to that conclusion for themselves.

Focus enables me to work free of internal interference. The interference is still there but it has been tuned out and replaced with a more appropriate focus. Our three key coaching principles of Awareness, Responsibility and Trust are required to bring about an appropriate focus and to enable me to discover my balance between Performance, Learning and Enjoyment.

SUMMARY

Once our work requires us to achieve results through others we are those people's coach. This is irrespective of whether the relationship is formal or informal. Coaching, like leadership is all about communication, but our purpose in communicating is not merely to pass on information or instruction. When coaching, the intent behind our communication should be to encourage a quality of thinking and insight untypical in most workplaces today.

With coaching at the heart of our communication approach we can more readily adapt our style dependent on the needs of the situation and the individual and in recognition of our own preferences.

Sometimes as leader or a coach we may chose to give people the answer. Sometimes we might argue that we are obliged to give people the answer as it is surely wrong to leave people struggling. I think this is fine as long as it is a conscious, judicious choice. All too often we tell and instruct out of habit but whenever we tell or give people the answer we have missed an opportunity to build capability.

Coaching, on the other hand, presents a range of benefits. Interference is diminished as I learn to focus on more useful things. Learning, enjoyment and, crucially, performance are all enhanced as people begin to take greater notice of what is happening to them and around them. Even recall improves because people have learnt things in their own way and in their own time.

This level of focus, so vital for success in any endeavour, is achieved by coaches raising awareness, generating responsibility and building trust. These three key principles of Awareness, Responsibility and Trust (ART) underpin all good coaching.

Telling, instructing and even demonstrating present few of these benefits as they are each ways of doing people's thinking for them. Many coaches espouse a style called directive coaching, but I feel this is just *tell* in disguise, particularly in the hands of the inexperienced coach. The great temptation from a directive approach is the danger of clouding the coaching session with SMOG:

S	Should do
M	Must do
O	Ought to do
G	Got to do

SMOG is the enemy of ART and flies in the face of the notion of generating responsibility.

This section of the book is entitled How to Coach, but we're three chapters in and have yet to look at what you actually say or do to run a successful coaching session. This has been a deliberate ploy as I was determined that we give adequate coverage to the principles and concepts which must be understood before we can move on. You cannot build a house on weak foundations after all.

In this next chapter I'll explain how you can use questioning as your main communication tool in coaching and how, alongside listening and observation, it provides the way to bring about the levels of focus that we need.

I'll also provide an outline of a questioning framework for you to use at the outset, but one which you'll be able to adapt for yourself given the principles you now understand.

CHAPTER 4

PEAK COACHING MODEL PT 4 – THE COACHING ARROW

Socrates has a lot to answer for I reckon. It's perhaps he that we coaches need to credit for the essential notion of 'ask don't tell' that features in most coaching philosophies.

This simple idea also provides the glue that sticks the components of the Peak Coaching Model together: To remind you:

- To answer your coaching questions I will need to focus on the variables in my situation (more on this later)
- Once focused, I will experience feeling aware, responsible and trusting
- Because I feel this way, I will experience much less interference and much more performance, learning and enjoyment
- In this way more of my potential will come through to achieve sustainable high performance

Thus the ability to ask the right sort of questions is vital in the successful coach's toolkit.

In Socrates's view anyone should be able to challenge anyone else with a question and it seems clear that this idea also serves us well in a coaching context, where the job of the coach is to challenge people to move forward and make changes for themselves rather than instruct, teach, guide or advise.

Question: Why, normally, do we ask questions?

Answer: To get answers

But coaches do not always get answers. In fact sometimes the biggest indication that a coach's question has given a coachee some fresh insight may be a wry smile, a shake of the head, a far away look or complete silence. Perhaps there is another reason for coaches to pose questions.

I believe that the efficacy of coaching questions lies in their power to promote thought. Our ability to think is what distinguishes us from other species. Unlike Pavlov's dogs, between stimulus and response we humans have a moment to think; a moment in which we will make a choice about how to respond in a certain situation. It follows that if we can increase the quality of thinking we should increase the quality of the end result or decision and consequently our performance.

Coaching – particularly asking questions – produces a higher than normal quality of thinking because, as we've seen, it encourages the raising of non-judgemental awareness. As I become more aware of the variables in any situation and, just as importantly, my feelings about them, I begin to understand things better and see more options for change.

> Before you try to change anything, increase your awareness of how it is

> **Timothy Gallwey**

A simple example may help. I was once doing some work in an open plan office and got talking to the Director's PA about coaching. She told me that she thought she could really do with some coaching herself as several times a day she was required to say 'No'. This might be in response to requests for appointments, comments for the media, invitations to events and a whole host of other demands on her boss's time which her job required her to deflect. She explained that she found this very difficult as she did not consider herself a naturally assertive person.

I explained that as I was going to be around all day, we could easily do some coaching around this. I asked her to come and find me immediately after the next time she'd had to say no.

After only a few minutes she was back. 'How did that feel?' I asked. I asked this because, knowing that focus follows interest, I wanted her to begin to focus on what she was noticing *for herself*.

'Oh, it was horrible', she replied, 'I felt all flustered'.

'How do you want it to feel instead?' I asked. I asked this because, knowing that focus needs to be appropriate, I wanted her to get focused on what she wanted to happen rather than what she wanted to avoid.

'I'd like to feel . . . calm', she said.

'Okay then. For the rest of today I want you to notice how calm you feel each time you have to say No'.

She came and found me each time this happened throughout the rest of the day and happily reported feeling calmer on each occasion. No telling or instruction had been needed from me at all and whatever she was learning about calmness was going to stay learnt. This was simply as a result on helping her focus on an appropriate critical variable.

CRITICAL VARIABLES

A variable is anything that changes during or between activities. A critical variable is one which can impact on the outcome. The weather might vary over the course of a day in which I make four sales visits, but that's unlikely to make much difference to my success rate. My passion for my product might equally vary between appointments and this could have a massive impact on my success.

Going back to our PA, she had noticed that the critical variable of calmness was a key element in how able she was to give an assertive response.

I had no idea that this was the critical variable for her, and if I was advising her I might have suggested she needed to be more strident or authoritative, but this was not what she was noticing.

When coaching people on repetitive tasks, inviting your coachees to identify a critical variable and then simply to pay attention to it is often all that is required to produce lasting improvement. When coaching on more complex issues or on occasions when you cannot be present when the activity is being undertaken, you might have to do a bit more work and the coaching sessions may need to be more in depth, but in principle your task as coach is exactly the same.

In the next section of the book we'll uncover some of the obvious critical variables for a range of work issues you might expect to coach people through.

For now, we'll turn our sights to using coaching questions to identify critical variables and promote a focus on them.

CRITERIA

There are perhaps three things that need to be present to upgrade an ordinary question into a coaching question:

The question must force the coachee to pay attention

In the above example the only way the PA was able to tell me how calm she felt in saying no was to pay attention to the things that indicate calmness or not. Was her breathing steady and calm? Was she speaking clearly and concisely? Was she aware of feeling any tension anywhere or did she feel relaxed? Paying attention to those things raised the quality of awareness and once that was done change and improvement took care of itself. Notice also that our PA was fully responsible and empowered to work it out for herself. This would not have been the case if I had resorted to instructions such as 'Don't get flustered, keep calm', 'Be sure to speak clearly and try not to stutter' or 'Stop getting so tense!'.

This works equally well in all sorts of situations. I remember coaching someone who felt nervous about attending networking events. I asked him 'What makes you most nervous?' and he explained that it was the thought of having to initiate a conversation. I then asked 'What quality do you need to use most in that situation?' He said it was something to do with taking an interest in people. We then simply agreed that at the next event he would occasionally ask himself 'How much taking an interest' am I doing?

Once again increased awareness and focus leads to natural improvement, owned by the coachee, and therefore more likely to endure. At no time did I need to instruct and at no time did I get judgemental, e.g. 'You *should* take a greater interest in the people you network with'.

The question must bring about a tight focus

The coaching just outlined would have been much less effective had I asked my coachees only to consider 'how does it feel this time'. The focus is too wide, there are simply too many variables in the situation. A coaching question needs to promote a real focus, not unlike adjusting the lens of a microscope. Questions that start with 'How much' or 'How often' can be particularly useful.

On another occasion I was coaching a team leader who was having difficulty asserting herself at meetings. I could have suggested that she recalled some recent meeting and asked 'How assertive were you?' This would have brought about a degree of awareness, but not enough to hone in on some specific things she could change, so I asked 'How often does that happen? Is it the same in all meetings? What feelings do you experience? How much of a particular feeling do you experience? And so on.

Coaches I train often ask 'How do I know what to get the coachee to focus on?' The answer is simple: you won't know, but the coachee will. The trick is to remember that focus follows interest and people will focus most readily on what they *actually* find interesting not in what we, as coaches think they should find interesting. In my coaching sessions, once we have established the issue to move forward and formulated some aims, I will often ask 'what do you most notice about your situation?' as we begin to look at how things currently stand. I trust that the people I coach know instinctively where to look for answers and I also trust that they will recognise quickly where they may be barking up the wrong tree.

The question must provide some feedback to the coach when it is answered

Although as we've already seen, the primary purpose of coaching questions is to promote thought rather than generate answers, responses to questions can provide a useful feedback loop to the coach. Had the PA told me that she felt perfectly calm when I could see her blushing terribly I would have known there was further work to do. Had my team leader told me that she had been twice as assertive as usual when I asked her how assertive she'd been but was unable to tell me what she'd said, to whom, on what occasions, etc. I would similarly have known there was more work to do.

CONSTRUCTION

We need mainly to ask *open* questions as these tend to require more thought before an answer can be formulated. As we've already seen How much and How often type questions can be particularly effective in promoting high quality awareness and focus.

There is also a place for *closed* questions in terms of getting coachees to confirm specific facts or commit to specific course of action. For example, 'Are you going to talk to your boss next Thursday as we've discussed?'.

PROCESS

The process is very simple. The coach asks the question and then notices the response by way of listening carefully to the content of the answer and by monitoring the accompanying body language. The coach then asks follow on questions until it is clear that the coachee has developed the depth of insight required and is showing signs of wanting to move the conversation on.

FRAMEWORKS

Finally we need to look at what questions to ask and in what order. Most coaches use some variation of the mnemonic GROW which divides a coaching session into four main areas:

Goal	What do you want?
Reality	What's happening now?
Options	What *could* you do?
Will	What *will* you do?

This model is useful in guiding a coachee from a broad understanding of what they're trying to achieve long-term to a clear plan of action with detailed process steps. However, experience suggests that things are rarely quite so straightforward and coaches need to be very flexible in using the model and be prepared to bounce back and forth as they follow the coachee's thinking. It is a big mistake to follow GROW slavishly.

There are a number of variations on a theme and lots of models out there but in all cases we must recognise that they are simply useful aide memoirs.

Frankly, any fool could reel off the questions found in any of the good coaching books and gaze in a semi-interested way at the coachee as they answered them. This is not good coaching and I doubt whether the poor person being coached would rate such an experience as helpful in any way.

For my book *Coaching in a Week* [19] I replaced GROW with ARROW – with Aims instead of Goals, a Reflection stage after Reality and a Way Forword instead of Will – because I sensed many coaches were using GROW on auto-pilot and I wanted to be sure my readers would think about the model. I will further examine the coaching ARROW here.

Coaching questions must raise awareness, promote choice and build trust. Three key principles without which GROW, ARROW or any other model is useless. The easiest way to do this is to be clear about the *intent* behind the question. Is it to enhance awareness, responsibility or trust or is it to manipulate the coachee into providing the right (i.e. the coach's) answer?

Keeping the underlying principles in mind enables us to work safe in the knowledge that we're asking sound coaching questions without having to worry about some of the semantics of question formulation.

Nevertheless, we need somewhere to start and so in the rest of this chapter I'll outline the ARROW model and give you some example questions that have proven to be effective.

AIMS

Tell me what you want, what you really, really want.

Spice Girls

In my view a coaching session however lengthy or short or however formal or informal needs to start by establishing some aims. We'll need aims for the session itself and an overall aim for the coaching issue. I might have an overall aim of becoming computer literate, but a coaching session aim of exploring ways of working with long documents in a word processing package.

I like to use the word *aims*, but you can easily substitute it with goals, objectives, targets, standards or whatever other euphemism organisations use to essentially describe *where are we trying to get to with this?* I also like to use the word *aims* because it captures the variety of intentions that people might express in a coaching session, the three main types of aim being dreams, performance goals and processes. Table 4.1 provides an example relating to a Customer Relations department:

Dreams provide the *inspiration* to want to achieve something, a reason why if you like. However, because they are not wholly within our area of control, we can lose focus if we see them coming under threat. I'm unlikely to be able to focus on using the software if I'm getting uptight that someone else might be in line for the team leader promotion.

Table 4.1

	Department	Individual
Dream	• To be recognised as the best after sales service provider in our industry	• To be promoted to team leader
Performance Goal	• To respond to all customer contact within 24 hrs, 100% of the time	• To resolve each case in my workload within 7 days of receipt
Processes	• Policy • Procedures • Resourcing, etc.	• Use of case management software • Familiarity with policy and procedure, etc.

Performance goals therefore become useful in providing a *specification*. In other words we can define what success will be like. If my goal to close my cases in seven days is a stretching one and we assume that effective caseload management is a consideration for promotion to team leadership then this is a good thing for me to concentrate upon.

Ultimately though I must bring my focus to the here and now and deploy a number of processes to be the *mechanism* for my success. To follow the example through, it's only by effectively using the Customer Relations processes that I can achieve my performance goal and thus give myself a chance of achieving my dream.

Just returning to dreams for a moment, another reason I like to use this term is because as well as describing a lofty, long-term aim, it also conveys a sense of vagueness which some you coach may express. If someone were to say 'I want to be a better manager', we would have to recognise that this was a dream aim, and that we would need to develop it – through coaching – into a performance goal in order to increase the chances of success.

Performance goals need to be properly described but I'm not going to go into that here. Suffice to say that as well as goals which are SMART:

- Specific
- Measurable
- Achievable
- Relevant
- Time Bound

we need ones which are also:

- Positive
- Challenging
- Understandable

Your goal should be just out of reach, but not out of sight.

Denis Waitley & Reni L Witt

The connection with coaching principles is now clear. By raising my awareness of my aims, I can use my Reticular Activating System to notice the things that will lead me towards them. The coaching ARROW helps me to do this because in the initial *Aims* section I can gain clarity around the dreams and the performance goals and then by the time we get to *Way Forward* I will have a number of processes on which I can focus in order to bring them about.

EXAMPLE QUESTIONS

What do you want from this discussion?

I like to ask this – or something like it – first as it establishes the issue or situation that the coaching session is going to address.

What are you trying to achieve long term?

This question gets close to the dream type aim we discussed earlier and it's important that we enable coachees to raise their awareness of this as it is by remembering our long term aims that we can keep going when things get tough.

How much personal influence do you have over that?

I've lost count of the number of times that someone has said to me 'I want you to coach me on stopping my boss being such a monster' or words to that effect. Unfortunately we can't coach vicariously and the best I could do was to help those people deal with the effect that their boss's behaviour had on them. We can only coach people on aspects of situations which are within their field of control.

What first steps could you take?

Are they challenging but achievable?

How will you know if you've succeeded?

What timeframe is involved?

These questions enable us to move from a long-term, dream aim towards a shorter term performance goal.

REALITY

By coaching people through the Reality stage, we're encouraging people to build a deep understanding of their current situation. By doing this we're raising awareness and thus they'll begin to notice critical variables on which to usefully focus. Furthermore, because we have established a hierarchy of aims they'll tend to notice those variables that are in keeping with these aims. Since focus follows interest we want to have primed people to be interested in variables pursuant to their aims.

To coach people through this stage effectively however, it is necessary always to bear in mind that in truth there is no such thing as objective reality there is only subjective perception.

What does this say:

OPPORTUNITYISNOWHERE

Opportunity is nowhere or opportunity is now here? It entirely depends on one's perception. This gives us one or two areas we need to be careful about in coaching at the reality stage.

Let's say you're coaching someone and you've reached the Reality stage. Your coachee begins to tell you about the current situation as they see it and you inevitably begin to form your own view. Unless you're careful it will be very tempting to perhaps interrupt and say something like 'oh yes, I know exactly what you're going through, the same thing happened to me last month. See, what you need to do is . . .'. All that's happened here is we have taken responsibility back and slipped into telling mode. Besides which who's to say that you've made a correct interpretation? Even if your coachee is facing literally the same circumstances you did, they're them and you're you! You can't be inside their head and know exactly how it feels for them. True awareness raising means people have to come to their own con- clusions about what's going on, not to have it described for them.

I believe the Reality stage to be the most vital of the five in the ARROW model for it is here that there is most scope for awareness raising. If pushed for time I think it better to reschedule a further meeting than to deal with reality half-heartedly. In fact I have often found that raising awareness and bringing people's focus back to the here and now is often all that it takes to produce some performance improvement.

People often ask me 'but what if the coachee just can't see the problem?'. A coaching law is useful here:

8TH LAW OF COACHING

Curiosity is more useful than judgement

Suppose I have had complaints about Jim, a member of the Customer Services team who many customers find unhelpful and abrasive, but who sees himself as performing well. Here's how a non-coaching reality discussion might go:

Matt   So, how are things going in terms of complaints Jim?

Jim   Yeah great, no problems

Matt   Well that's clearly not the case Jim. Look I've been getting complaints about people finding you abrasive. It's just no good

Jim   Me abrasive? It's Jenny you want to be talking to, she's abrasiveness personified. I can't believe you've brought me in here to discuss this.

And so it would go on.
What about a coaching approach?

Matt   So, how are things going in terms of complaints Jim?

Jim   Yeah great, no problems

Matt   How do you know there are no problems?

Jim   Well, we don't get many complaints. I don't think so anyway

Matt   Actually that's interesting. How many complaints have we had this quarter?

Jim   To be honest, I've had a few, but that's really just customers being unreasonable isn't it?

Matt   Hard to say, what sorts of things have been said?

And from here Jim and I could go on to have a much more productive conversation because I am intent on raising his awareness, keeping him responsible for his actions and I'm doing this in an environment of trust.

EXAMPLE QUESTIONS

What's happening now?

A nice broad question, the answer to which will reveal the critical variables your coachee is noticing.

How much/How often is that happening?

The only way a coachee can answer this question is to think more deeply about the situation they're describing. In other words to become more aware.

How does this make you feel?

Who else is involved?

What happens to them?

Here we're encouraging the coachee to think broadly and to build up a complete picture of what's going on.

What have you tried so far?

What results did you get?

My experience suggests that these last two can be extremely powerful. I've often found that when people realise that the reason they've lived with a problem for a long time is because they've never taken any action, they can suddenly feel quite mobilised and the coaching session can stop.

I must stress again that these are only examples and that with practice you can expect to be able to think of many more of your own.

REFLECTION

So, we're clear about where we are going – aims – and we're clear about where we're starting from – Reality. But are we? I've done a lot of coaching as an internal coach and a lot of work more recently as an external provider. The biggest difference I have found is in the quality of trust that can be established. When I'm hired as an external coach the matter of trust needs to be thought about before the contract is signed and I've found the answers to my coaching questions to be very honest from the outset. When I was an internal coach however, I often had the feeling that I was getting only superficial answers to my questions; it was as if people were holding something back. In retrospect this was due to a lack of trust in both me and the process of coaching.

It is for this reason, that the coaching ARROW includes a Reflection stage, and it's a stage that will be particularly useful to those of you coaching alongside a line management responsibility for the same people. It may be that it's only towards the end of the reality section that our coachees begin to relax and realise that all that's going on here is an effort to be helpful and realise their potential or just solve a problem. But if people have been a little guarded in their answers up until this point there's a danger we might move forward from here with an underdeveloped understanding of the issue.

EXAMPLE QUESTIONS

How big is the gap between 'Aims' and 'Reality'?

This is about taking stock of how big or complex an issue we're facing. Coachees might conclude that they're close to their aims and just a little more work will get them there, this can be a great fillip for them. At other times they'll realise that they're a long way from where they're trying to get to. Well, that's okay it just means that we need to establish some further short term performance goals to act as mile stones along the way.

How realistic are your aims?

Following on from this it can be useful to revisit the aims in light of the answers to the reality questions. People may have an overly optimistic view of what can be achieved in a single coaching session or be creating lofty aims to paradoxically prove that coaching doesn't work.

How certain are you about the reality of the situation?

How could you find out more?

Our reality questions may have revealed that our coachee is working with very little information and is effectively working on intuition. Their intuition may be perfectly correct but is there any value in going back and checking up? Could our coachee benefit from contrasting their perception of reality with anyone else's?

What assumptions are you making?

There's an old cliché, when you ASSUME you make an ASS of U and ME. All very amusing but the point is that so much of what we believe to be 'true' and believe to be 'possible' is based on pure assumption.

I constantly find myself coaching people who'll say 'they'll never agree to that', 'It won't work', 'it's too expensive' and so on. I'm forever responding with 'how do you know that's the case?' in an effort to encourage people to challenge these negative assumptions.

We'll see in the next section on options that getting people to take their thinking beyond these assumptions can have a profound effect.

Have you been totally honest with yourself?

I would ask this question only rarely but have found it a powerful challenge if I sense I'm getting only superficial answers to my questions.

What's *really* going on?

This question appeals to people's intuitive sense and is a useful way of getting to the heart of the matter when the coaching conversation is perhaps losing direction.

When I've asked it, the usual response is a smile and a sheepish look followed by a description of the real coaching issue.

The Reflection stage is included at this point because it's logical to review things immediately having gained clarity around aims and reality. It also helps spell ARROW! Nevertheless, I would encourage you to reflect, summarise and revise throughout the coaching process. Reflection is a key component of learning, but not something that our frenetic working lives always accommodate. Also, if coaching through a particularly complex issue, it can be useful to stop the initial coaching session after the Reality stage and allow your coachee to reflect in their own way and in their own time. It's likely that the options and way forward questions you'll reconvene to discuss will be far more useful this way.

OPTIONS

The biggest challenge at the Options stage is to get people to think beyond the norm; to think outside the box as it is popularly termed. Gestalt psychologists refer to *Einstellung*, a tendency to limit our thinking by keeping it within existing boundaries.

An orthodox western education will not have taught you how to think, but how to absorb facts. It will also lead you to view things that need thinking about as 'problems' which must require 'solutions'. This creates an over reliance on logical, left-brain thinking which doesn't always serve us well when situations require creative, innovative thinking instead.

We have created a paradigm; this means literally a world view or a firmly established set of beliefs about how things are. As coaches we can do wonders by creating an environment in which people can break outside of their own paradigms and thus gain access to new ideas and insights.

EXAMPLE QUESTIONS

Remember that by the time we get to this stage we have probably created a clear set of aims and developed an understanding of the reality of the situation.

With this done we can now ask:

What could you do about all this?

At this stage anything goes, allow your coachee to voice any idea at all, no matter how wacky and avoid at all costs the temptation to judge an idea as workable or not. This just closes thinking down again. Your aim should be to generate a large *quantity* of ideas, worrying about the *quality* comes later.

What else could you try?

You might think that if your coachee had any more ideas they would have already told you about them in answer to your first question, but this is rarely the case. As we've seen, people tend to limit their thinking which means that in answering the first question people have probably told you about tried and tested options that have been around for ages. Asking the what else question begins the process of looking for new ideas.

What if you had more/less . . . ?

The people that you coach will be working within constraints, typically time, status or budget. These things cannot be ignored but can create barriers to thinking. In coaching it can be useful to free people from these constraints to see what happens.

I was once coaching someone who worked in a business advisory role. She was struggling to meet her targets which were to do with meeting the clients in her portfolio. One of the problems she had identified at the Reality stage was the amount of time she spent travelling between appointments. We had discussed some options, but these were pretty unimaginative like catching up on phone calls whilst in the car to save time and so on. I decided to ask 'What would you do if you had more money?'.

'Well, with more money,' she began, 'we could get the clients to come here and pay them a mileage allowance. That way I wouldn't be wasting time travelling from appointment to appointment and could probably get to see twice as many clients in a day as I do now. Actually we get paid mileage anyway so there's probably not much extra cost. I'm going to suggest this at the next team meeting!'.

Now, the idea may have proven to be impractical, but that's not the point. My question had thrown up new possibilities and other ideas could flow from that at the team meeting. At the very least my coachee was now upbeat and animated and had taken responsibility for solving the problem again. I could also ask 'What if you had more time?', 'What would you do if you were the boss?', or even 'what would you do if you had even less time?'. The purpose of these questions is not to pretend that such constraints don't exist, rather it is to create mobility of thought.

Whose advice could you seek?

What suggestions would they have?

Once again the idea here is to create a different viewpoint. It's surprising how often people say to me, 'my old boss would know what to do', or they'll cite their parents or a family friend who was always a wise old sage. I believe that if we ask these people the question in our imagination our own intuition will actually provide the answer. We often seem to seek advice when we know in advance what we're hoping or expecting that advice to be.

What would you do if you knew you couldn't fail?

This question is designed to challenge that most pervasive of all internal interferences; fear of failure. It is an example of an incisive question as detailed by Nancy Kline in her wonderful book *Time to Think* [11] which I can heartily recommend if you find these ideas intriguing. The point again is to free people from the limiting assumptions which constrain their thinking.

Would you like another suggestion?

When I introduce these questions on our training programmes, my participants often think this example has been put in to catch them out, 'surely that's just a tell in disguise' they'll say. You can see it that way of course, but it is not a tell because responsibility is kept with the coachee where it belongs. They can always say no thanks.

In most cases your coaches will be only too glad to have another option to the ones they've already generated and I would argue that it's wrong to withhold an idea if you think it could help. You do need to be cautious though because as a manager or leader your ideas come with an element of gravitas, it may also provide an opportunity for a coachee to claim it was all your fault if things don't work out. For these reasons I would recommend that you don't offer your own ideas until your coachees have thoroughly considered their own options.

Lastly, I'd just like to give you advance warning of a couple of pitfalls that are very common in coaching people through the Options stage. The first of these is *stopping at the first option*. It can be very tempting given the pressures of time to move on when a coherent idea has been expressed, but really that's just the start. It may be that the first option proves to be the one to take forward in the end, but take time to explore other options first. As we've seen thinking gets stuck and it can take a bit of an effort to help people take their thinking to different levels. Similarly *stopping at the* right *answer* is very common. This usually happens when the coachee expresses an idea that you as coach feel is the right one to pursue. The trick is to hold off on judging any options as right, wrong, good or bad, until all options have been properly considered.

WAY FORWARD

The primary purpose of coaching in any context is to bring about change and improvement, but there can be no change without action.

If, after a period of coaching, we have not left our client or coachee with a genuine desire to move forward; to take meaningful action then our intervention cannot be judged wholly successful.

But taking action is often easier said than done. Human beings are known for being overcome by inertia and procrastination, especially where fear of failure enters the equation.

The reason behind this is often that we want to stay in what is popularly known as our *comfort zone*. We are in our comfort zone when we know and understand what's happening to us, usually because it's happened many times before. This does not necessarily mean that our comfort zone includes only pleasant experiences, in fact often the reverse. We can often keep ourselves in destructive relationships and unhelpful situations simply because they're familiar and we know what to expect. It's the classic 'better the devil you know' mentality. However, whilst we remain in our comfort zone we are not exposed to new experiences and therefore do not grow and develop.

We can recognise the need therefore to move out of our comfort zone, but if we do this too far or too quickly, or without adequate support we might move into our 'panic zone' where everything feels so strange and uncomfortable that we feel over-whelmed by it all and rush to get back in our comfort zone as quickly as possible. The alternative to this is to turn to a coach who will guide us out of our comfort zone into our learning zone where we can get the benefit and learning from new experiences without the panic! The key aid in doing this is a carefully con-structed action plan.

Our job at this stage then is to encourage our coachee to pick a way forward that they can commit to and develop the required action plan. We need to figure out what action is required, how it is to be carried out, who needs to be involved and so on. A sys-tematic approach to finish the session will help to ensure that those we coach can commit to a definite course of action and move in a controlled way outside of their comfort zones and benefit from new experiences.

EXAMPLE QUESTIONS

So, what *exactly* are you going to do?

When *exactly* are you going to do it?

Here you must watch for people wriggling. We humans get very stuck with the status quo and don't like change even when we can see the benefits. You may find that your coachees have talked a great fight in your session up to this point and then dilute their ideas with expressions like 'We'll see', 'After lunch/tomorrow/this busy period/the holiday season'. As coaches we need to work hard to encourage people to take action otherwise we end up with vague wish lists.

Who needs to know?

How and when will you tell them?

What resources do you need?

How will you get them?

These questions – and you'll doubtless be able to think of many others – all serve to put detail around the plan of action. It's about making sure that our coachees leave the session utterly clear about what to do next to make things happen.

Will this take you towards your aims?

Now we can come to tying up the loose ends and this question checks that your coachee is still moving towards the stated aims. If you discover that they're not it doesn't necessarily mean that the way forward is inappropriate, it could equally mean that the aims were ill conceived in the first place and that this has only come to light because of the quality of awareness rising throughout the coaching session.

What do you need me to do?

A great coaching question which keeps responsibility for learning with the coachee and positions the coach as a source of help.

What is your commitment to this course of action on a scale of 1–10?

This final question is designed to establish the likelihood that, outside of the coaching session, your coachee will follow through. In my experience a 7 or upwards suggests they will, whilst a 6 or less indicates they won't. But this does not mean that the coaching session has failed or even been unhelpful. It simply means that there's still something holding them back. It's likely to be one of three things:

Lacking clarity. It might be that the solution seems too simple to be true or challenges our coachee to reconsider some beliefs, e.g. 'I think I know what to do. I guess if I just shut up when I've asked for the business and wait for the customer to speak, I'll stand a better chance of getting the sale. But what if they don't say anything? Surely it's my job to take the lead'.

Lacking conviction. Alternatively our coachee may be utterly clear about what needs to be done but doesn't believe it will work, e.g. 'The solution is obvious, we need to put an appraisal system in place so that we can identify the high and low performers. But what's the point? We've tried that before and it only lasted about three months. Besides the Union will probably object'.

Lacking courage. Clear about what needs to be done and convinced it will work, our coachee may still lack commitment if they don't feel brave enough to put their plan into action, e.g. 'I realise that in order to tackle my time management problems, I need to tell my boss that he's dumping too much on me. But he's a big imposing man that frightens everybody! I can't imagine raising this with him'.

Asking 'what would have to happen to make it a 10?' is a very effective way of finding out where the commitment is falling down. In essence you're uncovering a coaching issue within a coaching issue. You could schedule another session to tackle these and set some aims around clarity, conviction or courage and then return to the original issue.

SUMMARY

In this chapter we've seen how crucial the ability to ask well constructed coaching questions is to your success. However, it is very
dangerous to think that asking questions is really all there is to
coaching. All of the other things you'll read and learn about in
this book are equally valid components of doing the job effectively.
Also, please don't think that everything has to be a question. It
can be infuriating for a coaching session to turn into an endless
series of questions. A coaching session is not an interrogation.

Sometimes, where there are high levels of trust between coach
and coachee, awareness raising instructions as opposed to questions
can work really well, e.g. 'Tell me the point when you feel completely calm', 'Come back to me when you've identified when the
nervousness starts', 'Recall the circumstances in which you felt
most assertive last week'.

You'll have noticed that in the examples given and in the suggestions for constructing questions that there is no mention of
asking 'Why'. This is because Why questions can tend to make
people want to justify their actions and look for answers in an
analytical way rather than in an open, non defensive way. It's also
worth watching out for any tendency to want to use leading questions. Often where I as a coach have particularly strong views on
how my coachee should proceed I find my questions turning into
'Don't you think you ought to . . .' and 'Wouldn't it be better
if . . .'. These are just commands in disguise and serve only to
reclaim responsibility from the coachee.

The ARROW model provides a great way of organising the
questions in a coaching session but you'll need to learn to use it
flexibly. Our minds work in unique ways and thoughts travel in
all sorts of unexpected directions. Just because you ask a reality
question does not mean your coachee won't start generating
options. If people's thinking is racing ahead that's okay provided
each element of the model has been adequately covered, but you

can do this in any order. In fact you should feel encouraged if this happens as it is a sure sign that the trust is there and people are focused on their thinking not your coaching.

You'll probably follow the example questions here quite closely to begin with, but soon find yourself working at the level of the headings and devising your own questions. In time you'll be thinking about raising awareness, generating responsibility and building trust and the questions will flow quite naturally.

CHAPTER 5

THE MODEL IN PRACTICE

COACHING V OTHER INTERVENTIONS

You now know a great deal about coaching and are hopefully comparing and contrasting it with other learning methods you know about. This reflection is crucial to becoming an effective coach as it enables you to coach with integrity in a way that suits you, rather than only ever following a formulaic approach.

Let's see if we can deepen that insight by looking in some detail at the similarities and differences between coaching and other ways of developing people at work.

Coaching v training

To be an accomplished trainer you'll need to know about learning styles, differing speeds of learning, engaging the learner by asking questions and so on. The good news is that as a coach you will definitely need to draw on any skills you have in these areas.

The bad news is that a lot of other things you might do as a trainer will be counter productive as a coach. The most obvious of these being telling and instructing. In training – particularly technical training – these are vital skills and we use them to pass on information and check that we have been understood.

In coaching we're more concerned with helping learners find their own way forward and are probably best advised to avoid telling and instructing as far as possible. This is because when we tell or instruct we assume responsibility for making the learning happen, we deny our learners the opportunity to think for themselves and we end up simply passing on our recipe which is unlikely to be quite as appropriate for our learner anyway.

Coaching v mentoring

We're in danger of hair splitting here but in terms of approach, there is little to distinguish coaching from mentoring as both are concerned with realising potential. Nevertheless, there are some differences in context which might be important points of clarification for work-based mentors or coaches and those whom they help.

The word mentor comes from Homer's epic poem *The Odyssey*. Before going to fight in the Trojan wars, Ulysses entrusted the care of his household and of his son, Telemachus to his trusted friend Mentor. Most mentoring schemes at work have a similar intent in that a mentor is usually someone who has 'been there, done that' and, as a senior member of staff, is assigned a mentee or protégé to take under their wing. Mentoring schemes vary with their degrees of formality but are often concerned with pointing out the unwritten rules and providing mentees with a confidential sounding board. A coaching approach within this setting ought to provide great results.

Coaching v counseling

In academic terms the differences are again slight, but in practical terms the perception of the differences can be great and it can be important to clarify these with staff before launching a coaching programme. There will be those who see counseling as being for the chinless, the weak-willed or the ill. They may see coaching in the same light and thus be reluctant to participate openly in coaching sessions. Of course counseling is none of those things and neither is coaching but perception is reality as we've seen and it will be important to talk these things through.

You may also need to bear counseling in mind if any coaching session you undertake has a highly emotional content. We cannot legislate for what may happen when we start to ask people questions and their answers may take us to places that we, as coaches, find uncomfortable. The best advice would be to find out about your organisation's welfare policy in advance if you feel there could be deeper issues behind a work performance problem. We must know our limitations as coaches and pass people on to other forms of help if and when appropriate. Having said all that it is rare in my experience for coaching on performance issues to take such a dramatic turn but you never know.

Are any of these distinctions important? Not really, not once you're up and running and coaching regularly. You'll be concerned with raising awareness, generating responsibility and building trust and less worried about what particular approach you may be using. In learning about coaching however, I believe it is vital to keep the differences in mind as there is potential for mentoring and training in particular to turn into a telling session.

THE INNER GAME OF COACHING

In looking at the qualities of an effective coach we can quickly identify key skills and knowledge in the areas of questioning technique, listening skills, monitoring body language and so on. These things represent the 'outer game' of coaching, but what about the inner game. What goes on in the head of the novice and not so novice coach as they attempt to deploy their coaching skills to best effect?

The principle of Potential − Interference = High Performance applies to coaching as much as any other endeavour. There are several sources of both external and internal interference that occur frequently in those coaching in a work environment. In my experience the most common sources of external interference are as follows:

Pressure of other work

Unless you are a dedicated coach and that is all you do, you are likely to have to organise your coaching around a host of other responsibilities. It is inevitable that the time you have allocated towards coaching could come under pressure from deadlines, crises, staff shortages or any other short-term emergencies which bedevil all working lives. One option is to cancel the coaching and attend to the emergency, another is to ignore the emergency and honour the coaching commitment. Neither is wholly satisfactory but the point is to recognise that the quality of your coaching will diminish in direct proportion to the time you spend worrying about trying to do two things at once. A cancelled coaching session is better than a hopeless coaching session provided the coachee is given a reasoned explanation.

Existing relationship

It can be difficult to be coach and manager to the same group of people. We may sometimes have to be the artful coach and the arch disciplinarian at the same time. The key seems to be in establishing a relationship of trust and treating people with respect whatever the nature of the conversation.

Poor environment

I believe that you can do what I call coffee machine coaching, in the middle of a busy office, shop or factory floor and get a good result. However, this tends only to be the case where the issue is straightforward and the coaching largely concerned with restoring focus. Most other times you'll be better off with a quiet, private space where people can get comfortable thinking and talking and, just as importantly, you can tell that they are. Similarly, I have come across these sources of internal interference many times:

I have to get it 'right'

Let's be honest, the danger of a book like this is to overemphasise the use of models and structures to the point that I imply that there is only one right way to coach. I apologise if that's how you're feeling right now as you read this, it was never my intent. Coaching is not a system, a framework, a methodology or a technique. It is an approach to the development of people founded on a positive belief in their potential and executed by raising awareness, generating responsibility and building trust. As such there are any number of models and questioning sequences that are useful. In the same way, you'll draw upon your own unique background, prior knowledge and previous training to influence your coaching style. The only 'right' way to coach is the one that suits you and that serves the needs of your coachee. It's hard to be focused on the needs of your coachee when you're trying to stick to a prescriptive approach and you're just putting yourself under unnecessary stress.

I have to solve a problem

When they start out a lot of managers who coach become disappointed if a coaching session does not result in a tidily resolved problem. Worse still is the expectation that every coaching session should produce some kind of epiphany for the coachee and that if it wasn't life changing, it wasn't successful. Here we must bear in mind the second key principle of Responsibility. In the same way that you can lead a horse to water but not make it drink you can coach a member of your team flawlessly but not compel them to take action. That is their choice. Time is also a factor. Whilst there may not be a solution reached at the end of a coaching session your awareness raising work is likely to have created some thought patterns and insights that produce results later on. Good, solid coaching will always bring some benefits.

I have to be credible

Yes you do, but your credibility will come from being an effective coach. The temptation is only to want to coach those people who work in your own technical arena or who report in to you, but this misses the point. There is no reason why a nurse couldn't coach a surgeon or a cleaner coach an airline pilot. Rather than worry about not being credible, why not focus on asking the best coaching questions you can? Notice what happens when you concentrate on delivering great coaching rather than worrying about whether you appear credible.

Having said all that, if coaching is poorly understood there may be a perception that coaches have to be expert. If this is the case I think it wiser to have some discussions in teams about what coaching does and doesn't involve rather than restrict the numbers of people who may coach.

I have to do lots of coaching

This is a real danger in organisations that have defined specific coaching roles. In order to justify their existence these people go on the hunt for people to coach or worse still insist that line managers 'send' people to them for coaching. Coaching works best when made available to the right people, at the right time and for the right reasons. Coaching for coaching's sake is likely to be counter productive and just create resentment. I feel so strongly about this that I offer it as a coaching law:

9TH LAW OF COACHING

Coaching should be driven by demand, not supply

You already know the way to lessen the effect of all of these interferences. Find a good coach who will raise your awareness of the barriers and the qualities you would rather have in their place; who will encourage you to take responsibility for improving your coaching and who will do all of this in an atmosphere of trust.

This will enable you to focus on the right things and your coaching skills will improve as a result.

COMMON MISTAKES

I want to take some time now to outline some of the common mistakes that work-based coaches often make, particularly in the early days.

Perhaps the most common is to lose sight of the objectives of the coaching session and allow it to turn into an overly informal chat or a moaning session. Now don't get me wrong, each of these things can be cathartic and they have their time and place, but it's not coaching. We none of us have the luxury of too much time and coaching sessions need to be controlled and focused and to run within an allocated time slot. I don't recommend open-ended coaching sessions; they create complacency. There's clearly a need for flexibility though so if you've told a coachee you can give them an hour, I'd block out an hour and a half in the diary.

It is also quite common in the beginning to find coaching questions getting skewed and turned into a 'tell' in disguise. A question beginning 'Don't you think you ought to . . .', or 'wouldn't it be better if . . .' are simply prefixes to your own ideas and create the kind of SMOG we looked at earlier. Remember you can always ask 'would you like another suggestion?'.

However, it is just as wrong to assume that as coaches we must always ask questions. There can be nothing more infuriating for people than to constantly face a barrage of questions. If some one asks you what the team target is, tell them. Don't ask them what they think it is. This is especially important when people are working under stress, individually or collectively. If people are reaching out for some help because they're in trouble we should help if we can. It can appear terribly smug to just continually ask questions until they come up with the answer you're thinking of. Always remember that when people are drowning they'll want a rubber ring before a swimming lesson.

It isn't wrong to tell and knowing about coaching doesn't mean that you won't ever tell, instruct or demonstrate again. What it does mean is that you'll be using the right communication approach for the right reasons. In time you may even begin to develop awareness raising, coaching style instructions such as 'Tell me about the quality you'd most like to have available to you in your next client interview' or 'Make a note of each time today that interest is greater than boredom'.

Finally let me underline that at the start of a coaching session the issue is not the aim. Let me explain. Say someone presents the issue of 'I want to find my work interesting again'. This is simply the issue or the dream level aim and we know that we have to develop a performance goal around that such as 'By the end of next month, I want to have found three new aspects to my work that I find interesting'. We can then identify some options or processes and away we go. Whilst if we leave it at just 'I want to find my work interesting again', we're unlikely to make any real progress.

COACHING QUALITIES

Once again drawing on the collective wisdom of my training programme participants, let me present this list of coaching qualities as being typical:

Effective listener, good communicator, well organised, able to ask probing questions, patient, honest, empathetic, approachable, enthusiastic, likeable, respected, trusting and trustworthy, good sense of humour, believer in people, positive, tactful, discreet, sensitive

It's quite a list and at first glance might suggest a job of super-human proportions, but let's consider the listed items in more detail. If instead of listing 'the qualities of an effective coach' we produced a list of the 'qualities of an effective HR Manager, Chief Executive, Foreman, Supervisor, Team Leader or any job which requires results from others, would anything fall away? It's likely that we'd produce a bigger list with lots of technical elements but the relationship qualities are likely to be almost identical to the coaching ones with which we began.

I draw two conclusions from this. Firstly, as I mentioned earlier, your team already view you as their coach. They want you to have all of these qualities and bring them to bear in your leadership role. Secondly – and this I hope is good news – assuming that you're performing adequately in your management role, you have all the qualities you need to be an effective coach at work. I suggest that all that's been missing is a little technical detail around exactly what coaching is and isn't and how to frame coaching questions, etc and you've got more than enough information in this book to satisfy that requirement.

Were you wanting to pursue a career as a Life or Executive Coach you'd need a lot more training but you have what you need to coach your teams to high levels of performance and you always did have it.

Notice that aside from the first two or three items on the list, most of the qualities are to do with personality or attitude rather than technical skill. We saw in the last section that an over concern with coaching correctly simply creates interference. The list of coaching qualities reinforces this view as it shows that our coachees are probably more concerned with *how we are* than *what we do*.

Notice also that there is no place on the list for technical expertise or a background in the underlying problem. Coaches need expertise in coaching, technical expertise is not necessary. Of course, in a work situation you are likely to have at least some familiarity with the work of the people you coach but don't get hung up on it. In fact there's a danger that such familiarity creates a temptation to tell.

Certainly the list presented here is far from exhaustive and I'm sure you could add other qualities of your own. It is interesting to consider by whom would you most like to be coached and why? When I ask this question people often tell me that it would be a teacher, a parent or a manager from their past. They'll tell me that such people believed in them no matter what, were encouraging and supportive and always encouraged them to be their best. These are the 'golden seeds' that Handy refers to in *The New Alchemists* [6].

A good exercise is to refer to the list of qualities – this one, or your own version and to begin to prioritise the items perhaps in terms of your own development areas. You could award yourself marks out of ten and decide whether to concentrate on developing weak areas or reinforcing strengths. You may want to consider some formal skills training and we'll look at this later alongside coach supervision – an increasingly popular development model and a common one in the 'healing professions'. For now let me just emphasise that coaching is a skill that can be developed greatly from being coached. As we've seen you'll be affected by interference and concerned with performance, learning and enjoyment the same as any other performer so why not have someone coach you in these areas of your coaching. Establish an aim, check the reality and . . . you know the rest. Perhaps you could lend a colleague this book and begin to develop the skills together, coaching each other as you go.

LISTENING

Let's pick up on one area of skill that is vitally important, and that is listening. All helping interventions are based on effective listening. Marriage guidance counselors listen, doctors listen, lawyers listen (sometimes) car mechanics listen and even salespeople – if they want to win business – listen to the customer's needs. By the same token, the quality of your coaching interaction will hinge in many ways on your ability to be a good listener. It's not the only skill you'll use, but it is the most important. It warrants a coaching law:

10TH LAW OF COACHING

As a coach you'll need to listen, ask questions and think, but you cannot do all three effectively at the same time.

Our coachees will know instinctively if we're listening effectively or not. We are all highly sensitive to this. The positive side is that as we tune in and give our coachees our energy and concentration the quality of their answers and thoughts will improve dramatically.

Effective listening serves many purposes throughout a coaching exchange. First and foremost, it encourages the coachee to open up. Many managers are at great pains to get the physical setting right for a coaching session, arranging a private, quiet room and so on, and then neglect the emotional setting. They fiddle with papers, check their watch and make notes to the detriment of both their own listening and their coachee's thinking. Knowing that we're truly being listened to is a liberating experience that can be hard to appreciate until one has experienced it and sadly it is uncommon at work.

Secondly, an ability to listen well enables us to reflect back to the coachee both the content and the mood of their answers to our coaching questions, for example 'so you're saying that you don't believe your boss will support this', or 'You're telling me you're totally committed but that doesn't come across in your tone'. Remember always that the purpose of such reflection is not to catch them out, but to encourage higher awareness. If we don't listen well we won't know the right comment or question to offer next. Similarly, this level of listening will enable us to pick up on moods and feelings and help you both identify the source. You'll also pick up any inconsistencies and invite your coachee to consider why that might be.

From the coach's point of view – given that coaching is an exercise in communication – many of the critical variables that you'll want to focus on to perform well will be in the communication of your coachee, Words, pitch, tone, and speed are all useful things for coaches to notice and will enable you to encourage a deeper focus in your coachee.

Let's now consider some ways of making the listening task easier. We must firstly give our coachees our full attention. This means putting aside thoughts and feelings that are not relevant so you can concentrate on the coachee. We need to maintain eye contact to encourage them to express themselves. All the usual common sense advice applies: nod your head, make encouraging noises, and use the coachee's words to demonstrate that you are listening. Be aware of both your own and the coachee's body language. Be particularly aware of seeming impatient if you disagree with what is being said. Concentrate on what is being said, not on what you want to say next or the next coaching question to ask. You can always take a moment when they have finished speaking to consider your next response.

The challenge is to make a conscious effort to do these things; there is nothing inherently difficult in any of these ideas. Poor listening is usually the result of having developed unhelpful habits. Interrupting, for example, is a habit that is often developed by managers who have to constantly fight to make themselves heard during meetings. Nothing taints responsibility and trust quite like interrupting but a great coaching question to ask yourself next time you're aware of doing it is 'What I am assuming that makes me interrupt?'.

It is similarly common to want to put words into the other person's mouth. There is a temptation during a coaching conversation to jump ahead when listening, assuming we know what is about to be said. But the chances that they were going to use the words we have put into their mouths are slight. If we are wrong, we have once again interrupted the coachee's thoughts and taken responsibility back. We've probably all met people we believe have 'selective hearing' and we're all guilty sometimes of hearing only what we think is important. It's worth noting as well that we speak at an average speed of 125 words per minute, yet think at about 500, so we are often jumping ahead of the coachee and filling the gaps with irrelevant, distracting thoughts.

Can you be certain that you appear interested at all times? We judge speakers and the words we are hearing according to our own personal interests, beliefs and attitudes. We tend to 'tune in' to subjects that interest us and switch off to those we find boring. Next time you are listening to a coachee talking about a subject you find uninteresting, restore your focus by wondering how long can I listen before my mind wanders?

Of course listening is not easy and work provides an environment with a host of distractions. This could be by a noise like the wailing of a police siren or a sight like someone passing the door behind the coachee, so you may find you miss a whole section of what someone is saying by the time you bring your attention back. You can also be distracted by your reactions to the coachee. You could be too busy judging the coachee rather than what they are actually saying, worrying instead about their accent, their mannerisms, their gestures or their clothes.

At the same time it is not advisable to try to fake effective listening by, for example, maintaining fixed eye contact while obviously thinking of other things, or showing false enthusiasm by asking too many questions, interrupting or being to eager to respond. Be ready to admit to a listening failure, whether in hearing or understanding. As we've said, people do know when you've stopped listening to them and it is better to just admit that you lost concentration and ask them to repeat themselves than plough on regardless. Finally, remember that as a manager who coaches it will be challenging for you to remain detached from the situations your coachees describe in the same way an external coach could. Hearing something with which we disagree makes it is all too easy to switch off or get angry. When we start to make judgements or plan our counter-attack we are likely to have stopped listening.

RUNNING A COACHING SESSION

Running a coaching session is an exercise in applying common sense and as we've said before, provided your intention is to raise awareness, generate responsibility and build trust you cannot go far wrong. Nevertheless, we'll take time here to consider some of the key things to get right, before, during and after a session.

Before the session

Much will depend on whether the coaching is pre-arranged or spontaneous, but in any event it is wise to consider how the coaching is initiated. Ideally the coaching will have been arranged in response to a request from the coachee as this is most in keeping with the key principle of Responsibility. Of course sometimes you'll need to initiate the session and this is okay as long as you realise you may need to work harder on establishing the necessary levels of trust.

Planned session or not, you'll want to agree timings and objectives for the session and think about the location. In my view coachees are best placed to decide on whether they would prefer a formal, private setting or something a little less structured. Privacy is vital, but the coffee area can be just as good as a meeting room with two chairs facing one another.

If coaching is a new initiative in your organisation you may also want to take time at the outset to establish what coaching is and why you're introducing it at this time. External coaches refer to this phase as contracting, i.e. establishing roles and expectations and it is a useful approach to follow.

During the session

Most of this you know already, but for sake of clarity: You're going to be asking questions to establish aims, consider the current reality, reflect and adjust, generate options and commit to a way forward. In other words you'll be using the coaching ARROW, albeit flexibly. Your coaching questions will raise awareness, generate responsibility and build trust and thus create a mental state we might call focused. When your coachees are focused they will be working free of interference and with a sense of performance, learning and enjoyment in balance.

Above and beyond this you'll probably want to record any agreed actions and confirm the next steps before bringing the session to a close.

After the session

The great advantage that you have over an external coach is the ability to easily monitor and follow-up. It can be so useful for a coachee to have ongoing contact with you as they put their plans into action particularly if they're trying to break old habits. Never forget to celebrate success no matter how seemingly small the achievement.

Follow up sessions provide the ideal opportunity to reflect on progress so far, perhaps revising some goals and other aims and putting new milestones in place. It is also a chance to encourage your coachees to pay great attention to their current reality; raising awareness and finding new variables on which to focus.

In time you'll find that your coachees accept more and more responsibility and come to a coaching session having thought through most of the ARROW model in advance. The nature of such a session turns into one of seeking your endorsement for the action points they want to progress.

SUMMARY

This chapter has been about the real-life application of the theories and concepts covered previously.

We've seen how similar coaching is to other helping interventions such as counseling or mentoring. The contexts and situations when each is applied probably differ, but the skills and behaviours required are almost identical. Good coaches tend to make good counselors or mentors and vice versa. Conversely we saw that coaching is very different to teaching or instructing. These are tutor centred, coaching is learner centred. Coaching is about helping people to learn rather than teaching them things.

Looking at the inner game of coaching we saw that coaches are no more immune from interference than performers in any other sphere. The good news is that coaching responds to coaching and if you get coached as well as give coaching you'll find it easier to focus on the right things. A further benefit is to deeply reinforce the value of coaching by being seen to practice what you preach.

The common mistakes that occur when you're new to coaching seem linked to the inexorable pull of tell conditioning. You're trying to replace possibly years of conditioning to the tell style with a new approach that probably seems counter intuitive. In fact nothing could be more intuitively sensible than coaching people towards their best or we'd all still be tying our children's shoe laces for them. There is little in this book that you didn't already know at some level and the challenge of coaching is not in learning to do new things, it is in stopping doing old things.

We looked at coaching qualities and saw that from the coachee's perspective it is personal qualities such as integrity and a positive approach that count for more than technical skills. At the time of writing there is tremendous pressure for anyone who coaches in any setting to be suitably 'qualified'. There is nothing inherently wrong with this unless we ever start believing that a qualification can replace the personal qualities. The key skill is undoubtedly listening and this is an area that most of us can develop. Stephen Covey, author of the well-known self help guide *The Seven Habits of Highly Successful People* [3] suggests 'Seek first to understand, then to be understood' Imagine the effect on our coachees' thinking when they realise this is what we're genuinely trying to do.

Taking these skills and ideas into a coaching session means a piece of communication that is almost guaranteed to prove fruitful. A little structure can help to reinforce the value. Before the session starts in earnest we need to make sure that both parties are clear about what will happen and about the overall aims and intentions of the coaching approach. We need then to use the ARROW flexibly, remembering that awareness, responsibility and trust are far more important than just reeling off the questions. If you're working with the same people whom you coach, turn this to your advantage by making the effort to follow up and find out what they've achieved and learned.

This first part of the book has been designed to equip you with the tools you'll need to coach at work. We've covered a range of ideas from the highly theoretical to the downright practical. I want you to use these in any blend that suits you.

There's no substitute for practice and no shortage of willing coachees I expect, so you might want to test your general skills before returning to the next part which looks at coaching in very specific circumstances.

PART 2

HOW TO APPLY COACHING

INTRODUCTION

In this part, I want to examine the situations in which I have most frequently been asked to provide coaching support and which I'm pretty sure will be the situations in which you'll be asked to help also. The areas are:

- Sales
- Presentations
- Personal Organisation
- Performance Review
- Career Development

In each section we'll consider how the Peak coaching model typically works in those settings and look at sources of interference, critical variables on which to focus and so on. I'll also include other models and ideas and suggestions you can use to help your coachees if they get stuck. You'll understand by now that in no way do I want you to just tell them these tips and ideas, rather the idea is to build up your own background of what it means to perform in these areas so that you can formulate great coaching questions, evaluate options and discover appropriate points of focus.

There will be little detail around the mechanics of these activities as there are literally hundreds of books and other resources to cover these areas. Equally – assuming my clients are typical – organisations are experiencing diminishing returns from orthodox approaches to developing skills in the area of sales, performance review, and so on.

This is not to say that such mechanics aren't important, it's just that experience suggests it is not mastery of external matters that distinguishes the high performer from the ordinary performer. Instead, it is how well people are able to deal with the mental obstacles inherent in these tasks that will determine their success. As coaches we can play a huge part in bringing this about.

CHAPTER 6

SALES

INTRODUCTION

I believe that sales are the life blood of any business. No matter how wonderful the product or service, no matter how sophisticated the policies and processes, a business is doomed if it cannot win new work. Even in the public and not for profit sectors there is an element of sales or selling. Charity fundraisers have to persuade their local contacts to choose their charity. Government agencies pitch for funding and to win assignments. This is all selling.

Selling covers a multitude of activities. For some it is rooted in the image of the door to door salesman with a briefcase full of vacuum cleaner accessories. Others take a much wider view and include activities concerned with public relations, brand awareness, exhibitions and the things more commonly thought of as marketing than sales. For the purposes of this chapter, however, I'll use the term sales to describe all of this. Whether you're coaching front

line sales people or middle office marketers you'll find ideas here
to help you to help them fulfil their potential.

I referred in the Preface to my experience of introducing sales
to the stuffy old world of high street banking in the early 1990s.
Did everyone want to go from being a bank clerk to a salesperson?
Definitely not. Did everyone have the potential to do so assuming
the desire was there? Without a doubt. Selling is a world full of
myths and obfuscation perhaps the most common of which is the
limiting belief that in order to be a successful salesperson one must
have 'the gift of the gab'. The primitive Celtic word for mouth
was Gab; the expression is used to describe those who talk a lot.
Anyone who knows anything about sales, however, will tell you
that it's much more important to listen than to speak and consequently even the most introverted soul can make a great salesperson should they wish to.

Sales is a fascinating arena in which to examine coaching. It
is very easy to measure results in a sales environment: either sales
and leads increase or they don't. It's one area of work that is relatively straightforward to quantify.

The work of the sales professional, on the other hand, is a
complex thing. It can be pressurised, lonely and exhausting. There
are deadlines and targets which no sooner are they accomplished
than they're replaced with fresh and more challenging versions.
There is the law of averages to contend with that says however
effective your approach you'll inevitably encounter a lot of rejection. This requires a strength of character and a tolerance for the
word No, that does not feature in any other sphere of work that
I've experienced.

INTERFERENCE

Our positive belief in the potential of people has us working on
the assumption that the salespeople you coach have the capacity to

be a high performer if we train and coach them properly. We'll assume also, for our purposes here, that the people concerned have had some sales training and are performing to some extent already. Let's firstly examine the typical sources of interference that most salespeople experience to a greater or lesser degree and at some point or other.

External

Lack of product knowledge

As we'll come to see a detailed knowledge of one's product or service has no direct correlation with sales success, but a lack of it doesn't help. Good salespeople know their stuff but use this knowledge wisely. This can be taken to mean by answering customers' specific questions rather than bombarding them with detailed technical knowledge upon their first enquiry. Equally a lack of product knowledge is likely to lead to the internal interference of lack of self-confidence which in turn will lead to a reluctance to make the sales call or approach the prospective customer. Coaching can reveal any worries in this area and then you and your coachee can work out the best way of filling the knowledge gap.

Poor systems

Again we are talking about the fundamentals but many a great salesperson has been thwarted by inadequate systems. We need a solid database of existing customers and prospects that is regularly cleansed. This means updated with current contact details and purged of those contacts who have told us they no longer wish to be contacted. It can be ego bruising for even the most robust salesperson to have too many calls or approaches go sour because they're contacting the wrong people. Coaching can allow the salesperson to become aware of the impact of poorly maintained systems and processes and encourage them to take responsibility for making improvements.

Poor sales management

There could be a systems element to this regarding a lack of information around targets and performance to date, but I'm thinking more about the human side. Good salespeople don't want to be managed, they want to be supported, new salespeople need time and space to develop their confidence. All too often the sales manager was appointed because they were previously the best performing member of the sales team, but the skills of sales and sales management are quite different and imploring the team to 'do what I used to do' is a bit of a blunt instrument.

Poorly articulated targets

Sales targets that are too high are demoralising and targets that are too low are patronising. How do we get the balance right? I think by involving the sales team in a coaching session around this. What were the targets last year and how did we do? Where did we achieve our best successes? What was the most effective campaign and so on? The team can then begin to develop its own targets for the coming year which you can compare with the ones that have come from on high. If they're different at least you can discuss with the team the business drivers behind them and thus get some involvement and responsibility. Also, you might be delighted to find that the team's own targets exceed the ones they've been set.

Internal

Sales is about winning

Competition is often used as a motivator in sales and, in fairness, good salespeople are often highly competitive individuals, but there is a problem. Using competition as a measure of success means we are always judging performance in *relative* terms, i.e. have *we* done better than *them*? We might be better off judging our success in *absolute* terms, i.e. what is the very best that we could ever do? I have also discovered that a will to win can so easily turn into a fear of failure particularly in a team situation. Use competition and winning for motivation but not as a source of focus.

You need a certain personality

This is a limiting belief that does no one any good, but it is regularly reinforced. Good salespeople are born not made, you have to have the gift of the gab, etc. sadly become self-fulfilling prophecies when things aren't going well. I think that good selling is merely a transfer of enthusiasm from seller to buyer and a belief in one's product or service coupled with a zest for talking about it will outweigh any innate abilities one may or may not have.

You have to close the deal

Or in other words a sale is only a sale when the customer hands over the money. But, hang on, there's also brand awareness, customer service, reputation management and a host of other useful business outcomes that can come from any kind of sales conversation, to say nothing of the learning that can come from an unsuccessful sales pitch if we're focused on it. Of course we need to hit targets and get results but the only way we can do this is by focusing on the customer's needs. An obsession with closing creates a sort of desperation which I for one can spot a mile away and I'm sure I'm not untypical.

PLE IN SALES

As we know, these sorts of interferences will inevitably be around and the task of the coach is not so much to remove them as to help the coachee find something more useful on which to focus. Let's return to the PLE triangle. Sales is the lifeblood of any business as it creates revenue. Public sector and even not-for profit organisations will have a similar need for money in and so will have a sales like function in some way, shape or form. This creates pressure as everyone else is relying on sales and it underpins the business or service plan. No surprise then that Performance is stressed in sales almost to the exclusion of Learning and Enjoyment. Some sales departments and teams are characterised by a fairly macho environment where learning and enjoyment would be seen as weak and a sign of not working hard enough. But would you rather have your sales teams hitting targets almost effortlessly with smiling faces or by working all hours and hating every minute of it? Would you rather have your salespeople come to you saying they've realised why last month's figures were poor or trying to change the figures to disguise that fact?

CRITICAL VARIABLES

Let's consider the critical variables that will be apparent in most selling situations. You can expect coachees to mention these in some way when talking at the reality stage and focusing on them will help reduce interference and promote learning and enjoyment.

Outer variables

Rapport

In simple terms, rapport means getting on the customer's wavelength. It's a truism in sales that people buy people first but this will only happen when the customer likes and respects the salesperson. If, as a coach, you asked a salesperson 'How would you rate the quality of rapport in your next conversations?' what are they going to be focusing on to answer you?

Number and type of objections

Objections should be welcomed as it is the customer's way of telling us where our sales approach is going wrong. Rather than focusing on the fact that an objection means we might miss a sale, let's pay attention to the objections. Are they real or excuses? When do they tend to happen? How many would be typical? etc.

Buying signals

Lots of salespeople oversell, usually because of a need to display product knowledge. The customer has signalled their intent to make a purchase but the salesperson must finish their list of features and fails to spot the buying signal. Unless the features are relevant to the customer's need they'll switch off and the sale will be lost.

At the morning sales briefing why not suggest that everyone focus on spotting the earliest possible buying signal and see what happens?

Inner variables

Confidence

We all have good days and bad. We'll have days when nine out of ten customers will buy and days when the ratio will be the opposite. This can all have a big impact on confidence. What we need though is to become highly aware of the variable of confidence. Let's learn its subtleties, let's become sensitised to its nuances so that we can get at more of it when needs be. The only way to do this is to focus on our confidence levels, but remember focusing on them is very different to worrying about them and this is where coaching can come in.

Faith in the product or service

People need to believe in what they're selling if they're to produce sustained high performance. In complex businesses with a multitude of products or services we may notice differences from campaign to campaign depending on what's being promoted. A coaching conversation can reveal why the top salesperson on product A is finding it difficult to get results with product B. In my banking days I was asked to sell endowment mortgages and I was never completely comfortable with this and now those products have been exposed as generally poor investments. I was far from alone and some coaching at the time would have helped me deal with the problem and provided some feedback on the problematical aspects of the product.

Respect for the client

If I asked you 'How much respect do you have for each client you handle today?' you'd notice how they conduct themselves, the things the say, their situations and the reasons they give for wanting your product. You'll naturally start making subtle changes in your own responses without any need for further instruction from me at all.

AIMS CASCADE

Let's now have a look at typical set of aims that might emerge from a sales related coaching session, see Table 6.1. Remember that the people you coach will have a variety of aims and part of the coaching process is to organise these in such a way as to provide clarity and mobility in moving towards them.

As ever, the critical variables and hence the sources of appropriate focus are found at the level of processes. The dream will provide a backdrop, and the performance goals a definition of success, but with these things clear we'll need to move on to processes to make changes and take action to bring these things about.

WOULD YOU LIKE ANOTHER SUGGESTION?

In this section I'll set out some hints, tips and other ideas to help in your coaching sessions, particularly where your coachees get stuck and you want to offer some help.

Establishing rapport

We know that the level of rapport we establish with customers is a critical variable in sales and a crucial area of performance, but

Table 6.1

	Salesperson	Sales Team	Sales Division
Dream	• To be the top performer this year	• To top the regional league	• To be the most profitable division in the group
Performance Goal	• Achieve 10% increase on last year	• Average 5% increase in sales on all product lines	• Increase net profit by 2% whilst maintaining cost of sales at current levels
Processes	• Questioning technique • Product knowledge • etc	• Effective use of systems • Sales training • Appropriate communications • etc	• Effective use of systems • Sales & Marketing training • Monitor effectiveness of sales and marketing policies • etc

how do people establish rapport or repair it if things are not going well?

Rapport is a somewhat exotic English word derived from the French verb *rapporter*, meaning to bring back, to refer. The English meaning, a relation of harmony, conformity, accord or affinity, indicates the importance of rapport to communication.

Rapport is the link between the models of the world of different people. In creating rapport we agree to enter someone else's model of the world, and to let them into ours. We both benefit from the exchange because we both enlarge our model of the world by including someone else's experience in it.

It is for this reason that just being with a warm, trustworthy and trusting person can help us relate to customers. It is why no prescriptive sales technique will be universally successful; it is the salespeople themselves who are more or less effective.

One of the signs that people are in rapport is that they have become like each other in some way. When we enter someone else's world we begin to match some aspects of them. The possibilities are endless but some examples are posture, gestures, balance, voice, language and so on. It is astonishing how closely people in real life match each other when they are in rapport. Look around in a pleasant social situation, and watch the matching shift with the rapport.

If we are in a sales situation where rapport would be useful, and it isn't there yet, we can begin the process by matching some aspects of the customer's communication and usually this is enough to start the process of rapport going. It's also worth noticing that good rapport may not necessarily be comfortable or cosy. If the customer is upset or angry, rapport may consist of taking on a bit of that distress or anger.

Questioning

Models of customer thinking and behaviour in the buying process – for example the one laid out in Tom Lambert's excellent *High*

Income Consulting [14] – all state that customers have a point of view and expect it to be considered. This means that the notion of ask don't tell that we coaches have embraced is a very useful start point for salespeople as well. It means that before we start bombarding our customers with our encyclopedic product knowledge we need to take time to understand their requirements. Not only so that we can genuinely understand what they need but also to show that we care and are not just pushing our current product of the month. I remember being in the market for some double glazing and inviting reps from several firms round to our house. Most of these people left me glazed rather than the windows and were shown the door in a few minutes. Then a chap arrived from a small firm without briefcases full of brochures and prices lists. He asked us questions concerning our budget, the style we wanted, our requirements for safety and so on. Eventually, he said that he thought he had just the thing and fetched a cut away model from his car. He then explained how his product met all of our requirements exactly. Yes it was no doubt the only cut away model he took around, but the point is that he'd taken time to understand our unique needs first. No surprises for guessing who got the order.

Open questions beginning with Who, What, Where, How, When and Why are best for encouraging a dialogue with customers and encouraging them to give lots of information and information is essential to successful selling. Closed questions like 'do you want a new kitchen' or 'would you like to save £10 on your mobile phone bill' are clumsy and spotted as a sales pitch from miles away.

It's often best to put yourself in the customer's shoes. Who do you like to buy from and why? Who would you never buy from? What shops or suppliers do you return to time after time and what does the sales force contribute to this loyalty?

A picture is building up here. We need to pay attention to the critical variables in the customer's communication in order to establish rapport. This can then be deepened by asking questions designed to establish the customer's exact requirements. With this done we can start to outline our solution, which to the customer will seem almost tailor made.

Presenting solutions

Notwithstanding what we've said so far, there comes a time in every salesperson's life, and indeed a time in every sales conversation, when we will need to present our product or service to the customer.

My wife was recently in the market for a new mobile phone. She is not one to be seduced by new technology but was keen to have a phone which would be loud enough to hear ringing in busy places, and that wouldn't switch to voicemail too soon. We went into one shop and the salesperson described the handset he thought suitable:

> With this phone you get GSM tri-band technology for communication around the world. It has an integrated VGA camera incorporated into a flip-phone design. You can use either MP3 or MIDI ring tones for your incoming calls and you get MMS messaging features for sending pictures, animations, wallpaper, icons and ring tones. It's got IM for talking to friends and family in real-time and downloadable themes, screensavers, icons and ringtones for personalisation. Oh and you can also get downloadable games using WAP 2. Unlike a lot of phones at this price, it's got a built in mixer to mix unique MIDI ring tones and a built-in speakerphone. You also get date book and phonebook synchronization and 256 MB of memory.

We did not buy this phone. Experience at other outlets was similar and we were beginning to feel exhausted when another salesperson described his idea as follows:

> This is the loudest handset we have and you can set the volume yourself which means you can have it ring as loudly or quietly as

you like. If you're happy with that I can adjust the ring off time to 30 seconds by calling your network. Is that ok?

There are three elements to any product or service:

- Features – what the product *is*
- Advantages – what the product *does*, i.e. how the features are useful
- Benefits – the advantages that apply to a *particular customer's* situation

The key to presenting solutions is to concentrate on benefits, as in the second example above. It is also best to use simple, customer friendly language and avoid jargon or too much technical detail. All this can come, if necessary, *after* sale.

Handling objections

Fear of rejection is a massive source of internal interference for most people and one which can really drag even the best of sales-people down. We hate the word No in this context and despite the fact that we've all been on the sales course and been told it's not you that's being rejected but the product, it's still hard not to feel slighted when the customer declines our offer or begins to question or object to everything we say.

There seem to be two kinds of objection. There are technical objections like 'too expensive' or 'won't fit with what I've got already' and there are excuse objections like 'I'll need to think about it' or 'I'll have to discuss it with my partner'.

Let's think logically about why either type might occur. We've taken time to establish rapport so we're on the customer's wavelength and it's unlikely that they're just being awkward. We've asked questions designed to uncover what they need and presented a solution that fits. It seems most likely that we have not made a strong enough case in benefits terms or there are aspects of the customer's situation which we don't yet know. We need to go back to our questioning approach to find out more

> You say it's too expensive. May I ask what you're comparing it to?

> Of course you'll want to think about it, what other information do you need?

Questions like these not only enable you to find out more and put a better case forward, but also honour the customer's right to buy in a way that suits them. I appreciate that a lot will depend on the exact nature of the sales situation, whether it's high or low value sales, phone based or face to face, complex or simple, but any approach that shows respect for the customer will eventually give greater rewards than strong-arm tactics or deals of the day.

Closing

There is probably more rubbish written about closing than any other part of the sales process. There are books and seminars detailing hundreds of different closing techniques with names like wrestling holds and it's all nonsense. If you've followed the advice here and established rapport, asked questions, presented benefits and explored objections the close should be automatic and you'll either get the sale or you won't. In the end it's up to the customer and they can choose not to, no matter how compelling a case you've put forward and no matter how sensitively you've done so. Move on. Everyone knows the success ratios in sales are not brilliant, but you're now one step nearer to your next agreement.

However, there is one element on the closing process that does seem to elude people and that is asking for the business. There is absolutely nothing wrong with saying 'So, can we do the paperwork?' or words to that effect provided we have matched our product or service to the customer's need. So many sales come unraveled at the end, not because the salesperson has been ineffective, but because they've left the final move to the customer and some customers just aren't comfortable with this.

As with many things we've looked at in this book we now have a sequence that goes from building rapport to closing the sales. It's worth stressing again that sequences don't always pan out so neatly in real life and you'll probably need a blend of all of these ideas throughout a sales conversation. I must also stress that an ability to listen intently to your customer is the best tool you've got.

ROLE OF THE SALES MANAGER

It's not unusual for coaching to be used to support the transition from sales to sales management. This is not always a comfortable transition as the skills and attributes needed for sales management are in many ways different from those required for selling success. It's a common transition though because it's a natural career path when there is perhaps no scope for an account management type role and promotion is often the only reward available when a salesperson has reached the top of their salary scale. If asked to coach a newly appointed sales manager towards high performance, particularly if they were previously part of the direct sales force, you'll need to keep the following points in mind.

Sales management is about leading not following. Sales managers need a strong sense of purpose and to be aware of what needs to be done. Whereas sales can be a solitary role, the sales manager needs to take an overview of the work of the whole team and will need to find new variables on which to focus.

Effective sales managers are invariably good communicators (and likely good coaches as well). They need to explain to people precisely what's expected and to provide regular feedback and encouragement. Salespeople work in the relationship business and there's an inevitable emotional aspect to their work. The effective sales manager will recognise this and work with a flexible communication style. Furthermore, there is often a need to be an effective mediator whether this is concerned with mediating internal conflicts to stop good people leaving or mediating between the sales, finance and administration functions.

There will be a need to lead by example and be a good role model. In seeking to generate an atmosphere of high performance the sales manager will need to be seen performing well, looking for formal and informal learning opportunities – including learning from missed targets – and promoting a sense of fun and enjoyment. Such an atmosphere will encourage awareness, responsibility and trust throughout the team and the makings of a coaching culture will be in place.

As leader of the team, the satisfaction for sales managers resides in seeing others attain their goals, which again can take some getting used to. Any drive for personal glory may need to be replaced by a determination to remove the sales team's obstacles and barriers, to help them grow and learn and to see each of them succeed in their jobs. Sales managers need to be assertive and resourceful to equip the team with the tools and technology they need to beat the competition and hit targets. Sales management is a true coaching analogy in that it's no longer about playing an active part on the field of play but roaring the team on from the sidelines and doing everything to support their efforts.

SUMMARY

Sales is a great arena in which to hone your coaching skills. Salespeople are generally performance oriented individuals and will gladly accept your offer of coaching in the hope of even a small improvement in results. There'll be some challenges in the outer game and if you've got unenthusiastic people trying to sell a product or service they don't believe in, using a sales process they consider unethical, then your chances of sustained high performance are slim indeed. But let's assume instead that you have a decent product or service, take a customer oriented approach and have a keen and willing sales team. You can coach around the inner game of selling and achieve remarkable results. Here's a couple of testimonials to that fact that we're very proud of at my firm:

> Since the training he has brought success to his new role and is a much more confident person. With this renewed confidence he has changed the way of working and has changed long standing systems. He is more effective in training colleagues and is also coaching himself through any issues.

> **Specsavers**

> Since the training the company have successfully used coaching skills in the training department. Through this the department has been extended and a new job has been created. Skills have been passed down to all branch managers; with new ideas on coaching their front-line sales staff have seen an increase in sales between 1%–2%.

> **Hays Travel**

People love to buy but they hate to be sold to. The best areas of focus for anyone involved in sales or marketing is on the needs of the customer. For the Head Office Marketer this might mean product trials and focus groups whereas for the front line salesperson this means paying real attention to the customer's communication, looking for buying signals or sensing objections.

When coaching through the Reality stage it is likely that fear of rejection or despair at the number of 'Not today thank you' responses will emerge in some way as sources of internal interference. Help people to realise that a No is only a No today and that provided they've handled the situation professionally there's no reason why we cannot contact the prospect again some time later. Even if the leads to sales conversion ratio is as little as 1 in every 10 and this generates £100 profit, then every sales call contributes £10 of profit. We must remember that there is a learning and enjoyment opportunity in every call we make, some will result in a sale others won't. The buying decision is in the hands of the customer, the sales approach is totally within the control of the salesperson and is thus a much more useful area of focus.

Use coaching to help your sales staff focus on their team and personal goals. They'll need this to sustain them through the inevitable dry patches which even the best experience. The goals and targets need to be taxing but not out of sight. The sales team themselves are best placed to know where the balance lies.

CHAPTER 7

PRESENTATIONS

INTRODUCTION

In the world of work, there is no greater distinction between the effects of the outer and inner games than in making presentations.

Those newspaper surveys of top 10 fears invariably include a fear of public speaking at some point, with some ranking it higher than a fear of spiders or even death. Am I to conclude that many people would rather die than give a talk or presentation?

Let's take an example. Suppose Sam works for a web design firm and has been asked to run a short session on 'search engine optimisation' for the local business club. Sam has done little speaking in public, has had no training, and might seriously consider death the preferable option. However, the presentation is not for a few weeks so there's time to get prepared.

Sam sources a two day presentation skills course. He learns about visual aides such as projectors and flipcharts and he learns about how to give his presentation a beginning, middle and end. He learns how to write prompt notes on index cards and how to prepare for audience questions. On the second day he makes a presentation on 'My favourite hobby' to the rest of the group and gets feedback from the students and the tutor. Unfortunately most of this feedback is on the training items which Sam failed to implement and this reinforced his view that he is hopeless at presentations.

The problem is that the training Joe received was all concerned with outer game stuff – what he *does*. The reasons for Sam's fear are all inner game concerns – how he *feels*. Clearly presenters do need to understand structure and use of visual aides and so on and indeed I intend to give some hints and tips on some those areas here, but it is the mental side of making presentations that distinguishes the high performer from the also ran. Happily it's also the mental side of making presentations that coaching can most readily help.

I have often been asked to coach presenters and the most common complaints that are raised as we begin to talk are:

> I'm okay presenting to a small group from my own team, it's when I get in front of a large group of strangers that I struggle

> I'm okay presenting to a large group of strangers, it's when I get in front of a small group from my own team that I struggle

(How can traditional training deal with polar opposite views like this?)

> I know that I have a tendency to speak too softly, but I can't seem to break the habit

> The harder I try, the more nervous I get and the more things go wrong

> Every time I get to the tricky bit, I lose my nerve

In this chapter we'll seek to uncover the interference which creates such thoughts and replace it with more useful variables on which to concentrate. We'll also see how we can balance the need to perform with some learning and enjoyment as well in order to ease the tension and ensure a successful presentation.

INTERFERENCE

I believe that everyone has the potential to deliver an effective presentation. Giving a presentation is not a natural thing to have to do and many people would probably rather not. The idea of coaching for presentation performance is not to attempt to turn everyone into an entertaining after dinner speaker, but rather to generate a level of comfort sufficient to get the job done. Having said that, many people begin to get a buzz from presenting and get to quite enjoy it once they can begin to operate free from interference. Let's look at the common sources of both external and internal interference when it comes to presenting.

External

Too much or too little time

In an ideal world we would plan a presentation based on audience requirements and then establish a realistic timeslot to accomplish this. In the real world it happens the other way around. We are invariably given a time slot and then left to work out how best to make our point in that timeframe. Inexperienced presenters tend to worry that they've got more to say than time allows or agonise about drying up with nothing more to say with ten minutes still to go. In truth there is neither too much time nor too little time, there is simply whatever time there is and the trick is to be able to plan a presentation with enough flexibility to speed things up or slow things down to fit the time available whilst still achieving the presentation's objective. We'll look at some ways to do that shortly.

Equipment

Now, I will admit to being something of a dinosaur as far as presenting goes and for years eschewed PowerPoint and similar for fear of it failing on the day. There's only so much that can go wrong with flipchart and pens and any problem can be rectified within moments. I have lost count of the number of times now I have sat in an audience watching armies of technical types fiddling with laptops and projectors and frowning a lot whilst the presenter shifts awkwardly from foot to foot in the corner. The more sophisticated equipment you have the greater the chance of something going wrong and, *more importantly from our point of view*, the greater the chance that fear of something going wrong will interfere with our potential to make a great presentation. Nevertheless, there is an expectation these days for smart, professional presentations with audio-visual clips and so on. We can meet this expectation and minimise the risk of problems with effective planning and preparation, as we'll see.

Environment

You can't present well to an audience that are too hot or too cold. You cannot present well if you can't be properly seen or heard. Have you planned to move around the room distributing notes only to find that there's no space? What if the catering people start delivering the coffee when you're less than halfway through? The most gifted and confident presenter could fall foul of any of these and coaching can help guard against complacency and create a plan for expecting the unexpected.

Internal

Nerves

Let's deal with the cliché first: I agree that a little nervousness is a good thing. It guards against being too casual and stimulates us to do our best. However, if the people I coach are anything to go by, the experience is more like outright fear than a little nervousness. It seems to me that this fear is a fear of failure or rejection in some way. Will the audience like me and what I say or will their eyes glaze over as they yawn through it? Will I forget what to say and look really foolish as a result? Will I get my notes mixed up and say the wrong thing at the wrong time? And – if making a presentation as part of a pitch for new business – Will I give a poor presentation and fail to win the contract?

When we begin to entertain these thoughts we might experience a tightening in the stomach, dryness of the mouth, perspiration or any number of other physical symptoms as our bodies invoke the primeval fight or flight response. People telling us there's really nothing to worry about doesn't help. The brain cannot distinguish between a real or an imagined fear and the physiological response will be the same.

Fear is generated when we consider the past or the future. Only the present moment is totally free of fear. Coaching people to focus on the here and now will prove to be a marvellous antidote to fear.

Prior experience

Does this sound familiar?

> The Head of Finance was supposed to give the presentation of the first quarter's results, but she was sick that day and so I had to do it. I hate giving presentations but there was no one else available and so I said I'd give it a try. I didn't have much time to prepare but I had a look through her slides and it seemed to make sense, so I wrote a couple of notes on index cards and just thought I'd go for it. Things went fine until some of the board members started asking questions and then I realised I didn't really know the results well enough at all. I felt myself going red and then I dropped my notes on the floor. Afterwards the guy from Marketing said I should have just issued a memo instead of making a presentation. I always knew I was hopeless and I'm dreading having to do one again.

Oh dear. A *lack of confidence* has led to a *hesitant effort*. This has generated *poor results* and *negative feedback*. This is likely to lead to a *lack of confidence*. It doesn't matter where this cycle starts the result is always a huge source of internal interference which will follow us around doggedly.

Negative self-talk

Let's imagine we have two account managers from large consultancies preparing to give a presentation in response to a tender invite from a major prospective client. In this scenario their brief is the same, they will each present to precisely the same panel of people and have each be given the same amount of time. The outer game, so to speak, is virtually identical.

We join them sitting in the reception area waiting their turn, each lost in their own thoughts:

> If we get this it will be a miracle. I've been up since 6am and I feel worn out already. I'll bet they'll ask me some really awkward ques-

tions. What if they ask me about client testimonials, we've never worked in the sector before? I'll be glad when this is over.

It'll be brilliant if we get this. We've not worked in this sector before so I must be sure to emphasise how objective we can be. Glad I got an early night. I bet they're in their now dreaming up difficult questions! Well, they won't catch me out and even if they do I'll email a response later, that'll impress them.

Who would you back to win the assignment?

How we talk to ourselves has a massive effect on what we can achieve as it determines what we focus on. In other words each of the presenters described above is likely to prove themselves correct.

In extreme cases even success can be dismissed with self-talk along the lines of *'Oh that was just a fluke. It's so unlike me I'll never be able to do it again'.*

We can often achieve great results in coaching by simply encouraging people to think in a more optimistic way.

PLE IN PRESENTATIONS

To those who put making presentations up there with death and fear of spiders, the idea that we could learn and enjoy whilst performing a presentation seems madness, but there are learning and enjoyment opportunities for even the most terrified of presenters. You can learn about the fear you experience, what drives it and how you can deal with it. You can enjoy the feeling of relief that the presentation is over and give yourself a reward for having managed it.

But let's not dwell on the negative. Where is the balance of PLE to be found in giving a presentation? By definition giving a presentation is giving a performance and there's usually some degree of pressure to do it well. To perform in a presentation means to achieve a given objective which can range from simply providing information to making a sale. Too many presenters focus on simply delivering their message in a way that suits them irrespective of the needs of the audience.

Making a presentation is a great learning experience. You can learn about organising information, presenting ideas visually, using your voice, thinking on your feet and a host of other factors that can translate to many other areas of working life.

As you begin to learn to focus on more useful variables, your presentation will go better and you'll enjoy them more. There's a great buzz to be had from a little shared humour or when someone thanks you for your thoughts afterwards. It can be very stimulating to be seen to have some expertise and find yourself answering others' concerns. You'll undoubtedly want to set some goals around what you want the presentation to achieve but why not set some learning and enjoyment goals as well?

CRITICAL VARIABLES

Remember, a variable is anything that changes each time a task is undertaken and it's a critical variable if it can impact how well the task is performed. There are hundreds of variables in giving a presentation and dozens of critical ones, so in this section I'll confine myself to outlining the more typical and leave you and your coachees to explore the others.

Whilst the critical variables I'll describe are all useful things to focus on and adapt to *during* a presentation, there are greater advantages in focusing on these things *before* the presentation, at the planning stage.

Outer variables

Audience Profile

The people on the receiving end of your presentation are the single most important factor on which to concentrate. This is the case whether you're doing five minutes at the staff meeting or a half-day at the annual conference. Always plan and deliver a presentation with the audience in mind. Who are they? What jobs do they do? What are their expectations? How experienced are they? What do they know already? Try to find this stuff out in advance but keep in mind the need for flexibility, there's always a chance the chief executive will drop into your slot on the staff induction day.

Schedule

Following on from this is the need to consider carefully the time-slot and general logistics for your presentation. If it's first thing in the morning it's almost inevitable that some people will turn up late. If you're on first thing after lunch your audience is likely to be feeling a little sleepy. If your slot is at the end of the day, you'll find people will be checking their watches, anxious to begin their journeys home. Your presentation will need to reflect these circumstances.

Perhaps you're one of a series of presenters and again you'll need to consider your place in the running order. If you're on first you'll need to finish with a strong summary so that people will remember your message even after hearing many others. If there have been two or three speakers before you, you might need to do something a little engaging to regain attention. This is particularly the case if the first talks have been poor and the audience has been exposed to 'death by PowerPoint'.

Room layout

A few minutes focusing on the room layout can pay huge dividends later on. Find out in advance if you have any control over how things are going to be set up. If not, at least you'll know what you're working with. If people need to do a lot of note taking, tables are best. If it's a large audience though this might be impractical and so you might decide to produce a handout instead. Will your audience be able to see and hear you properly? If you have posters and other visuals with you it might be best to place them at the side or the back of the room, so that you can draw people's attention to them at the right times.

Inner variables

My feeling is that the outer variables can be easily handled with a little bit of common sense and some forward planning. As always with coaching we find that it's the inner variables that hold the key to real presentation performance.

Confidence

Pay attention to how confident you feel from the moment you get the presenting assignment. As you sit down and start to figure out what you're going to say, do you find you're feeling better about certain parts of the topic than others? If so, can you feature more of the material you like or do you need to do more homework on the weaker areas? As you deliver your talk do you notice your confidence levels changing? Most presenters say that their nerves settle after a few minutes. If you feel like this, make sure that there's nothing too complex or controversial to cover at the beginning this gives you a chance to get into your stride before handling the trickier bits.

Familiarity with subject

Similarly, it's worth asking yourself – or the presenters you coach – 'On a scale of 1–10, how familiar are you with this topic or subject?'. If it's an 8 or 9 what would have to happen to make it a 10? If it's a 4 or 5 what would it need to be on the day to get the job done? Is there time to build your familiarity to that level?

Monitor your familiarity with the subject throughout the session as well; it will be helpful learning for next time.

Comfort in handling questions

Most presentations feature questions from the audience at some point. Some presenters like to take questions as they arise; others prefer to handle them all at the end. Either way, many a presenter has told me that this is the bit they most dread as it is when they are no longer in control; you never know what question will be asked. This is only partly true and if, after focusing on your comfort in this area, you feel uncertain, then you can make predicting audience questions part of your preparation. Alternatively, and if time allows, you can get a few colleagues together for a dry run and see what questions emerge. This will also give you feedback on the timing and how best to incorporate questions and answers.

AIMS CASCADE

For the aims cascade in this section we'll consider three different types of presentation that the people whom you coach may be involved in. The first, information giving, refers to any presentation where the purpose is to inform. This may be in-house to other members of staff and to do with say, financial results or business change. Alternatively it may be to an external audience as part of say, a seminar organised by a business club or networking group. A business pitch is where the presenter seeks to persuade a panel to do business with their organisation and the third type, staff training, is where the intention of the presentation is to enable staff to be able to *do* something as a result.

As ever the success of your coaching will be linked to how well you can help your coachees to focus on the variables found at the level of processes. The list that follows in Table 7.1 is by no means exhaustive.

Table 7.1

	Information Giving	Business Pitch	Staff training
Dream	• To have everyone leaving saying it was a great presentation	• To win the business	• To have all participants able to do what they should
Performance Goal	• To convey 3 key benefits	• To highlight our unique selling point	• To give at least 2 examples per learning point • To provide a practice opportunity for at least 3 participants
Processes	Production of session plans, production of speakers notes, production of visual aides, venue set up, rehearsal, audience questions, body language, vocal delivery, etc.		

WOULD YOU LIKE ANOTHER SUGGESTION?

Your coachees will thank you most for helping them develop a mastery of the inner game of making presentations. Nevertheless the following outer game tips may prove useful.

Preparation

'Fail to plan and plan to fail' goes the old cliché and I have found this to be particularly true – to my own cost on many occasions – when it comes to making presentations.

The first big tip is to plan and prepare the preparation with the audience in mind. You'll probably have all sorts of topics within your presentation subject and one idea is to write each of these topics on small cards and then begin to work them into some sort of logical order. You might put them in groups of must, need or like, i.e. things your audience must know, things they probably need to know and those things it would be nice for them to know. You can then organise the presentation, making sure it's the musts that get prioritised. This is also a good way of building some flexibility into your presentation as you can deliver the likes if there's time or leave them out if not.

Next you'll need to prepare the venue, or at least go and have a look in advance so you know what the set-up is. Check that there are enough electrical sockets for any equipment you'll use and find out if you'll need any extension cables. Electronic equipment is notoriously prone to fail when you need it most, so check that the laptop projector is working properly and is compatible with the computer you intend to use at the time. If you've been asked to email a presentation ahead of time for someone to load onto another laptop, it is wise to have a copy with you on disk just in case. Personally I still carry copies of my really important presentations on acetate as a back up solution should things go wrong.

You'll also need to prepare yourself which includes leaving plenty of time to get to the venue and deciding what to wear. If in doubt I would err on the side of the formal. You can always take off a jacket, but you can't do much if you turn up in casual clothes and everyone else is in business dress. The best advice is to dress in the sort of clothes the audience would expect a presenter like you to wear.

Structure

So, you've decided what you want to say, now it's time to decide how exactly to say it and in what order, etc. A good presentation will have a definite beginning, middle and an end. It is no use just standing up and launching into detailed explanations, audiences need to be primed about what to expect and, if they're to retain the information, given adequate summaries and key points. A great example is the way a typical news bulletin would be organised. We get the headlines, then the detailed stories and then the head-lines again by way of summary. This is an excellent structure that would apply to almost any presentation situation.

The first few minutes of any presentation are the most vital. As with so many things there is never a second chance to make a first impression and an audience will tend to decide whether to 'go with' a presenter or not in the first few minutes. I have found the following acronym a useful way of ensuring an effective opening:

I	Interest	Grab their attention, with something dramatic or witty
N	Need	Explain the benefit of listening
T	Title	Give it a relevant title
R	Range	Explain what you'll cover

O   Objectives   Explain *why* you'll cover those things and state
                      what the audience will know or be able to do
                      as a result

There are any number of ways of grabbing interest and attention at the start. Dramatic music, a video clip, a controversial statement or question or even a moment of silence will all stir an audience's attention. Humour is great as well but be careful. It's got to be something you're comfortable with and be sure to steer clear of anything even remotely likely to offend. I'd also avoid anything along the lines of 'I'm not very good at presentations . . .'. This is not what your audience will want to hear and creates a very negative focus.

Decide on your own form of notes. Its best to avoid a script as such but small cards or papers with key words as prompts tend to work very well.

If you are going to give the audience handouts make sure you have enough copies; there's nothing worse than a presenter borrowing or reading a participant's notes. Leave handouts to the end if you don't want them read during the presentation or give people a moment to read if you hand them out while you're presenting.

Using visual aides

Strong visual aides will help people to understand and remember your points. Most of what people learn is taken in through their eyes not their ears. Consider using wipe clean boards, charts and posters, flip charts and computer screen prints. Also remember that you and any co-presenters are a kind of visual aide.

Beware of the curse of *Death by PowerPoint*. A series of slides packed with information is not a presentation. A presentation, by definition, requires information to be actively conveyed. Use PowerPoint to embellish and support your verbal presentation but never to replace it. Has anything ever become so cheapened by misuse than PowerPoint? Reluctant presenters have become seduced by the ease of producing material in this way and believe it to be a substitute for a genuine attempt to deliver information with warmth and energy, but people have had enough clipart and beaney men to last a lifetime.

Similarly, it's great to use multi-media clips in your presentations, but do so only if it enhances your material. It's too easy to get carried away with the technology and end up doing things because you *can* rather than because you *should*. Once again a presentation designed with the audience's needs paramount should guard against this.

If using a flip chart or white board use different colours to create and maintain interest and group items in threes – people seem to remember information in triplets. Pre-prepared flips need to be 'spot on' – no spelling mistakes or smudges! Flips produced as you go can be as rough and ready as you like!

Check you have plenty of flip chart paper and that your pens work! Do not leave the lids off pens for too long – they will dry out and you might accidentally write on your clothes. Use slides carefully. Too much information on slides or overheads can ruin an otherwise excellent presentation. Remove visual aides once they've been used, i.e. turn off the projector or turn over the flip chart page.

In many ways it's a question of getting back to basics. Visual aides should be bold and interesting and large enough to be seen from the back of the room. Once you've produced some in draft review them for clarity, relevance, visibility and quality.

Using questions

Asking the audience questions is the simplest yet most effective way of getting an audience involved in a presentation. When people are involved they are more likely to remember what your presentation was all about.

Remember the two basic question types. Use open questions, Who, What, How, etc to open up a discussion and encourage debate. Use closed questions, Can you . . . , Would you . . . , etc, to clarify points with a yes or no response. Generally it is best to use 'overhead' questions, i.e. questions to the whole group that anyone can answer. However, occasionally you may want to use a 'direct' question, i.e. to a named person to draw them in or seek a specific view.

Sometimes you might want to ask a 'rhetorical' question, i.e. one which you ask and answer yourself. For example,

> Who cares about customer relations at Bloggs and Co? Well, every-one of course . . .

Remember you're asking questions of the audience to get them involved and add variety to your material. Don't ask the audience questions to soak up time and don't ask the audience a question if you're unsure of the answer. There's a chance someone will take the opportunity to make you look foolish.

Of course questioning works both ways and you can expect and should build in questions from the audience. As part of your preparation think about the likely questions and decide what response you will give and practise giving the answer. Asking the audience to get involved in this way will make your presentation much more interesting and involving. You cannot control what people may ask but you'll need to handle everything professionally. Try to keep calm, even if the question seems aggressive or akin to a personal attack. If you don't hear or understand the question ask the person to repeat it. Don't get irritated if you feel the point in their question has already been covered or say something smug like 'well if you'd been listening earlier . . .'.

Finally, be honest. If you don't have the answer, make a note of the question and find out later.

SUMMARY

Speaking in front of groups is not natural and all public speakers get nervous to a greater or lesser degree. The trick is to take this nervous energy and direct it to your advantage. Many people argue that a level or nervousness and adrenalin is essential to succeed.

Recognise that you are not alone and that people will want you to succeed. Ninety percent of the audience would not swap places with you for all the money in the world and will empathise with you and respect you for doing your best.

Speak about what you know. This will build your confidence and make you less nervous. If you're asked to speak on a subject you don't know a great deal about, try to do plenty of research beforehand.

Prepare thoroughly. Produce first class material and then rehearse, rehearse, rehearse!

Visualise yourself giving the presentation and it going well. Mentally, practise moving around, using your visuals, handling questions and so on.

If you feel 'butterflies' take a deep breath. Strange as it may seem, pauses and silences in presentations are quite natural and can actually be a very powerful way of making a point.

Use visual aides. They mean you don't have to talk the whole time, they direct attention away from you, they act as a reference point and you process nervous energy organising and using them.

Break up the presentation with audience participation – ask them questions and get them to complete short exercises.

Boost your energy by eating chocolate or having a sugary drink 15 minutes before you present.

Raise your awareness by practising your presentation in advance and getting feedback particularly on any mannerisms, e.g. idle scratching or repeating certain words. Just being aware of these things is usually enough to make them disappear.

Ask yourself 'What's the worst thing that could happen?' and then do all you can to make sure it doesn't.

....

CHAPTER 8

PERSONAL ORGANISATION

INTRODUCTION

What I write about in this chapter used to be called Time Management but this is a misnomer. There is no such thing as time management. Time cannot be controlled or managed it just passes. The only thing people can control is themselves and how they use their time.

I consider time management an anachronism from a bygone age. A time of predictable work-patterns and jobs comprised of regular repetitive tasks. I know of few working lives that are like that now.

Nevertheless, there has never been a greater need to be organised, to be on schedule and able to prioritise. Let's be clear, it'll never be possible to do everything and to try creates intolerable stress. You and your team will need to decide what to do on the basis that time spent doing one thing is time that is not available for another. To make these decisions well requires a high degree of focus – the very quality that coaching most helps promote.

Training in time management will produce *some* results. People will return from the training with a host of hints, tips and techniques which will help save minutes or even hours here and there, and if they can stick to it this can add up to quite a saving in total. Coaching for personal organisation will produce *great* results because it will focus on the habits and patterns, unique to each individual, that obscure a focus on results and rob them of precious time.

I will not advocate a particular electronic device, leather bound diary style system or indeed any prescriptive framework because these things tinker at the margins of the outer game. Instead, the intention of this chapter is to examine how coaching can help people to develop a working pattern that is theirs, which they own and accept responsibility for.

I know of countless people that have attended literally dozens of training courses in time management the results of which have inevitably faded over time. Like weight loss diets, each of these courses promises to have the magic answer but this never materialises.

The only true way to achieve mastery over one's personal organisation including the wise use of time is to recognise that the answers come from within.

INTERFERENCE

As ever, we need firstly to consider those things which militate against our potential to be organised and in control. I do not hold with the idea that some people are just a mess and cannot exert any influence over their working pattern. I think this sort of victim mentality just holds us back. What I do realise is that many of us are plagued by bad habits and unhelpful self-talk when it comes to personal organisation but that these can be powerfully challenged by a dose of good coaching.

External

Organisational culture

Too many organisations value effort over results. At one of the bank offices where I once worked there was a large section devoted to administering very large lending proposals. The work of the section was complex, important and risky and as such tended to attract some of the brightest and most talented members of staff. I recall being told of the 'jacket on the chair' mentality that existed. This meant arriving at work before the managers and being certain not to leave before they did. In between times it meant being at the desk looking busy and productive. Management behaviour reinforced this effect by seeming to link promotions and other rewards to hours worked rather than quality of results.

I see signs of this still today and I fear some people hold back from changing unproductive habits for fear they will no longer look good and miss out on effort based rewards.

Work systems

Many work systems are out of date, unwieldy, and inefficient, requiring tasks to be completed twice or repeated needlessly. All too often the technology exists to revise these systems but people are too busy to research the technology or implement a solution. The reason people are too busy is because too much time is taken up using ineffective systems . . . and so the cycle continues.

Work-life balance

I have coached many people on work-life balance issues and I've noticed a recurring theme: people are always somewhere else. If they're in the office they're thinking about missing out on being with the family at home. If they're at home they're fretting about what they didn't get completed at the office before they left. They're never fully focused on any of their responsibilities and consequently unable to discharge them as well as they might.

> If you want to be in the room, be in the room
>
> **Nigel Risner**

Coaching cannot create more time in people's lives but it can enable a focus on the priorities.

Inner

Lack of assertiveness

I think that the word No is the most powerful in the English language, but one which is often underused by overly busy, stressed out people at work. We know we can't possibly take on any more work and yet we accept that new project. We know we're not at home nearly enough and yet we agree to the extra hours. Of course there are pressures to do this: Not wanting to let people down, guilt, fear of missing out on promotion and so on but sometimes it's simply a matter of not being able to say No in an adult, business like and assertive way. We'll examine this in more detail later.

Procrastination

If you're prone to procrastination you may want to leave this section until later. On a serious note, procrastination has scuppered many an accomplishment but I know of few people who are entirely immune to its influence. Do you leave the files containing your major projects towards the bottom of your in-tray while you 'just sort out some bits and pieces'? Do you hold off starting that preparatory work, knowing that if a few more days pass you'll be motivated by the pressure of a deadline? For the confirmed procrastinator there is always another threshold. After tea-break, after lunch, tomorrow, at the weekend, next week, next month, next year, when we've won that next contract, when next quarter's results come through, etc, etc, etc.

One of coaching's most potent effects is to encourage taking action. It suggests that whatever it is you need to do you can start it now. Freed from the immobilising effects of procrastination people begin to move forward, to deal with things and see 'to do' lists shrink. This is marvelous stuff.

> Whatever you can do, or dream you can, begin it! Boldness has genius, magic and power in it. Begin it now.
>
> **Goethe**

Perfectionism

Let's be clear; I'm not talking here about attention to detail which is an important quality in a great many areas of work. Rather I am talking about that need for everything to be just so that is generated by the person rather than the circumstances. The figures that have to be produced on a colour-coded spreadsheet when a scrap of paper was all that was required. Lugging the laptop and projector to the conference venue to show one slide. What's worse is when senior figures foist their perfectionism on the team and people have to do things through gritted teeth all the while knowing they could be spending their time more productively. Perfectionism is fine if there is plenty of time to get everything done but there isn't. We need high quality output of course but not in a vacuum. Sometimes there is a bigger picture to consider. Remember the teachings of the Italian economist Pareto:

> In any series of events which you do 80% of the output arises from 20% of the input
>
> **Pareto**

I interpret this as meaning we need to look for the maximum gains. Where can we expend our efforts for the quickest results? This is only possible though with a clear understanding of priorities.

PLE IN PERSONAL ORGANISATION

Turning now to keeping PLE in balance when wanting to make improvements in personal organisation. As we've seen, those who struggle in this area are often held back by bad habits. Habits are tenacious creatures and are not vanquished easily. It's very difficult to change a bad habit purely by force of will as all you reluctant smokers and serial dieters will know. In this case you're simply trying to perform by trying really hard and you'll get tired and frustrated. What is needed is a balanced approach. Let's say you're trying to bring more structure to your working day by trying to get into the habit of working with a daily plan. It's almost certain that there'll come a point when you won't be able to produce a plan or decide not to. Rather than berate yourself over it, why not consider it a learning experience. Why did you give up? Was it just easier to react to what was happening on the day? Were others' work patterns making things difficult? Did it just all seem a bit much like hard work? The answers to these questions will be quite insightful and enable you to adjust your approach. Similarly, make it fun. Reward yourself when you've avoided a bad habit for a spell. Draw a picture of your bad habit as a monster on your jotter or whatever then draw an arrow each day to remind yourself that you're winning the battle.

CRITICAL VARIABLES

Outer variables

Scope for planning

One of the obvious things that vary in our day to day working lives is the amount of planning involved in the various tasks and jobs to which we attend. There are complex projects requiring detailed planning and simple tasks that require none. Similarly, there are tasks that might need lots of planning but which time constraints force us to just get on with and simple tasks which take longer to plan for than to do. It's useful to pay attention to the planning element *needed* for a task and compare it with how much planning you *want* to do. This can be a good awareness raising exercise and help you understand your own preferences and style. With that understanding comes the opportunity to develop alternative styles and approaches.

Urgency v importance

Do you respond to the urgency of the task or its importance? You'll likely say both and you'd be right insofar as there'll be tasks within your working day or week that are both *urgent*, i.e. need to be done quickly, and *important*, i.e. make a significant impact. But there are other combinations as well. There are tasks that are *urgent but not important* such as interruptions and probably most meetings. Then there are those tasks which are *important but not urgent* like planning, self-development and proactive marketing. Finally, most would agree that there are some things we do which are *neither important nor urgent* but which we still spend time on; Internet surfing, redundant reports, etc.

Usually the level of importance stays constant over a period of time but the degree of urgency obviously increases as deadlines loom. This means that we can begin to get on top of our personal organisation by spending more time on tasks that are initially important but not urgent before they become important and urgent. We can usually find the time to do this by ruthlessly cutting out anything neither important nor urgent.

Progress v maintenance

It is also useful to focus on the outcomes of the tasks we attend to. Do they enable us to make progress in some way or do they just maintain the status quo until next time. An example may help. Our up and coming course dates appear in about four separate places on our website. Each time a training date passes or we schedule new dates, I have to go in and make four separate changes. This is a maintenance task. If however, I were to learn a little more about the software it would be possible to make a single change that updated all relevant fields at once and have expired dates removed automatically. This would be progress. The problem is that the latter course of action is important but not urgent and as such gets submerged under a lot of urgent and important work. Unless of course I chose to make this progress task my priority.

Inner variables

Attitude

What is your attitude towards time management and personal organisation? Some people approach personal organisation with a frightening zeal that borders on obsession. I worked for many managers like this and they were never detached from their leather bound planners or their electronic equivalent. In fairness, these people did achieve a lot provided they were clear about priorities.

For others the whole idea of time management or personal organis-ation strips all the fun and spontaneity out of a working day. They like to respond and react to what's happening in the moment and eschew any methods of imposing order on things for fear of ending up in a sterile, boring environment.

The latter type can be thought of as 'in time' people. Their tendency to live in the moment makes them exciting to be with but frustrating to wait for; which will often be the case. Others are 'through time' people. They live life on a time continuum and always know where they are on it and what's happening next. They tend to work towards detailed plans and are invariably punctual.

Neither view nor tendency is right, wrong or indeed fixed. Paying attention to your own preferences will raise your awareness of changes you need to make to suit your own style.

Distractions

We all know that we should work with concentration and focus and avoid distractions, but it's easier said then done. But I want you to stop trying to avoid distractions and instead notice how often you get distracted. This sounds odd I realise, but it's an idea entirely in keeping with our coaching principles. By noticing your distractions you'll become more aware of them and you can then choose whether or not to do anything about them. This is more useful than berating yourself for becoming distracted. Sometimes simple tactics can be hugely beneficial. Try turning off your computer's automatic email alert. Put your phone on voicemail or ask a colleague to take your calls for a spell. Can you take some work to a cubicle or meeting room to get some quiet time?

Assertiveness

Do you recognise yourself in this description?: Assertive people get what they want, need or prefer without belittling or putting down others. They ensure that the needs and wants of both parties are met and ask for what they want whilst recognising that others have the right to say no. Assertive people have their own opinions and values but express them appropriately. They are not afraid to say 'I don't know' or 'I don't understand' and they take responsibility for their own decisions. Assertive people are not afraid to decline responsibility for other people's problems. They use appropriate levels of eye contact in communication and adopt a firm posture, not slouching or slumping. Assertive people 'own' what they say, e.g. 'I'd like to suggest' or 'I've got an idea' and tend to favour co-operative phrases, e.g. 'What do you think?' or 'Shall we?' They are open about their feelings – be they positive or negative – and express any annoyance constructively without reverting to aggression.

Pay attention to these qualities the next time you want to communicate assertively.

AIMS CASCADE

All too often the subject of personal organisation at work is reduced to the idle wish or the vague dream. People even make jokes about it: 'I wanted to go on the time management course, but I haven't got time!'. Many people wish for more time or control in their working lives but few do anything about it. In extreme cases the organisational culture almost works against it. The modern phenomenon of stress envy, where people jockey for position in terms of who gets the most email or who works the longest hours, creates a difficult backdrop against which to develop your own personal organisation tactics.

We therefore need to develop some clear performance goals and identify the processes that will deliver the results we need. Focusing on these will help us break out of old habits.

Table 8.1 should give you some ideas.

Table 8.1

	Alleviating stress	Taking control	Getting results
Dream	To achieve a work-life balance	To be more organised	To meet all my deadlines
Performance Goal	To be home by 6pm 4 days per week	To revise my filing system before the end of the month	To have completed all work at least 24 hrs before it is due
Processes	Diary management, delegation, tidy desk policy, working to priorities, assertive behaviour, full use of technology, etc.		

WOULD YOU LIKE ANOTHER SUGGESTION?

A reminder once again that the pointers included here are by no means intended as instructions for the people whom you coach in personal organisation. Rather they are there to raise your own awareness of the subject so that you may choose the right coaching questions to bring about a positive result.

Assertive behaviour

The big prize in behaving assertively is an increased chance of our needs being met.

When we state clearly what our needs, wants, ideas and opinions are, we increase the chances that these needs will be met and our opinions taken into account. At the same time we will encourage others to do the same. Where no conflict exists these mutual needs can be met. Where conflict does exist assertive behaviour will help both sides to find solutions that are mutually acceptable.

By making our views and feelings known we will feel better about the situation whether we *win* or *lose*. There are no guarantees that we will win every time but when our needs are not met, we are more able to put a difficult situation behind us without it becoming a source of internal interference. We develop a healthy regard for our skills and our self-belief is strengthened. This creates a snowball effect in which acting assertively leads to greater self-confidence which in turn leads to more assertive behaviour. Having greater confidence in ourselves also means we are more able to trust others. We can recognise openly and honestly their strengths and weaknesses without perceiving either as a threat to our own position.

By increasing our control over our behaviour we no longer blame others or external factors for it. We stop handing over control to other people in situations where they know they can get us to lose our temper just by mentioning a sensitive issue. We control how we respond to incidents rather than just reacting.

We will be less afraid of failure or making a mistake. We will want to do more than simply react to situations as they occur. We will want to act to prevent certain situations occurring. We are more prepared to take risks but won't blame ourselves or others if the initiative fails.

Assertive behaviour prevents a preoccupation with not upsetting others or with losing out. We will experience less stress and tension because we are not so worried about what other people will think. This leaves us with more energy to use productively in other areas of our work.

The benefits of assertive behaviour are many indeed and go far beyond helping with personal organisation. It is relatively easy to learn the principles of assertive behaviour and with practice and support it gets easier to do. The following ideas should help.

To behave assertively, you'll need to aim to satisfy the needs and wants of all parties involved in the situation. You'll need to know what your rights are or you will find it difficult to judge if other people are violating them. Remember that you don't have to feel guilty about saying 'No' if you have good reason to do so, and you don't have to apologise for having an opinion.

Why not take the initiative sometimes instead of just reacting to situations? Why not get better at dealing with issues when they are small?

Body language is an important part of being assertive; keep your voice steady and firm, your posture open and relaxed. Keep in mind you have the right to make requests in an assertive way, but respect the other party's right to say 'No', or you risk becoming aggressive. In the same way, others also have the right to ask a request of you and you too have the right to refuse. When refusing a request though, remember to slow down, speak steadily and with warmth, to avoid sounding abrupt.

Finally, keep to facts, not opinions, and use statements that are brief and to the point.

Time stealers

In my experience of coaching people where personal organisation or time management is the theme, these are the most typical causes of time being soaked up on activity that makes no real impact.

- Meetings
- Telephone calls
- Interruptions
- Junk paperwork and email
- Emergencies
- Looking for things

Don't you just hate pointless meetings? How many of us have sat through meeting after meeting dreaming of being somewhere else? We need, I think, to become much more ruthless with how much of our time is spent in meetings but this requires a corporate effort with much senior support. We need firstly to consider whether the meeting needs to take place at all. We are social creatures and generally like gathering in groups, but is that really the best way for a particular decision to be made or information given? If we all had lots of spare time then fine, but when a half an hour saved here or there can make a huge difference let's not have meetings unless they're necessary and productive. Even if a meeting is definitely necessary can the agenda be organised in such a way that people can leave once they are no longer required? If you want a concise business-like meeting forget the coffee and biscuits and if you really want to challenge the meeting culture hold them standing up!

The direct dial extension and the mobile phone mean that the days of telling a switchboard operator or secretary to hold your calls are over, but responding to unsolicited calls can waste hours sometimes. Set up caller id so you can ascertain who's calling. Use voicemail judiciously, but be sure to follow up your messages. Consider using a virtual office service to screen your calls as a temporary measure whilst you attend to an important project. Set up a buddy system with a colleague so that they take some of your calls and you in turn take theirs another time. Try to make your outgoing calls in bundles so that you remain focused.

Even if you've mastered the telephone there'll still be other interruptions, principal among which is the uninvited visitor. This is the person who perches on the end of your desk chatting about last night's TV seemingly oblivious to the fact that you're trying to get something finished. If you're a manager or team leader you'll want people to feel able to speak to you but you need to make it clear that this does not mean idle chat. If someone asks you if you've got a minute ask them if they're sure a minute is all they'll need. It might be better to schedule some time for later on. Try not to make your work area too inviting. If you have chairs in front of your desk people will tend to sit on them. Having said all this I do not advocate being rude or discourteous to people. Making an overblown gesture of looking at your watch or sighing a lot is not helpful. It's more a question of mutual respect for each other's time.

Paperwork, etc

I don't know about you, but I'm still waiting for the much heralded 'paperless office' to arrive. We were told that the advent of email, SMS texts and the like would see an end to the piles of dog-eared files strewn around desks in organisations of all types. If anything things have got worse. There's only got to be one system crash before, understandably everyone starts printing off copies of documents and emails 'just in case'. Those same emails probably have only one or two lines that are relevant but come with three pages of prior messages and responses.

It takes a determined effort and that key coaching principle of responsibility to achieve mastery over paperwork but the results can prove worth it. Here are a few ideas:

Firstly, have your name removed from external mailing lists and any internal circulation lists that you really don't need to be on. This is classic progress v maintenance. It's very easy to just put stuff in the bin or hit delete, but every time you do that takes up time and causes irritation. Invest time instead on the one-off activity of stopping this stuff arriving in the first place.

The strap line of an old British Telecom advertisement from years ago was 'If it can be said, phone instead'. It makes sense for BT to have us using the phone more and it can make sense for your personal organisation too. Sometimes it can take a lot less time to pick up the phone to pass on information or raise a query than to compose and send an email or a letter. Of course written correspondence provides a record which can be prevalent in low trust organisations where people want to 'cover their backs' and it can mean avoiding the emotional content when say, passing on bad news. Fine if you've got the time, but most of us haven't.

Then there's the weekly report. Do you really need your team or colleagues to produce this report? Do you use the information it contains productively? Does its usefulness and value justify the time it takes to produce? What would happen if you no longer produced this report? The weekly report is up there with the weekly meeting in that these things can so easily become Spanish customs that become ingrained and that nobody thinks to challenge. Could questioning these activities produce a saving of time or energy for other, more important things?

Finally, a couple of ideas that are more quirky but can be most effective. If you're receiving a stream of unnecessary material, return it all to the sender. Experience suggests that you'll only need do this once or twice for the message to get through. The other one I like is what's known as the 'measles' test. The idea here is to place a dot on a piece of paper each time you handle it. Most people end up with paper covered in dots after a day or so – hence the measles. In truth, there are only four courses of action to take with a piece of paper or correspondence; deal with it straight away, delegate it to someone else, put it in the diary system, or throw it away. Putting something in the diary is fine as long as it is because you intend to take definitive action on it at the later time and not just to procrastinate. Throwing paper away is again something that most of us do too little of, perhaps fearing that we'll need it someday. If you do, you can be almost certain someone less in control of their time will have a copy and you can get it from them.

How do you like to see your desk? I remember coaching a client whose desk genuinely looked as if the proverbial bomb had hit. He tried to explain this away by claiming to be following a time management approach called the Linear Spread System. Others will justify a chaotic approach by claiming that an untidy desk is the sign of a tidy mind or that they can locate anything they need in a couple of seconds. I am doubtful of all of these claims and consider most of them excuses. I believe that an untidy desk or work area leads to high stress, missed deadlines, unneces-sary distractions and time wasted looking for things. I realise that everybody has a preferred working style, but I also find that a haphazard approach to work organisation creates a great deal of internal interference. It tells us that we are not in control and cannot be certain that everything is on track. It sends similar signals to those with whom we work.

Getting control over the paper that flows around your work is straightforward enough but requires a determined effort. Be deci-sive when dealing with incoming paperwork and try to handle each piece of paper only once. Avoid doing things needlessly like recording appointments in your diary, PC and wall chart at the same time. Restrict your working area to one piece of work at a time and don't use your in-tray as storage space.

Try to keep up to speed with filing paper away. A few minutes each day is better than a couple of hour's worth at the end of the month. Throw away any redundant information you find in files and encourage everyone to mark discard dates on documents. Put used files in an archive regularly and try to avoid keeping the same note in different files.

The telephone

Does this sound like you?

I rush to answer the phone as soon as it rings because it might be something important and besides it's good customer service isn't it? I suppose I do spend longer on calls than is really necessary, but a bit of social chit chat doesn't hurt. I must admit I sometimes have to make calls twice because there was something I forgot to say, and that sometimes we do interrupt meetings to take calls. I'll drop whatever I'm doing when I remember a call I need to make and I don't believe it's fair to have calls screened. I spend a lot of time having to deal with unsolicited calls which means I end up scattering my own outgoing calls randomly throughout the day. I write down messages on the handiest piece of paper available at the time, but this means that I sometimes forget to pass telephone messages on to others.

You've probably been guilty of at least half of these 'sins' at some point, but the idea is not to make you feel guilty, rather it is to raise your awareness of the type of bad telephone habits we can all so easily slip into. To take this further you might like to spend a little time on something important not urgent, and analyse say, a week's worth of calls. Consider how many unexpected calls you received and how many of these proved pointless. Note how many calls lasted longer than necessary and how many calls could have been dealt with by someone else. Most importantly, identify how many calls interrupted you when you were dealing with an important, high impact item.

If such analysis reveals that you need to exert more control, there is a variety of techniques for managing incoming calls. You can put phone on divert or voicemail when busy as long as this tactic is used sparingly and for the right reasons. Set aside a quiet hour during which you will not take calls and respect others' attempts to do likewise. Ask for calls to be put on hold during meetings. Be polite, firm and brief with unwanted callers and ask others to call back at an agreed time when you are less busy. Avoid tackling peripheral tasks while on the phone especially taking notes on loose bits of paper. Arrange for calls to be screened wherever possible or ask the receptionist not to give out names to cold callers.

You can similarly do a bit of *Reality* checking on the way you manage your outgoing calls. Was the telephone the best way of getting the message across? Did I achieve my objective or did I waste too much time on small talk? Did the call last longer than anticipated and was there anything I forgot to say?

At the *Options* stage you might consider planning calls or making outgoing calls in blocks. Can you prioritise your calls and set limits on the duration of each call? Collect any relevant documents before the call and check afterwards that you achieved your objective.

SUMMARY

This chapter has been all about personal organisation. If you prefer the terms time management or personal management, fine. I think that the principles hold true in any event. Fundamentally, those principles are concerned with identifying your own goals and priorities within a work context and taking responsibility for acting on them.

> The key is not to prioritise what's on our schedules, but to schedule our priorities

Stephen Covey

I believe that coaching around personal organisation will be far more effective than any number of time management courses because I sense that everybody knows the theory by now but something is holding them back from taking action. It's that internal interference again making us think that it's always quicker and easier to do something ourselves rather than invest time developing others. It keeps us 'fire fighting' and reacting to whatever is most urgent rather than taking a strategic view.

Coaching also recognises that an individual approach to personal organisation is required because prescriptive approaches rarely succeed. On a simple level this can be in terms of helping people to recognise their own natural peaks and troughs in the working day and organising their work accordingly and as far as is reasonably possible. On a more complex level this can be a matter of people becoming so aware in their situation that they realise they're in the wrong job. I worked with one colleague who could simply not cope with the idea of a pending tray at all. They realised that to work free of stress they needed to be in a job where the work was finished at the end of each day no matter what. Other people would find that an unacceptable restriction. We're all different and coaching recognises difference.

Some jobs have more scope for planning and time management than others of course. A team of contact centre advisors employed to handle a large volume of incoming calls will have little opportunity to act on ideas like urgency v importance and progress v maintenance at an individual level. Nevertheless their own observations and feelings about what works and what doesn't can be voiced at team meetings or other fora and this at least allows for a degree of responsibility and ownership. Coaching for personal organisation in such a setting can concentrate on promoting performance, learning and enjoyment and capturing the focus and motivation that this will produce.

Simple devices such as time sheets, to-do lists and plans can really help, but use them properly and don't let them become time wasters themselves. Daily plans must include time for unscheduled interruptions or they'll be unworkable.

Reviews of how we're doing must concentrate on what was *accomplished* rather than what was *done*. Don't be so busy learning your lines that you don't realise you're no longer in the right play. Focus on processes by all means but check progress against your performance goals.

CHAPTER 9

PERFORMANCE REVIEW

INTRODUCTION

Here are some appraisal comments from my own (often less than) illustrious past.

> Has many shortcomings, but these can be put down to his immaturity

> Output has been adequate, but then he has hardly been stretched

If the purpose of management is to deliver performance – and I believe it is – let's consider the usefulness of these remarks. I will firstly admit that they are both true as far as my memory can be trusted but would they have promoted an improved performance? The first is a kind of thinly veiled personal criticism that contains nothing I can act upon to try to improve. What shortcomings? What is it that mature people do that I don't? The second is like being damned with faint praise. It's a judgement and one which I could create quite a counter argument for were I so inclined. Such an argument would be unlikely to yield anything positive though, given the power base in the relationship.

People deserve better than this. A decent performance review in which the reviewee is given a voice and can engage in a meaningful discussion can provide a number of benefits to both parties and to the organisation as a whole. From the organisation's point of view, performance review provides a way to ensure it is on track and that objectives and targets are being met. It also means staff who are contributing to the success of the organisation can be recognised, not just those that are under-performing. Reviewees benefit too by understanding their role in the organisation and the impact their behaviour has on its success. They can also see their efforts and successes recognised, confident that the recognition is based on rational judgement, not emotion. A poor performance review provides none of these things. It is quickly reduced to a tick box exercise driven by administrators in HR departments and is a waste of time.

Towards the end of a session on training managers as coaches, I will often ask the group to call out ideas for situations at work in which coaching may be useful. Invariably, 'during appraisals/performance reviews' is the first response.

This is perhaps not surprising given that performance reviews are often the only time that managers can legitimately spend time talking with their staff about their work without accusations of wasting time on 'touchy-feely stuff'. A well structured performance review provides a real opportunity to learn from what's happened over a period of time and to consider goals and development plans for the period to come. These are two issues in which a coaching approach can certainly help to produce a positive outcome.

In essence performance review simply means a framework by which organisation wide goals and objectives can be distilled to the individual level and then tracked and monitored so that any help or development required to meet or exceed those objectives can be supplied.

A coaching approach to performance review enables the benefits to be realised and the drawbacks reduced. I am often asked to coach new reviewers on how to get the most from the process and we have consulted with many organisations on system design and implementation. In this chapter I'll outline how coaching principles can be applied to the whole process and consider the perspectives of reviewers, reviewees and the organisation overall.

INTERFERENCE

As ever we'll begin our detailed look at how coaching connects by considering the more obvious sources of both external and internal interference.

External

Time

When given the task of undertaking performance reviews few people say 'Oh good, I was getting fed up with having so little work, I can fill my time by undertaking some reviews with the team'. It's more likely that they'll be wondering how they'll ever find the time to do the reviews in a meaningful way. This seems to be the case for both reviewers and reviewees. If you've read the last chapter on personal organisation you'll recognise that undertaking reviews is one of those *important, progress* tasks that so often get subordinated to urgent, maintenance tasks. It's typical to look at spending at least a couple of hours with each member of your team at least two or three times per year. This can add up to a significant amount of time. There are ways though of minimising this. Look for every possible way to involve reviewees in the process even down to administrative tasks like booking the rooms and writing up the discussion notes. This both frees up your time and generates responsibility for your reviewees. Another way of minimising any disruption is to look upon performance review as a process not an event. By this I mean that an annual review meeting can be made easier by holding a series of interim reviews throughout the year. These interim reviews are more straightforward if you regularly discuss performance with your staff, coach them and give feedback and so on.

Organisation Culture

To be a process that can make a difference and add value, performance review needs to have genuine, visible support from the very top. Without such support, any performance review framework will quickly become seen as merely an administrative chore driven by the HR department. Performance review needs to be positioned as a line management responsibility; an essential part of building capability in the team. HR should be seen as the custodians of the scheme and there to arbitrate if there are difficulties.

Sensing a lack of senior management support is likely to create interference in the minds of even the most dedicated reviewer.

Consequences

People often wonder what reviews are for. This was easy to see a few years ago when performance related pay was popular because people knew that ratings received at a review would have a direct link to pay, bonuses, etc. Such schemes proved difficult to administer though and so it's more usual now to have pay reviews separate from performance reviews. Where this is the case it is vital that the performance review discussions are highlighted as a way of helping staff to understand what has driven their results to date and what they can do to improve. Whilst this may not directly affect their pay there are always indirect links to progression and advancement. High performers get recognised in some way eventually. Once again it's easy to see that without a clear understanding of the purpose behind the reviews it's difficult to commit to the process with any real enthusiasm.

Internal

Relationships

Undertaking performance reviews can throw up some tricky situations. You may find yourself being promoted to team leader and having to carry out reviews with people whom you previously worked alongside. This can be particularly difficult if you contributed to any criticism of the system and now have to act as a sort of poacher turned gamekeeper. Similarly you may find yourself reviewing the performance of people you consider friends and with whom you socialise. It's not easy, but you'll need to keep the two relationships separate and to focus on reviewing performance not the person.

You could also find yourself coaching reviewees who find the whole thing difficult. They may need your support if they find their manager overbearing and difficult to talk to or if they have lost all faith in their manager's ability to run the team.

Lacking competence

Undertaking an effective review of one's staff is a process – along with interviewing, coaching and giving presentations – that managers are expected to be able to do well simply because they are managers. It's almost as if these skills are expected to be awoken within you as soon as your new business card with the word manager arrives. However, all of these things require training if you're to carry them out successfully. For performance reviews you'll need to understand how to set objectives, provide feedback and know the variety of development opportunities that may exist. You'll also want to know how your organisation's system works and what you're required to do before, during and after the review meeting. I know from bitter experience that without adequate training, managers just do what they think best which normally results in a tick-box session from which nobody benefits.

Lacking confidence

Beyond matters of competence lie matters of confidence. We've already seen that performance reviews can cause difficulties in existing relationships and you'll need to feel confident in handling these things. You'll need confidence as well when it comes to handling poor performance. If everyone in the team is performing really well, the reviews are simple; it's when you have to address poor performance that problems arise. People may get upset or angry which is unpleasant to handle if you prefer to avoid conflict. People may be so disappointed that their performance continues to dip after the review and you'll need to give ongoing support. None of these is reason enough to avoid reviewing performance but they do require a confident approach. Some coaching for yourself before you undertake your reviews – particularly difficult ones – will help bolster your confidence and ensure that things go well.

Try to remember that I'm not suggesting that this interference can be fully removed. I believe instead that if we focus on the positive qualities we want to experience in the review situation that the interference will fade into the background.

PLE IN PERFORMANCE REVIEW

In my organisational life I used to really look forward to my performance reviews and invariably enjoyed the meetings. I didn't always come away with the ratings I'd wanted and there were sometimes things which were uncomfortable to hear, but I always left the reviews clearer about things than when I'd gone in. My subsequent involvement in the wider world of performance review has taught me that this experience, whilst far from unique, is hardly typical.

It seems that it's the performance in performance review that gets stressed. The review meetings are seen as essentially a task. For some this means getting through it as quickly and painlessly as possible and for others it means slavishly completing the forms. This is not what good performance review is all about. A series of performance review meetings are an opportunity for two people involved in a working relationship to come together to discuss progress. The value lies in the quality of these discussions not in the form filling or scheduling of the meetings. I think it perfectly possible to bring a little learning and enjoyment into this process alongside the need to perform, that is, to get the reviews done and to do them well. What can we learn about performance reviews by undertaking the meetings? You may discover that there are ways to further involve your reviewees to both save time and generate ownership. You may find that it's possible to use the reviews as an opportunity to learn more about each other. Review meetings are often valued by those who don't work closely together day by day. Try to look upon even difficult reviews as learning opportunities in which you can discover ways of handling emotional exchanges.

There's also room for enjoyment in review meetings. You can celebrate your reviewee's successes and draw a line under any trying times. Provided both parties are comfortable you can consider holding the review off-site. A change of scene can sometimes change the whole nature of a discussion like this.

CRITICAL VARIABLES

Outer variables

Ratio of input

It can be really useful to notice how much air time you take up in the meeting compared to the reviewee. Depending on how well established your organisation's system is and how familiar your reviewees are with the process, you'll probably want to spend a fair amount of time up front positioning the meeting and establishing how it should work, but then really it's over to them. Try to encourage your reviewees to give you a commentary on what's happened since you last met and notice any times when you've been speaking for a long period without their contribution.

Performance v person

Perhaps the quality which most distinguishes the really effective reviewer from the average is the ability to manage this particular dynamic. The more you are able to concentrate on matters of performance and avoid matters of personality the greater the likelihood of a productive outcome. I've listened to countless tales of review meetings that have come unstitched and invariably this happens when the talk turns to matters of personality. Telling someone they have an unhelpful attitude will simply be met with resistance – we all believe our attitudes are appropriate – whereas explaining that you heard a customer passing comment on their way out of the building is the basis for a discussion around what might have caused this. Notice how often you stray from *performance* into *person* and encourage your reviewee to notice this too.

Reviewee's reaction

Of course the biggest variable during reviewee meetings is the reviewee themselves. It's conceivably possible for you to run all of your review meetings in an identical way but each will result in a different outcome because of how different reviewees may react. Notice the reaction some of your feedback generates. Is the reviewee sitting forward and animated or quiet and withdrawn? Which aspects of their work seem to be most interesting for them to talk about and which seem to be dull? This awareness raising exercise can be very revealing and far more useful to you than simply trying to follow a text book approach.

Inner variables

Detachment

This is linked to the outer variable of performance v person and is a question of noticing the degree to which you feel detached from the discussion versus the feeling that you're getting drawn into an emotional exchange. This can be a particularly useful variable to focus on when you know in advance that a review may be a little difficult. Perhaps there are areas of under performance to discuss or some bad news to pass on. Why not set a performance goal along the lines of 'I intend to keep my detachment level at a minimum of 8 out of 10 during this meeting'?

Focus

Where is your focus during a review meeting? We all know it should be on the reviewee and their performance but does it stray to what happened before the meeting and what will be happening later? Are you focused on trying to understand the reviewee's point of view or are you just rehearsing your counter argument?

Quality of listening

Finally, pay attention to the listening that goes on throughout the meeting. Maintain eye contact and use verbal and non verbal prompts to encourage the reviewee. Take as many notes as you like but remember it's difficult to write and listen at the same time so consider whether it would be better to pause for note taking. Notice what happens to the quality of input from the reviewee when you really quieten your own mind and do nothing other than just listen.

AIMS CASCADE

There are three main parties within any performance review system: the reviewee, the reviewer and the organisation, the latter term recognising all layers of management beyond the reviewee's immediate boss. Each of these parties will have their own aims in terms of what they would like from the system and some examples of these are shown in Table 9.1 below.

A good system will ensure that these needs are compatible and a good performance review is about balancing the needs of the different parties. Yes it's important that reviewees find the whole thing a positive experience, but at the same time they should leave

Table 9.1

	Reviewee	Reviewer	Organisation
Dream	To have my attributes recognised	To increase performance in the team	To drive performance
Performance Goal	To mention 3 personal achievements and request support for personal study	To run a meeting where the reviewee has 80% of the input	To implement a performance review system, applicable to all staff, by the year end
Processes	Body language, assertion, gathering evidence, etc	Questioning, Listening, meeting management, etc	Research, project management, staff communication, Negotiation, etc

a review meeting clear on the strengths they need to develop and the weaknesses they need to address.

The table shows that as the high level aims or dreams are developed into processes, people skills become key. Successful performance review does not come from system design, important though this is. Instead it is largely a matter of the quality of relationship that can be established between reviewer and reviewee. Consequently coaching in this area is usually a matter of restoring focus on the key communication skills of questioning, listening and using assertive, adult-like behaviour.

WOULD YOU LIKE ANOTHER SUGGESTION?

Ultimately then, it's all about people, and we can further simplify the idea of performance review by suggesting it is a means by which people in organisations can find answers to five key questions:

- What is my job?
- How well do I have to do it?
- How am I doing?
- How have I done?
- How can I improve?

We can now take each of these in turn and look at how coaching can help us provide meaningful answers.

What is my job?

Traditionally, defining job roles is a management task. In large organisations this may be done with a certain degree of formality and result in written job descriptions or role profiles. Such formability is often driven by the need for a consistent approach to defining the parameters of a job to support say, a job evaluation exercise.

In smaller organisations this would be akin to using a hammer to crack a nut and it would be more typical for a manager or business owner to sit the employee down and outline their tasks, duties, expectations and so on. Whilst this less structured approach may create problems later on if the business grows, it does afford maximum flexibility and ensures that people can readily change the dynamics of their role if the need arises.

Increasingly we're seeing that the latter approach is something larger organisations need to consider given the rate of change out there. Whilst we'll still need the documentation for the reasons described above, a coaching approach can allow us to explore staff member's own perceptions of their roles and responsibilities, gain access to any creative ideas they may have and encourage them to take ownership for their role.

Working together to define a job avoids getting caught in the minutiae of job descriptions or complex role profiles. It allows us to discover what an individual needs to do to be effective and make a contribution. And remember being effective means doing the right things, not just doing things right.

How well do I have to do it?

Defining how well a job needs to be done is admittedly a little trickier. The answer to this question is most commonly articulated in performance review documentation as Targets, Standards, Key Performance Indicators (KPIs), etc. 'Goals' is probably as good a generic term for these things as any, so let's look at how coaching can help us get this part of the process right.

Most people know the mnemonic SMART and the following – taken from my book *Coaching in a Week* [19] – is a variation on that theme:

M	Measurable	How will you know if you've got there?
A	Achievable	Is it within your reach?
C	Challenging	How motivated are you to achieve it?
S	Specific	Do you know exactly what's required?
P	Positive	Is it about what's desired, or what's to be avoided?
R	Relevant	How does your goal contribute to a bigger picture?
O	Observable	How will you demonstrate your success?
U	Understandable	Is the goal described in clear, simple terms?
T	Time Bound	By when will it be achieved?

Notice that the points for each criterion are expressed as questions. The idea being that the coach/reviewer should use them as the basis for discussing goals not imposing them.

Once again a coaching approach will ensure ownership by the reviewee because they will feel some sense of choice and control over what they're committing to.

Personally I think it best to write these goals down on the performance review forms in some way, but only if they're going to be looked at and reviewed! I like to see review forms that are dog-eared, torn and covered in amendments as this indicates they've been *used* as opposed to being tucked away in a drawer, which indicates merely that they've been *done*.

How am I doing?

To be able to tell your people how well they are doing requires you to commit to a regular timetable of reviews. Half-yearly or quarterly is common but each individual is best placed to advise you how often they would like their performance reviewed. Even with large teams frequent performance reviews do not have to become a time consuming burden. The trick is to encourage individuals to evaluate their own performance and come to you with their own evidence.

Evidence can include customer or colleague comments, statistics, timesheets, sales figures or whatever the two of you decide is important and relevant.

Don't be too quick to dismiss self-evaluation either, most people become surprisingly circumspect when describing their own performance. As coaches we should recognise that nobody is closer to the job than the individual performer and as such they are best placed to provide a commentary on what's been going well, less well and so on.

Above all recognise that considering performance and providing feedback (see below) should be an ongoing part of any manager's day to day activity. Likewise don't wait for a performance review before recognising mistakes or organising a training course. If any kind of learning is required then the sooner it is recognised and provided the sooner performance can improve.

Finally, it's probably best that I use this heading to highlight the value of giving praise. Whatever else we do, we coaches should use performance reviews as an opportunity to provide praise where due and thus reinforce self-belief.

> The only time people do not like praise is when too much of it is going toward someone else.
> **Martin Luther King, Jr.**

How have I done?

Irrespective of the number of reviews undertaken during the year, there will still be a need to tie up loose ends with an annual appraisal. Here you are answering the question, *How have I done?*

If you've followed my advice so far, you'll find that this becomes a relatively straightforward process where you can simply agree a rating and link it to pay or bonus if your organisation works in this way. This means that more time can be spent on looking forward to *How can I improve?* And you can both think about new goals and development plans.

Experience suggests however that this is often not the case and that too much importance gets attached to this annual event. I stress again that good performance review needs to be seen as an ongoing process not an annual event and I believe that taking a coaching approach will promote that perception.

Without coaching at the heart of our approach to managing performance we risk fostering the sense that the performance appraisal is a one sided judgement of the person rather than a joint evaluation of performance.

How can I improve?

Everything we've looked at so far can be likened to rowing a boat; trying to steer a course ahead by facing backwards! Whilst we can and must learn lessons from past performance, the real value of performance management lies in considering how we can mobilise people's potential to improve and make progress. Thus it is at this point that coaching takes centre stage.

A well constructed performance review is likely to unearth three main types of development need. I might need to develop my *knowledge* in some way, e.g. learning how to use a software package or I might need to develop my *skills* in say, effective communication. These first two types of development need are arguably best addressed by the more orthodox means of, say a face to face training event.

But if the review uncovers development needs related to *behaviour* or *attitude*, such as becoming more assertive or handling pressure more effectively, then working with a good coach is likely to yield much more effective results.

By and large it seems that performance review systems are often seen as a waste of management time and of little practical use. However, my feeling is that if performance reviews are undertaken in the spirit of coaching then there is a real opportunity for learning and advancement.

SUMMARY

This chapter has concentrated on coaching as it relates to the performance review *process*, but even more important is the underlying *behaviours* that need to be in evidence.

Any performance review framework will quickly become a key part of an organisation's culture and it is therefore vital that the senior management team demonstrate effective behaviour at all times. In addition to providing feedback and coaching, they should be seen to be acting as coaches, communicating effectively being open to upward feedback and learning from mistakes.

In many ways a good coaching session can be thought of as a performance review without all the bells and whistles.

Similarly, if we take the ARROW we can see that it doubles as an effective review structure and will ensure we discuss all areas.

A	Aims	What are the key targets and objectives for the coming period?
R	Reality	What's happening now, and what can we learn from that?
R	Reflection	How big a gap between these two points?

O Options   What changes can we make, or development can we provide to improve performance?

W Way Forward   What is the plan of action and when will we get together to review it?

I was talking at a seminar recently about the need for coaches to work hard at helping the people they coach to raise their levels of awareness.

'Surely,' suggested one participant, 'their awareness will be raised if we provide good feedback'.

Now normally I would disagree and say that you can only offer feedback on what you *see* and *hear* but that unfortunately performance issues are often due to how people *feel* and you can't give any feedback at that level.

However, it was an intelligent suggestion that got me thinking and I produced the following mnemonic for effective feedback:

P Precise   Make sure the feedback contains information that the receiver can choose to act upon. Saying 'that was good' however well intentioned does not offer the receiver any clues about *what exactly* was good.

U Understandable Normal rules apply. Simple, unambiguous language that can be easily understood.

N Non Judgemental Good feedback is informative not evaluative. This is crucial in coaching where being judgemental can create a lot of negative interference.

C Constructive   Whether the feedback is on something that went well or badly, it should be possible to offer the receiver some thoughts on how things could be better next time.

| **H** | Honest | We serve no one's best interests by avoiding or fudging performance issues. |
| **Y** | Yours | The best feedback is owned by the giver. |

All too often feedback is personalised and judgemental and results in resentment and defensiveness. Asking coaching questions encourages reviewees to think for themselves and take responsibility for developing their own performance.

CHAPTER 10

CAREER DEVELOPMENT

INTRODUCTION

Running a coaching session under the general heading of career development covers a multitude of scenarios. At one end of the scale you may be having a quick chat with an employee who is about to go for a three month secondment to another section. At the other end you may be dealing with someone who is now out of a job with your organisation and who you are trying to help secure an external position. In between there is coaching to perform well at interview or assessment centre, coaching for curriculum vitae (CV) and personal marketing material construction, coaching as part of a fast track development programme, and more besides.

Each of these scenarios includes an emotional element to some degree or other and this means that coaching is an approach likely to yield some impressive results. Coaching, as we know, deals with the 'inner game'. That opponent within us all that gets in our way at the most inopportune times. In the other areas we've examined, performance review, personal organisation, etc, we often get another chance. You might run a poor review or be badly organised for a day but you'll get another opportunity. On the other hand, certain aspects of career development, particularly interviews or assessment centres, create much greater pressure to perform. Do badly on the day and you might miss out on that job or promotion. The stakes are higher and those internal interferences of self-doubt and negative expectation can speak with much louder voices than in more day to day situations.

Coaching for career development has a big pay-off for the organisation as well as the individual in the current working climate. Career development has become an essential part of the deal these days – the so-called psychological contract. New employees, particularly young ones, are likely to join organisations expecting to be developed, to be exposed to high quality training and development and to see their CV build throughout their tenure. Then they'll move on and this is no longer seen as a sad separation as it was in the 'job for life' days. Organisations must meet this expectation and support the employee as they build their own employability.

Some may see this as recruiting for the competition and withhold from developing their staff for fear that they'll leave and go elsewhere. Some will but what's the alternative? We could do no career development and run the organisation with a partially developed workforce or we could pay lip service to career development and then make it difficult for people to leave. But unhappy people do not generally make for good performance.

> It's awful when people quit and go, but it's worse when they quit and stay.

> **Robert Holden**

In reality a team of people who are developed and who believe the organisation has their best interests at heart are far more likely to stay and give of their best. A recent staff survey at Hilton International found that 37% said that being offered development opportunities was the most important factor in deciding whether to continue their career with the organisation.

INTERFERENCE

External

Feedback

A session on career development will invariably include an element of performance feedback. When done informally, this is likely to mean you giving the coachee your views on how well they're doing, the strengths they deploy and the opportunities to develop such things in the future. More formal career coaching may include some feedback from the manager's own team collected perhaps by some 360° feedback tool. This is useful only insofar as the content can be presented to the manager as information as opposed to judgement and, as we saw in the last chapter, this is very difficult to do. Judgemental feedback such as 'your team think you are abrasive' is likely to be met with resistance however true the sentiment. But what if the person you're coaching really is abrasive and the team genuinely feel that way. Let me remind you that the 8th law of coaching states that curiosity is more useful than judgement. We might therefore ask 'What reasons might the team have for expressing this view?' What incidents might have created this opinion?' 'How can perceptions of abrasiveness differ?' and so on. This is likely to lead to a much higher level of awareness.

Outside influences

Without wishing to make sweeping generalisations or succumb
to stereotyping, it seems to me that people at work commit to
taking their career seriously around the same time they commit
to taking their life seriously. Often this means wanting to get on
at work at the same time as entering a serious relationship, buying
a home, starting a family or a variety of other serious commitments. The question is: are these things compatible? They may
or may not be and we can find out from an effective coaching
discussion but the point is that a *feeling* of being pulled in two
directions is likely to make it difficult for the coachee to focus
on what they *really* want. This has to be acknowledged and dealt
with.

Clash of values

As a young man working in a bank I could not have told you what
the organisation's values were if my life depended on it and frankly
I could not have cared less. My concentration was on doing an
adequate job and emptying my pay packet into the hands on the
nearest publican! As I progressed though I began to understand
that a part of the more senior roles I now held was to represent
the organisation to my team, colleagues, customers, and so on and
to form of view as to whether my own values were in line with
those of the organisation. I found it very difficult, for example, to
feel committed to the move towards customer service via call
centres as I value one-to-one service. I could understand the business case, but that didn't mean I had to agree with it. Senior roles
require people to uphold organisational values and where these
are at odds with personal values a lot of interference can be
generated.

Internal

Arrogance

This is an interesting one and not a factor we've discussed so far. The simple fact is that some people really are too arrogant to believe that they need help in developing their careers. They believe that what they've done to develop their careers thus far will serve them well in the future. I remember sifting through some internal applications and being appalled at the apathetic way some very talented people had applied for a significant promotion.

At other times it's a question of people believing they've 'done their time' and that they should be in line for promotion or development irrespective of their level of performance. This 'time served' mentality is still a big part of the culture in many organisations.

Of course sometimes a little arrogance is used to mask some insecurities. Some people might feel that as 'managers' and 'leaders' they should be fantastic role models with brilliant career plans that almost magically come true. In truth, even the most accomplished performer has nagging doubts and concerns about their ability and will value being able to explore these concerns in a climate of trust.

Fear of failure

To put oneself forward for a promotion, to apply for a place on a development programme or to think about moving on all have an element of risk. It might not happen. It is often easier to keep ourselves small and stay in a comfort zone which although not wholly satisfying is, by definition, safe, comfortable and known. Unfortunately this type of thinking can lead to sabotaging our own success. I have heard many people tell me that 'there's no point preparing for this assessment centre as they've made their mind up anyway' or 'This is my fifth interview this month, I'll be devastated if I fail again'. As coaches we can promote a much healthier focus than this.

Limiting beliefs

Here's a selection:

- I don't have the intelligence to be a Director
- I don't have the qualifications to be a manager
- I'm not tough enough to work in that section
- As a boss I'll have to have all the answers
- I'll never be able to learn all that I need to do the job
- People like me can't expect a position like that
- I cannot make a difference
- I cannot lead

I consider every one of these to be utter rubbish. None of them are facts, they are all simply beliefs but they are beliefs which limit rather than liberate talent and this serves no useful purpose. We must remember though that such beliefs are formed on the basis of some evidence which makes people think that way. As coaches we need to challenge the validity of that evidence. We need to spend time at the Reality stage of the ARROW sequence exploring how it is that people know they're not intelligent enough or cannot lead. On what evidence do they base such assumptions? Under this kind of spotlight many of these limiting beliefs can be challenged.

PLE IN CAREER DEVELOPMENT

There is an argument to say that certain aspects of career development, such as interviews and assessment centres, as purely about performance and that the notion of enjoying these occasions and being alive to what we might learn from them is completely unrealistic. I'll return to this idea later, but for now let's look at other parts of career development activity where we might more readily seek PLE in balance.

Putting together a CV is a good example. First and foremost we have to perform the task. Plan out what we want to include, type it up and print it out. But what can we learn from this process? Take some time out to find out about CV construction; there are many excellent booklets on the subject. Why not have a quick conversation with your colleagues in HR to see what they look for in a CV? Putting a good CV together is often the art of brevity. What can you learn about communicating briefly but compellingly that you can use in other areas of your work? Similarly, constructing your CV should be an enjoyable process. It is after all, a celebration of your accomplishments. Given a pile of CVs to review I'm convinced I could tell which had been produced carefully with a positive frame of mind from those that had been produced at the end of a hard day, when the aim was to just get it done.

One of my first ever coaching assignments was to help redundant workers find new employment as part of an outplacement programme. The need to perform – to find new work – was acute; these people had bills to pay and families to feed and yet we were determined to create some learning and enjoyment as well. The need for learning was very important because sadly, nobody could guarantee that this would be the only time the people concerned would have to use these job search skills. The need for enjoyment was also paramount as potential employers want upbeat motivated applicants, not downhearted victims, however justified they might be in feeling that way. Rejected applications and unsuccessful interviews were discussed and we would even contact the firms concerned for feedback. Then we moved on and looked ahead. Similarly, successful applicants would be asked to share what they learnt with the rest of the group before leaving to take up their new role.

Going back to my first point I would even argue that it's possible to learn and enjoy an interview or an assessment centre. In fact when I coach people who find attending these things terrifying that's what we concentrate on. The overall aim is obvious; to be successful, but establishing some aims around aspects to enjoy and things to learn about can provide a more useful focus, particularly as the internal interference builds up. You could even think about undertaking an assessment centre or securing an interview when you don't actually need to. This creates a great learning and practice opportunity without the pressure to perform.

CRITICAL VARIABLES

Outer variables

These are perhaps easiest understood by thinking about a typical one to one job interview and so this is the backdrop we'll assume here.

Professionalism

Try to understand the nature of the sort of interviewer you are dealing with. Hopefully you'll be dealing with professional people who after a little small talk will be straight down to business, asking straightforward questions that enable you to demonstrate what you can do, but this is not always the case. You might come up against an interrogator who tries to see if you'll wilt under pressure or the pop psychologist who seems preoccupied with asking you questions about your family or early childhood experiences. Unfortunately not all interviews or assessment centres are run by highly trained people, sometimes it's a matter of all hands to the pump or line management insisting on undertaking all recruitment and selection themselves without support from HR. Your tactics in all of these situations need to be around remaining calm and confident and to give factual, professional answers. Become aware of your own levels of professionalism as this is directly within your own control. We'll look at some specifics later on but for now consider adopting an upright posture with plenty of eye contact and projecting a positive outlook.

Ratio of input

Much of the job search literature makes recommendations regarding the ratio of input between interviewer and interviewee and 80:20 in favour of the interviewee appears typical. I think this is fine as a rule of thumb but it assumes that you will always encounter a professional interviewer which, as we've seen, is not always the case. Some people out there love the sound of their own voice and you're probably best advised to give them some airtime rather than interrupt because you want to hit the magic ratio. Also, think about the role for which you're applying. Lots of talking and extroversion may be great for a role in customer care but not so good for say, research and development. Try to behave during the interview in a manner in keeping with that required by the post.

Reactions

My suggestion here is that you take particular notice of how the interviewer reacts to you and the questions and answers you raise during your time together. Please note this is not an invite to obsess over whether you're saying the *right* things all the time, this will only create interference and tie you in knots. The idea is to increase the rapport between you and the interviewer by becoming more attuned to the things that you do or say that create a positive response. Never forget that it is the interviewer that is trying to solve a problem – they have a vacancy to fill and they are going into the interview hoping that you can demonstrate that you have all the qualities they seek.

Inner variables

Many people are guided in their career development decisions by what their intuition tells them; they need to get a sensation of 'this feels right'. I think this is probably a good thing to notice and focus upon so the following are variables related to this theme.

Desire

How much do you want it? As you sit down to fill in an application form or update your CV, are you filled with determination or excitement or does it feel like just going through the motions? Do you mentally rehearse the interview or assessment day going well or is it something you're putting to the back of your mind until the day arrives? I know this sounds strange and you might think that people wouldn't pursue career opportunities unless they wanted to but in my experience there's a surprising number of people who apply for a certain job because they think they should. Perhaps a manager has told them they ought to be seen to be taking an interest in certain roles or they feel under peer pressure seeing colleagues being promoted and so on. A coaching session in which such issues are manifested may be uncomfortable, but is probably best for all concerned in the long run.

Security

These days there is a lot less linear progression up a solid hierarchical structure than was typical ten or twenty years ago. To get a promotion or develop your career can often mean moving into a project role or in a fledgling department or even on secondment to a supplier or subsidiary company. These opportunities can come with some high financial rewards, but there is usually a higher degree of risk as well. If the project doesn't deliver the expected benefits or the subsidiary fails then you can suddenly find yourself with no role where previously you worked in an established department with a solid if unglamorous future. This of course is something to be weighed up, but listen to what your own intuition tells you. Many people are seduced by the trappings of high office; the salary, the car, the foreign travel or whatever and ignore the fact that they've been driven for years by the need to pay the mortgage and feed the family. If your intuition is screaming at you to be cautious listen to it. What could go wrong? Do you have a plan B? A little 'what if . . . ?' thinking now can save a lot of 'what have I done?' thinking later.

Sense of looking forward

I was working in London and was not enjoying my role at the time having just been through an office merger and being left in a job where I couldn't see much progress. I was given details of a vacancy which existed in a department based on the South Coast. I had the right qualities and experience but taking the role would mean uprooting and leaving behind friends, family, social-life and moving way outside my comfort zone. But the more I progressed along the application path the more I began to *look forward* to the opportunity and not backwards to what I was giving up.

I got that particular job and within a few months had applied for another, largely because people were telling me I *should*, but the same feelings weren't there. I was happy now and didn't want to move on just yet. Yes, I'd be getting more money and other tangible rewards, but I was still learning, performing and enjoying in my current role and didn't want that to stop. I got as far as a one-to-one interview but luckily came up against a skilled interviewer who must have spotted my lack of true commitment. I didn't get that particular role and it's a relief to this day. I wish I'd paid more attention to my intuition and saved a lot of time, energy and heartache back then.

AIMS CASCADE

Those that come to you for support and coaching through some area of career development are likely to have their eyes on the big prize; get that job or win that promotion. In our terms they are focused on the dream and we need to get them focused on processes. The only way to get that job is to perform well at the interview and so we'll need to focus on preparing good answers to questions and adopting appropriate body language.

This theme of developing vague dreams into useful processes on which to focus is continued in Table 10.1 below.

Being able to focus at the level of processes provides a means by which the stress and nervousness inherent in these situations can be minimised. It enables people to concentrate on matters which are within their area of control. Certain aspects of our careers are out of our hands and we are better off concentrating on those things we can directly affect.

Table 10.1

	Getting an opportunity	Getting an interview	Getting selected
Dream	To get out of this dreary, dead-end job	To get invited for interview	To pass this assessment centre
Performance Goal	To have identified at least 3 suitable opportunities by the end of next month	To produce a professional CV and covering letter by the end of next month	To complete all the tasks within the allotted time
Processes	Job search Networking Register with agencies	Produce a draft Circulate for feedback Revise Send as appropriate	Find out about tests to be used Obtain some example questions to practice

WOULD YOU LIKE ANOTHER SUGGESTION?

Undertaking a job search

So, whether through your own choice or not, you're in the position of wanting to find a new job. Most people reach straight for the jobs section of the newspaper but this is not always the best tactic, as we shall see.

In the first instance it's best to do an audit of your skills and abilities at this stage. This is useful in two ways. Firstly it helps you decide on the sort of work and jobs that you are likely to enjoy and find fulfilling. If you're intending to leave your current role because you're bored, the last thing you want to do is go straight into the same situation with another employer. The second reason for auditing your skills is so that you can accurately match them to job requirements that appear in advertisements, etc. Grab some paper and pens and write down your recent work experience. Use this list to distil the key knowledge and skills that you have developed during this time. Remember to include personal qualities such as commitment, drive, and loyalty as most employers are really looking for attitude even though they advertise for skills and experience. Later in this chapter we'll look at using this information to develop your CV and covering letters.

With a clear understanding of your skills and qualities you can begin to seek out the right opportunities and to do this requires an understanding of the hidden job market. Imagine that you're an employer and a vacancy comes up for a senior management role. Before you pay hundreds of pounds to take out a job advertisement where would you first look for likely candidates? To begin with you'd ask around at forums and committees of which you are a member and of course at the golf club or other social groups. Taking on new employees is seldom risk free, so a recommendation from someone you know will be appealing. If that doesn't yield the right person you'll probably consult your file of speculative

CVs and letters that all employers inevitably receive, it's a very cost effective resource. If that doesn't work you'll probably consult a recruitment agency or take out an advertisement. All this means that when undertaking a job search yourself you are better off devoting time and energy to uncovering hidden jobs by networking and letting friends and family know that you are looking for new opportunities, than by firing off endless application forms. Some of these opportunities are so well hidden that even the employer doesn't know they have a vacancy! In other words if you can demonstrate some skills and experience that the employer can use to develop their business in some way you may find that they begin to create a role custom built for you.

Preparing CVs and covering letters

I think the best advice I can pass on here is not to have *a* CV. Whereas at one time you'd have prepared a CV and have had several copies made, in these days of instant word processing I think it better to have a template CV that you can modify to reflect the opportunity you're pursuing. In this way you can use a job advertisement or the knowledge you've built up about your target company to determine what to put in and what to leave out. You want your CV to read as though you have been computer designed for the opportunity in question.

There are hundreds of books out there concerning CV construction and layout and I won't go into detail here. Suffice it to say that your CV is yours and you need to decide how best to present your experience and history. Why not prepare one or two different formats and circulate these for feedback? Generally speaking though your CV should be word processed or at least typed – never handwritten. Use A4 paper of high quality and try to keep the finished document to no more than two sides. Go for a clear, clean layout. First impressions count for more than the detail at this stage. Always check your spelling and grammar and remember that your CV is an advert for you and your first chance to show a new employer or boss what you can do.

When you apply for a job or formal promotion you will invariably need to write a covering letter, even if one is not requested. Sometimes you might be writing a speculative approach and other times you may need to write a formal letter of application. In any event, just like your CV, your covering letter is a personal advert and needs to show you in the best possible light.

Once again go for a word processed document printed on high quality paper. Be careful that the letter is addressed carefully and as a general rule try to write to a named person rather than a 'Dear Sir or Madam'.

I think it best to avoid email if possible. The people to whom you're writing will probably be in receipt of hundreds of emails each day and it will be difficult to make your approach stand out. At some point your email will be printed out anyway and unless you're really IT literate it's difficult to ensure that your formatting won't go awry during printing. Best advice seems to be to prepare word processed documents with protected formatting that you can attach to an email if you have to.

No one is ever recruited or promoted on the strength of their CV and paperwork alone, the purpose of these documents is to create enough interest in you to invite you along to an interview or assessment centre. This means that you can prune any unnecessary detail from your documents and ensure that your key strengths stand out.

Attending interviews

Whether interviews reliably identify employees who will prove to be strong performers is open to question, but they remain the most popular of recruitment methods. I believe this is because the practice of recruitment and selection is essentially a human process and that interviewer and candidate alike appreciate the chance for a one-to-one (usually), face to face exchange.

Let's consider matters before, during and after the interview. It can be much easier to feel focused in the interview itself if you have prepared well beforehand. You need to re-read any materials you already have such as job descriptions and person specifications and be clear about how you will answer any questions based on these.

Find out about how the interview will operate. Will there be one interviewer or a panel? What is the exact location? Do you need to bring any documents? etc. It's also wise to find out as much as you can about the organisation or internal department you are hoping to join in order to be able to answer the almost inevitable 'What do you know about us?' question. Finally, make a list of the questions you want to ask. This demonstrates a business like and professional approach.

As part of your preparation – ideally within a coaching session – make a list of the things you'll need to decide upon before the interview, such as:

- What will you wear?
- What might help you to relax?
- What time will you arrive?
- What will you do while you wait?
- Will you accept a drink?
- How will you enter the room?
- How will you shake hands?
- How will you sit?
- How will you leave the room?
- What will you do after the interview?

Working through these issues in advance will give you a feeling of control and preparedness that will enable you to present yourself in the best light when it comes to the interview proper.

During the interview you'll need to think just as much about how you come across as what you say. The often quoted communication research of Albert Mehrabian suggests that in terms of first impressions, 55% is based on appearance, 38% on tone of voice and only 7% on what is actually said. You can infer from this that you need to ensure that you sit up straight with an open posture, that you look at the interviewer whilst talking and dress appropriately for the role in question.

Hopefully, the job or promotion will be yours but if not a coaching session can turn a disappointment into a learning opportunity by considering:

- How much talking did you do?
- What questions caught you out?
- How well did you highlight your strengths?
- How effectively did you demonstrate that you were listening?
- How did you convey that you wanted to work for the organisation or department?
- How did you demonstrate real enthusiasm?

An honest appraisal of your performance should reveal areas you can develop for next time.

Undertaking assessment centres

As I've alluded to throughout this chapter, assessment centres are becoming more and more popular and you can expect to have to attend one at some time particularly if pursuing a senior role with a large employer.

They can be daunting as you'll have a number of activities which will need to be completed in a short time frame. It is common for assessment centres to be held over one or two days, usually in a hotel or conference facility. From the organisation's point of view, assessment centres make sense in that they can see candidates perform in a number of situations and the averaging effect of this produces a much more reliable prediction of work performance than interview alone.

With focus you can turn the assessment centre to your own advantage as you get a chance to perform in a number of different ways and therefore have a number of opportunities to show what you can do.

Other than a face to face interview which we've already covered there is a range of other exercises which it would be wise to prepare to encounter. Psychometric tests are very popular and fall into two categories. There are aptitude tests which examine your abilities in, say verbal or numeric reasoning or personality profiles which seek to establish whether your behavioural style will be suitable for the role in question. It's also quite likely that you will be asked to participate in a teamwork exercise or group discussion. This may involve completing some physical task or require the group to reach a conclusion or decision following a discussion. Survival scenarios are typical and it's important to remember that the assessors are probably more concerned with how you reach your decision as a group than the actual outcome you decide. Trying to second guess the exact behaviours the assessors are looking for is likely to create interference in your mind so instead concentrate on working with enthusiasm, communicating clearly, keeping the group involved and being as natural as possible. Role play exercises are often used for customer service or sales roles and will normally examine your style of dealing with customers or staff in tricky situations. If you know in advance that you're going to be asked to undertake a role play exercise, ask a colleague to rehearse with you and have a coaching conversation afterwards. Other than these, you might encounter the work simulation or in-tray exercise. You'll be given a series of documents and be asked to choose your priorities and decide what action to take. Finally, you might be asked to prepare and deliver a short presentation. You may be given the topic in advance or it may be given to you with only a short time to prepare. This may be because presentations will feature in the job or because the assessors want to look at how you communicate. The chapter on coaching for presentations contains ideas that will help.

Alongside these formally assessed activities you may get a tour of the organisation, have lunch with senior management or meet with existing employees. Whilst you won't be being assessed as such during these times it's worth remembering that you are always making an impression, so make sure it's a positive one!

SUMMARY

So you (or the people you coach on career development) wake up one morning and decide your job and your work is no longer satisfying your needs. Time for a little career development. The lasting impression of this chapter ought to be that this is an area of working life in which the inner game figures most prominently. Whether the change you will navigate has been thrust upon you or whether you are seeking new opportunities a positive mental approach is your best chance for success.

Accept the need for change. Burying your head and wishing for the old days is rarely productive and places you in the victim role. Change is inevitable and you will inevitably have to deal with it. The question is will you take control or just respond to emerging circumstances? Responsibility means that in career development terms you need to take control of your work and career choices and recognise that no one else will do it for you.

Remember that actually you *can* teach an old dog new tricks and that even while you wait or plan for a new opportunity you can be learning and developing new skills to increase your options and, just as importantly, to keep you upbeat and motivated.

In the section on aims we considered the importance of developing dreams (vague aims) into performance goals and then focusing on the processes that will deliver those goals. It's vitally important that these goals are expressed as matters over which you have control or at least influence. One of the frustrations of pursuing the career or working life that you want is the number of other people that can have an effect. No matter. Take responsibility for what you can and as other matters crop up decide on positive actions that you can take to get you back on track.

Having said this a little reality checking and focusing on key strengths is useful too. Take time to identify your transferable skills. A transferable skill is one that is a genuine strength, that you enjoy using and that is marketable, i.e. a skill that others value. Look widely for these skills, there may be aspects of your social or personal life in which you have developed abilities that could be highly prized in another part of the business.

Much of this chapter was devoted to developing an effective CV or covering letter or any document which you submit alongside an application or response. It's important to remember that any such document is a form of personal advertising and as such needs to be eye-catching, interesting, easy to read and individual. You want something that will lodge in the recruiter's mind . . . but for the right reasons.

A big tip and one which you can implement straight away is to get into the habit of talking about achievements not activities. Whether writing your CV or fielding questions at interview it would be better to say something along the lines of 'I successfully rationalised the department's procedures and saved £3,000 per year' than 'I reorganised the procedures'. Coaching and being coached will not only help you become more aware of your achievements but also to feel at ease in claiming responsibility for them.

PART 3

HOW TO IMPLEMENT COACHING

INTRODUCTION

If you're reading this book cover to cover as opposed to just dipping in to the parts that interest you, you've reached a crucial point. We've examined the Peak coaching model in detail and this has given you a framework that you can use to bring about sustainable high performance from the individuals and teams with whom you work. We extended that ability in Part 2 by considering the typical work situations in which your coaching might be sought and hopefully developed your coaching skills in these specific areas. This may be enough for you. You may consider that coaching is a tool in your toolbox that you can reach for as needs be and this is fine. I hope though that you'll want to take it further. I believe that the true power of coaching becomes available when organisations seek to make it an essential part of the every day business of managing and developing people. Of course utilising coaching in this way has more implications than having one or two people trained as coaches. How would a coaching culture differ from the current culture and would it be appropriate given the business or service plan? How would a coaching approach affect management style? How could we train managers as coaches? At what cost? How would we know if the training and subsequent coaching are effective? These are not easy questions and there are no quick answers so this third part of the book is for those of you charged with making coaching happen in your organisation. My aim is not to provide a rigid implementation plan but rather to highlight the key points you'll need to consider to produce your own plan fit for the unique needs of your place of work.

CHAPTER 11

TOWARDS A COACHING CULTURE

INTRODUCTION

So what is a coaching culture and how would you know if you've established one? Professors David Clutterbuck and David Megginson at the Mentoring and Coaching Research Unit of Sheffield Hallam University define it as one where coaching is the predominant style of managing and working together, and where commitment to improving the organisation is embedded in a parallel commitment to improving the people [2]. This suggests that every area of organisational life from post room to board room should have coaching at its core. This makes perfect sense if we strip out some of the needless complexity that permeates working life and get back to basics. You provide a product or service to people who want it and charge more than it costs to provide it. The more often you do this the more money you make. You'll have people who make, serve, manage or support and the better they do this the more effective the business. Therefore, if through coaching we can help individuals perform better, then by extension, the business or organisation will perform better.

Of course if it were that simple everyone would feel as if they were working in a coaching culture, but most don't and there are some obvious barriers that must be overcome to bring it about. Managers must be trained in how to coach and not left to work it out for themselves simply because they *are* managers. Similarly, coachees need some training or at least quality information on what coaching is and what it isn't, what to expect from coaching and how to access it if they need it. The senior team, assuming they're driving or backing the move towards a coaching culture, must become advocates and role models in deed as well as in word. Each time a director leaves a coaching workshop because 'something important has cropped up' it sends the message that coaching isn't important and there's no real commitment behind it.

My aim in this chapter is twofold. I want firstly to examine in detail what we mean by culture and then to present a model of interpreting culture to try to create a compelling vision of what working in a coaching culture would be like. My hope in doing so is to create a dream aim worthy of the time, money and energy you'll need to make it happen.

WHAT IS CULTURE?

In his thorough treatment of the subject in *Coaching Across Cultures* [18], Philippe Rosinski offers the following definition:

> A group's culture is the set of unique characteristics that distinguishes its members from another group.

Rosinski's work is mainly concerned with how coaching must recognise and utilise cultural differences *within* the coaching relationship, but his definition is also useful in our attempts to understand the nature of a coaching culture.

The characteristics which comprise culture will have both visible and invisible elements. The visible ones will include the language and symbols while the invisible set will include beliefs and values. A coaching culture requires both. It is not enough to have a highly organised approach to training and development, a rigorous performance review process and so on, if there is still an intolerance of time taken to think and endless blaming whenever anything goes wrong.

The definition also mentions groups, and cultural groupings have many dimensions. Typically people recognise nationality, religion, gender and ethnicity as cultural groups but there are also groups whose culture may be defined by industry, profession, education, union membership, etc. The implication for establishing a coaching culture is to firstly define the group concerned. Is it the whole organisation or just certain departments? Is it for all staff or only for some? We must also recognise that people can belong to more than one group at the same time. It is perfectly possible to be both English and a HR Professional but which culture most influences your behaviour at work? At a basic level it is perhaps reviewing people's notion of who is 'them' and who is 'us'. No one will respond to working in a coaching culture they do not feel part of.

CULTURAL INDICATORS

In their book *Exploring Corporate Strategy* [9], Gerry Johnson and Kevan Scholes present a model called the cultural web as a means of characterising and analysing organisation structure. The cultural web consists of:

- Stories
- Routines and Rituals

- Organisational Structure
- Control Systems
- Power structures
- Symbols
- Overall

My feeling is that these elements can be useful in defining a desired culture as well as describing an existing one and to this end the rest of this chapter is devoted to taking each of these indicators in turn and outlining a coaching culture in the same terms.

Stories

Think back to your early days at work. Remember your first few days or weeks getting accustomed to your new surroundings and being introduced to the people with whom you would now interact on a day to day basis. If your experience was typical you would have been exposed to countless stories during this time. By stories I mean the conversations you have with people who tell you what it's like to work there. The conversations you hear in the staff room about the problems the finance department is having with sales or the fact that the latest change initiative is doomed to failure because some have worked there long enough to remember the last time it was attempted. The stories told in organisations tend to reflect the tacit beliefs of those that work there and these beliefs may be quite different from the ones senior management wish were the case. In the case of a coaching culture the stories should be of success and, just as importantly learning. They should reflect a belief that people's potential will come through if they are given opportunities and choose to take advantage of them. Wouldn't it be great if new recruits were told about the time that a training programme that was due to be shelved to save money was retained because of staff feeling? Let's have people talking about how great managers are at getting results from people instead of moaning about the fearsome task masters they have to work for. How about more stories of high performers – already very good at what they do – seeking out coaching and highlighting its worth to others?

In 2004 we did a large coaching skills training programme for a group of advisors from an organisation called *Back Up North*. The advisors worked with disadvantaged groups including ex offenders and substance abusers in an effort to help them return to employment. No easy task and a challenging environment in which to apply coaching. We had originally trained the senior management team in coaching as a management skill but were then asked to roll the training out to the advisors as it was seen to have huge potential benefits. We followed up with the advisor participants some months after the training and were delighted with the stories they were now telling. Here are just a few:

One advisor told us of a client who suffered from severe dyslexia for many years. The advisor began coaching the client following the training and the client was now visiting a centre once a week for help. Whilst this may not seem like a huge achievement by some standards, it represented the first ever meaningful action for this particular client.

Another advisor told us of his experiences with a client who was good at completing application forms and sealing an interview but had no luck getting the job. Following a coaching session the client attended another interview and got the very next job for which she applied.

There was also the advisor who had found many coaching applications outside of work, helping her husband with problems at work, supporting her bereaved mother and helping her daughter move house.

We understand that these stories are still told and the usefulness of coaching still highlighted despite the time that has elapsed since the training.

Routines and rituals

All organisations have their own unique schedule of routines and rituals which quickly become part of the fabric of organisational life. Some of these are very formal like audits or inspections, and are probably driven by a need for compliance with laws or internal procedures. Some of the strongest cultural indicators though emerge from the less formal, social routines. From my company days I can remember the importance attached to Birthday Cakes and Leaving Dos. If it was your birthday you were expected to bring cakes in for the team. To not do so was to risk being a social outcast for the rest of your working life. Similarly, when someone left, for whatever reason, work stopped in the afternoon for about twenty minutes while the most senior manager available would say a few words and crack the odd funny at the leaver's expense. It was then all off to the nearest pub for most of the night and everyone was expected to attend. We all valued these rituals because it said 'we value each other and want to acknowledge a life outside of work'. If senior management had tried to change either of these there would have been a revolt.

Some routines and rituals fall away if there is no real ownership. Team Briefings and Quality Circles, all the rage a few years ago, and now only really found in organisations where the staff themselves took responsibility for embedding them.

In a coaching culture the most obvious routine to expect would be regular, scheduled coaching sessions. However, this is not necessary to achieve a coaching culture and some signs may be more subtle. It would be fair to say that an organisation that has committed to regular performance reviews for all staff and that holds pre and post learning event discussions, for example, has placed coaching central to its routines and rituals. Similarly, an atmosphere in which employees are encouraged to recognise numerous opportunities for learning in their day to day work can be thought of as indicative of a coaching culture.

Organisational structure

As we moved from the agricultural to the industrial age organisations got a lot bigger. Farms turned into factories and there were
suddenly dozens if not hundreds of people to be deployed and
managed. Businesses looked for models of large scale organisation
and settled on the military as this was perhaps the best example
available at the time. This led to the rigid hierarchical structures
common in most areas of work throughout the last century. There
would be a small number of directors (generals) at the top deciding
on strategy, large numbers of workers (soldiers) at the bottom
carrying out the required work and various levels of management
(sergeants, captains, etc) in between to ensure the workers carried
out the work to implement the strategy.

This structure worked well for a time and is still quite common
today. It works well when the nature of the work is dealing with
extreme situations such as in the armed forces or emergency
services, but less well in our current times of change, turbulent
market conditions and sweeping technological change. Against this
background, organisations need nimble, flexible structures that
can respond to these shifting sands. The 1980s and 1990s saw the
advent of the 'flatter' structure and there was a large scale cull of
management ranks at the time. This evolution continues still with
virtual teams, project teams and matrix management replacing the
solid, predictable reporting lines of old.

All of this requires a contemporaneous evolution of management style and this is an area in which change has been less rapid.
A militaristic, command and control approach does not work on
a team of people whose make up changes every three months, who
report to two other bosses as well and whose education taught
them to expect a different approach. In Chapter 1 I told you of a
potential client who began the meeting by saying 'I want to bring
you in because I used to just shout at people to get things done,
but apparently you can't do that anymore!'. We didn't take the

assignment as my feeling was it was doomed from the start with that kind of attitude at the very top.

I don't subscribe to the notion that only a loose, informal structure is conducive to coaching. In fact I think that coaching could apply and be effective in any type of structure, given the commitment of coach and coachees alike. Nevertheless a coaching culture is likely to feature a structure that is more organic than it is mechanistic. I would expect to see a fairly flat structure with minimal levels of management. Relationships probably err on the side of the informal to the extent where people feel comfortable to seek coaching and discuss development issues. I see this extending across teams as well as within teams and have often found that in a coaching culture teams become more interested in collaboration rather than competition. Strong divisions between, say finance and sales work well in terms of concentrating expertise but can create a silo mentality and turn competition into conflict.

Control systems

In Chapter 1 we explored the idea of sources of external interference and found that many of those things that people cite as barriers to their potential coming through are often elements of organisation control. In fact the very word organisation implies control and working life would be pretty chaotic without it. Unfortunately control is now a word with negative connotations seen by many as the way management suppresses freedom at work.

In truth, control systems are a necessary part of working life and a way of measuring results and alignment with organisation plans. It is common to find organisations using both systems of output control and behavioural control. Output control systems are concerned with ensuring the necessary quality and quantity of work produced whereas behavioural control systems seek to establish ways of working conducive to the organisation's values and beliefs. Behavioural control systems are covert not overt. I have never seen a staff handbook with a section entitled Behavioural Control Systems, but reward policies, performance management systems, competency frameworks and discipline and grievance procedures are all examples of behavioural control systems and they may or may not contribute to establishing a coaching culture.

Control systems are a powerful indicator of organisation culture and close examination can be quite revealing. I would firstly look at exactly how many control systems there are. There would be no right or wrong number and much would depend on the nature of the organisation. A chemical plant would need many and an artist's studio few. Generally speaking though we might conclude that an organisation with many controls and checks in place is one with a largely Theory X view of people at work. I would also want to find out what is most closely monitored, whether the systems are based on what's happened or what's coming and whether the emphasis is on punishment or reward.

A coaching culture would be one featuring the coaching principles of responsibility and trust. Individuals would be responsible for the full completion of a task rather than an isolated part of a procedure. Work requirements would be expressed more in terms of targets and standards than detailed task breakdowns. Decision making would be pushed down the hierarchy to those nearest the client or customer but supported with the necessary training to make sound decisions. There would be generally fewer formal controls. At Lexus GB, with whom we worked in 2004, we found a small team of customer relations advisors who were fully empowered to decide on goodwill and other remedial actions in the event of customer complaints or dissatisfaction. Their job was to 'keep the customer in the brand' and they were given the resources to do this. This element of a coaching culture allowed them to respond appropriately to a customer base unlikely to have the patience to endure delays while actions were checked, counter-signed, reviewed or endorsed. Lexus is a luxury marque and the customers are high powered, assertive, strong willed people. In other words, this was coaching culture as business necessity.

Power structures

The way that power is derived and distributed in organisations is a very powerful indicator of its culture. The sources of power are many and various, official and unofficial, formal or informal and can be used for fair as well as foul means. Let's consider the more obvious categories.

'Knowledge is power' so the saying goes and now more than ever in this information age this is indeed so. Do people guard their specialist knowledge jealously or share it freely and willingly? The *written word* is a very strong source of power and can be used to inspire or belittle. Organisations have long recognised the power of *reward* and managers who have the discretionary power to reward performance or behaviour will often claim that the 'carrot and stick' is an effective tool for motivation. It's a blunt tool at best and may disguise the fact that what appears to be willing com-mitment is actually just reluctant compliance. The use of *physical* power is sadly not just restricted to the school playground and the increasing instances of bullying at work support this view. Of course, power is not just restricted to management and employees too can exert the power of *inertia* or *disruption* to thwart many a change programme. However, they probably need to be mobilised in number to have any noticeable effect and this is more difficult since the reforms of the Thatcher government.

There is also Position power, Expert power and Personal Power and these are more directly linked to questions of coaching culture. A manager who leads by exerting Expert power may well generate respect in an environment that values technical ability but creates problems in developing capability and independence in their team. Expert power requires expertise and with knowledge bases being constantly and speedily eroded by technological and other changes, there is a massive source of pressure to keep up to date. A team whose cultural expectation is for its leader to be the expert will become demoralised and uncertain where this is not the case. Similarly, many managers, often newly promoted ones, rely too heavily on their position of power, but waving a business card and job description in people's faces is unlikely to produce sustainable high performance and will probably produce the exact opposite. These are the power sources of the uncertain and the insecure.

A coaching culture has personal power at its core. Personal power comes from a combination of having a clear set of beliefs and values and behaving in accordance with them. Where the people whom we lead and manage can share and identify with those values they become willing followers and advocates.

In practical terms this means that coaching should be divorced from the hierarchy and coaches selected on their ability to coach rather than their seniority. It means that coaching should have a developmental as well as a remedial focus and be seen to be utilised by even the strongest performers. Senior management involvement is vital but this need not be as deliverers of coaching support themselves. Indeed those managers who have actually received and benefited from coaching can be seen as the most potent advocates of a coaching approach. The strongest use of personal power within a coaching culture that I can see is where a manager is prepared to take a coaching approach with their team irrespective of how they are managed by their own boss.

Symbols

I was once given a project that required me to organise my own resources in terms of desk, chair, stationery and so on. I got hold of the office supplies catalogue and ordered myself a solid looking desk and a nice comfortable chair with arms on. I then got on with the task in hand. Some time later a senior manager walked past and immediately stopped at my desk with a look of abject horror on her face. 'You have a chair with arms on!' she said. I looked down at the chair and confirmed that this was indeed an accurate observation. 'You don't get a chair with arms on until you're a manager!' she said and immediately spun on her heels to presumably go and report me for gross misconduct or some such sin.

Logos, office layouts, signage, job titles and so on are all powerful indicators of the essential nature of the organisation. In the above example status was very important to people and status symbols like office furniture, company cars and a job title that included the word manager were obvious signs that one had arrived at the required level.

There are even more stark examples in the living memory of many, including staff *canteens* but management *restaurants*, different uniforms to denote status and a tendency to use more 'proper' forms of address. There is nothing inherently wrong with any of these things and in more conservative, long established organisations such symbols may form part of the charm of working there and be a deliberate part of the reward strategy. From our point of view though, these things do not serve to promote a coaching culture.

Coaching is an essentially egalitarian principle and really only works when coach and coachee come together as equals. To establish a coaching culture may therefore require some dismantling of symbolic indicators of status. Do business cards really need titles on them at all unless they are useful to clients and customers? Why not make a company car available to the sales force who'll use them productively rather than give them to all managers who'll probably leave them in station car parks while they commute into work? How can we expect loyalty and discretionary effort from employees when managers and business owners award themselves inflation busting pay rises? This dismantling will need to be done carefully, over a sensible time period and with as much co-operation as possible. As we saw when we looked at motivation, these things have much more power to demotivate when tampered with than they do to motivate in the first place so it will be necessary to manage the change sensitively and ensure people have their 'loss' recognised. Nevertheless we must recognise that a coaching culture will not take root until there is a sense of fairness and of working on a level playing field in an atmosphere of mutual respect.

Language too is an important cultural indicator and I find it fascinating to listen to the ways that people describe to me the people whom they wish to coach. Team member, worker, employee, staff, colleague, subordinate. Each of these words has a unique resonance and thinking about how they are used can give an insight into how people might respond to coaching.

Overall

Each of the cultural indicators we've discussed so far will contribute to an overall view, sometimes referred to as the paradigm. The paradigm will capture the essence of the culture and will serve as answer to the question: 'what are you all about?' An NHS Trust we work with has *caring for people* at its core, the Ritz-Carlton hotel group has 'ladies and gentlemen serving ladies and gentlemen' as its motto and its paradigm. I stayed at their hotel in Berlin and could see this statement reflected in the routines, symbols and structures that I observed. A coaching culture will have people and learning at the heart of both its strategic approach and its operational processes.

I maintain the view though that the most powerful indicator of overall culture is leadership behaviour. People take their cue from what they see the top team *doing* not what they hear them *saying.* The greatest challenge then for those determined to establish a coaching culture is to win the hearts and minds of the top team. Senior management must be competent and confident in coaching and should attend any training and follow up sessions. They must espouse the value of coaching and ideally have experienced it as a coachee. They should ask HR to make the move to a coaching culture but retain responsibility and accountability for ensuring it happens.

SUMMARY

This chapter has presented the cultural web as a means of identifying barriers raised by an existing culture and of suggesting the key components that will form a coaching culture. We'll conclude by considering the practical steps that you'll need to take on your journey from one to the other.

I would firstly suggest some analysis of the existing culture. The cultural web lends itself readily as an agenda and structure for team meetings, focus groups, interviews or indeed a coaching session in which organisation culture will be discussed.

You will also need to understand your organisation's business or service plan and the strategic direction in the coming years. This will help define the exact nature of the coaching culture required and will be vital in securing the support of the senior team. Many a change initiative has failed through an inability of HR to make a compelling business case. We'll look at this in more detail later.

A coaching culture necessitates some willing and able coaches and you'll have to hire them in or train your own. I would clearly advocate training your own as it's more difficult to establish a coaching culture with a reliance on outside help. There are obvious logistical considerations of course and we'll look at the matter of coach training in the next chapter.

Make sure that effective coaching is rewarded. Recognition must be given to those who willingly take up the coaching challenge, especially in the early days, and it's not unheard of to find targets for coaching included in performance management plans. To begin with these will likely be around the amount of coaching taking place, but with experience you can begin to develop more qualitative measures that evaluate the *outcome* of coaching interventions.

I think it absolutely vital to celebrate success for a coaching culture to take root and the success indicators, I would suggest, include coaching happening naturally outside formal sessions, coaching outside reporting lines, improved overall communication and a movement towards more on the job learning and away from formal training courses.

CHAPTER 12

IMPLEMENTING A COACHING PROGRAMME

INTRODUCTION

This chapter is about taking the practical steps necessary to develop the coaching culture described previously. To make this as straightforward as possible I will describe an implementation approach that has two major steps: Training the coaches and running the sessions. The following four sections will deal with the issues surrounding the training of managers and leaders as coaches – a subject very dear to my heart – and if you follow the advice given you will have a pool of trained coaches to call upon which you can supplement with external coaches should you wish. The subsequent four sections deal with selecting coaches from your internal or external pool and deploying these coaches to run a coaching programme that brings about the benefits you have identified.

Implementing a coaching programme is a challenging project for even the most accomplished change agent. Unlike implementing new systems or processes, you're dealing with the 'hearts and minds' dimension of people at work and the emotional responses that this can produce. For coaching to really take hold there needs to be a fundamental shift in attitude for both coach and coachee. This may be neither quick nor easy if each is ingrained with a tell culture that probably took hold at school let alone work. You may see some behaviour change in the short term as coaches try out new skills and coachees try out some new ideas, but success in the longer term will come to those that play the long game.

In the last chapter I advocated getting commitment from the very top if a coaching culture is to emerge. I stand by this view but this does not mean that a coaching programme has to *start* at the very top. 'Monarchies do not start revolutions' so the saying goes and the executive team may unfortunately be too fixated by short term objectives to plunge fully into supporting a coaching programme. It may be more prudent to start with, say an upper management layer who can produce some hard, meaningful results to put before the executive and virtually guarantee their support and commitment thereafter. In short, start at the highest level you can that includes genuine support for what you're trying to do. You'll eventually reach a tipping point with enough advocates to ensure your coaching programme can gain wide acceptance and participation.

Following on from this, the other great challenge is maintaining momentum. There'll be a flurry of activity as you schedule coaching skills training programmes and an air of excitement as people embark upon their initial coaching sessions. But what will things be like after eight coaching sessions or six months down the line? You'll need to plan for the longer term as well giving consideration to how you'll communicate the progress and achievements of the programme and how you'll facilitate catch-up and follow-up training. You'll also need to think carefully about how you intend to measure your success. I give detailed advice on evaluation in the next chapter and cover a range of measurement tools.

We'll start at the stage of training managers or leaders to be internal coaches and, before we get into detail of buying or designing a training programme, let's consider how you can ensure your training intervention can have the greatest impact. In his pioneering book *High Impact Training* [15], Todd Lapidus proposes a simple yet highly significant question we need ask before we can begin. It is: Who is the customer of this training? The obvious answer is the training participants but perhaps on closer examination things are not so simple. The training participants may receive the training but do they want it? In my experience participants fall into one of three categories: prisoners, holiday makers or learners. The prisoners feel trapped and have usually been 'sent' by a line manager hoping that some training might make a difference. Holidaymakers go to any training event imaginable because it beats being in the office, and then, usually in the minority, the genuine learner is there because of a recognised training need and an enthusiasm for having it met. Perhaps it is the line managers of the participants that are the real customer, and this is often the case with other forms of management training like negotiation or sales skills because it is line managers who benefit if the training is successful. I propose that with training in coaching skills it is the *coachees* who are the real customer of the training as they are the group most profoundly affected by whether your organisation is able to train effective coaches or not. Thinking in this way leads us towards soliciting coachee's views of what the training should cover – which can only be useful – and making sure the training is geared towards outcomes not activities. It's very easy to design training which is fun and which generates great feedback, but will the training work and endure back in everyday life? Recognising our coachees as the ultimate customer of training in coaching skills also forces us to confront the truism that what happens before and after training is more significant than the event itself.

Let's look firstly at the option of devising your own in-house programme.

BESPOKE TRAINING

Devising a bespoke programme is probably the most challenging but ultimately most rewarding approach to providing training in coaching skills. There is no shortage of books, websites and other resources out there for you to do your content research and you will have the advantage of being able to link this to your exact circumstances.

If you've been asked to design a programme because external coaches have been doing effective one to one work with senior management, you'll have a wealth of learning and experience that can be factored in to the training and give it real credibility.

However, because effective coaching requires a change of attitude as well as a change of behaviour your training programme will need to be very carefully designed. A few models and a couple of quick exercises will not have a lasting effect. Long before deciding on particular elements of content you'll need to consider some principles of adult learning.

A useful reference point on this is the theory of andragogy developed by Malcolm Knowles [12]. According to the theory adults are self-directed and expect to take responsibility for their own decisions and adult learning programmes, such as training undertaken at work, must accommodate this fundamental aspect.

The theory has been so widely adopted in the field of training design that it seems like stating the obvious, but Knowles's work was very influential in establishing four core principles of adult learning. Firstly, adults need to know *why* they need to learn something which is why stating up front a programme's aims, objectives and rationale is so important. Secondly, adults need to learn experientially i.e. by getting involved. Thirdly, adults approach learning as problem-solving. Whilst children tend to take a subject orientation to learning – at least in formal education – adults prefer to contextualise their learning to real-life situations. The final principle is that adults learn best when the topic is of immediate value, with early opportunities to act on what has been learnt.

In practical terms then, andragogy means that training in a work setting needs to focus more on the learning process and less on the content being taught. Training methods such as case studies, role plays, simulations and business games are often extremely effective, especially where trainers are adept at taking on the role of facilitator rather than lecturer.

If we apply the theory of andragogy to designing a coaching skills training programme we can work within these principles and help ensure a powerful learning experience. There will be a need to explain *why* specific things are being taught so that as well as encouraging participants about how to promote focus, to take one example, we would also need to stress *how* focus can improve work performance. Asking groups to commit ideas or models to memory and testing their recall is of limited value. Training exercises should instead be task oriented and related to work where possible. The training design must take into account the wide range of different backgrounds of learners and similarly any materials and activities should allow for different levels and kinds of previous experience with coaching and developing people. Since adults are self-directed, training in coaching skills should allow learners to discover things for themselves, providing guidance and help when mistakes are made.

I have used the term training programme here to indicate that these principles apply to more than just a classroom based training course and are just as relevant to practice sessions, learning sets, pre and post course briefings or any other activities that you may consider to supplement formal instruction.

OFF-THE-SHELF PACKAGES

The second option is to look for a pre-designed training package. Most of the established providers such as Fenman or Gower have a coaching product and a little time spent on research should enable you to find a quality product that suits you and your audience's needs.

A good package will contain a complete set of resources to run the programme without you needing to supplement it with your own materials. Typically, the training approach comprises a two or three day face to face workshop followed by suggestions for facilitating follow up meetings. Those programmes that lead to accreditation also require the submission of a case study based portfolio or a work based assignment. The pack should include resources for all aspects including facilitator notes, participant workbook and overhead slides.

Make sure the workshop design features a variety of exercises that will appeal to different learning styles and ensure that each session is lively and upbeat. Some exercises have been around in coach training for a while, so check on any previous coach training your likely audience may have had.

The standard of materials and the production values in training packages are generally very high throughout and present excellent value for money, provided you know your audience and their needs. The one drawback is the possibility of the material falling into the hands of an inexperienced facilitator. A trainer running Induction or Customer Service one week and then asked to implement Coaching Skills the next may lack the coaching experience necessary to answer all delegate questions or to deal with some of the emotional content of practice coaching sessions. Some form of internal 'licensing' may be wise to guard against this.

TRAINING PROVIDERS

The third option is to work with a training organisation and this is a wise move if you have the slightest doubt that you can provide the training in-house. Training in coaching is a specialist area and definitely not a topic where the old adage of 'get a book and keep one page ahead of the delegates' will do.

I considered devoting this section to producing a list of the current training available in the market but decided this was not appropriate. The market for coaching skills training is extremely competitive and highly dynamic. Any list of the current provision would be out of date as soon as I went to print. I recommend a visit to www.coachingnetwork.org.uk for a detailed directory of coaching skills training.

In any event, a typical procurement process would see you requesting written tender responses and then inviting a short-list of providers to present their proposals in person. I would suggest that you need to explore the following considerations in deciding which firm has an offering that will suit your needs.

How flexible can they be? Training can have a large 'opportunity cost' if lots of people are away from the organisation at one time. Does the provider cover weekends or night shifts? Do they have any examples of other organisations whose managers they have trained and could you contact some of them to discuss their experiences? Can they meet your timescales and do they have the capacity to train the numbers you want in that timescale? Large training companies will have a pool of associates or freelancers to call upon but the quality can vary. Smaller companies will have a dedicated team but may struggle with a larger project. Ask for details of the exact nature of the training. What content would be included and what would the outline timetable or agenda be? Can the provider adapt parts of their material to more closely match your needs? How would the provider provide ongoing training in the future for new managers? Finally, what are the costs associated with any of the options they propose?

In choosing a supplier you'll want to be sure that you're comparing proposals on a 'like for like' basis so it is worth asking for proposals to follow an agreed format to make this easier. At the very least you should make sure that each proposal clearly states:

- The overall aims and objectives
- Links with the business objectives
- Detailed and comprehensive costs
- Adherence to your legal or ethical requirements, e.g. equal opportunities
- How the coaching skills training will be assessed or evaluated
- The level and nature of any follow-up work provided
- Programme content, style and appeal to individual learning styles
- That the need for flexibility in working, resources, materials timescales, etc can be accommodated
- That wider issues, e.g. changes to practices, systems, project management, etc have been considered

SUCCESS CRITERIA

Whichever option you choose, it's wise to decide up front the elements of a training approach you consider to be crucial and from which you will not deviate. Experience suggests there are several common elements worthy of your consideration.

To achieve the best from any development activity, particularly training in coaching skills, you'll need to look at line management involvement in the process. Do managers have the skills needed to monitor performance and support the new coaches when they return to work?

The organisation should make sure that a discussion takes place between the trainee coach and their line manager about the reason for selecting them to be trained as a coach and the links to the individual's own objectives. The more specific the manager and trainee coach can be at this point the easier it will be to measure whether the learning has had an impact on performance. The trainee should be given an opportunity as soon as possible to put their development into practice on returning to work to enable reinforcement of learning. This presents a challenge when the newly trained coach is undertaking coaching alongside their 'day job' and their line manager will need to be fully supportive of the coaching role if conflict is to be avoided.

In my view any coaching skills training course must include some practice sessions. Ultimately people learn how to coach by coaching; there is only so much that can be learnt by theory. Role play scenarios are one option but not an effective one in my view. It is difficult for the person *acting* the part of a coachee to answer questions and navigate the session in a realistic way. A better idea is to ask people to bring along real life issues to be coached upon during the course. However, this approach is not without its challenges. When people sit down with each other and start posing questions in a coaching style we cannot legislate for the answers that may come forth or for the direction the coaching conversation may take. Some of the sessions may become quite emotive and coach trainers need to feel comfortable with this and be able to intervene where necessary in a sensitive way. Most training providers will happily support a 'train the trainer' event if you consider this might be a problem.

Choose your training audience carefully. Coaching skills training can prove very popular and you may find yourself accommodating delegates that don't quite fit the audience profile. Be particularly careful if line management begin dispatching delegates who have no formal 'people' responsibility. Such delegates can assume that coaching is the preserve of management and of no concern to them and you may need to counter this by illustrating the range of contexts in which coaching may apply.

I trained as a coach in 1995. I was so taken with the concept that I began inserting coaching modules in a lot of the training I was delivering at the time. Looking back I now realise that this was probably unwise as I hadn't done much actual coaching at that stage. I can remember being caught out by questions like, 'How do you deal with people who don't want to be coached?', 'How can I be a coach and a manager at the same time?' and 'What if the coachee becomes upset?'. These questions require a practical, real-life answer rather than a theoretical response and as such trainers of coaches need to have had some real life coaching experience.

SELECTING COACHES

Before we move on let's return to the idea of deciding whether to use internal or external coaches. There are advantages and disadvantages which I've tried to summarise in Table 12.1.

Please look upon this list as merely some high level thoughts. I strongly recommend that you and whoever else has responsibility for commissioning coaching produce a similar matrix for yourself.

Personally, I err on the side of using in-house coaches as I believe this is more conducive to establishing a coaching culture. Great care must be exercised though in choosing the right coaches and this is sometimes overlooked. I know of one organisation with a number of long-serving middle managers whose positions became redundant. This group was immediately identified as spare and ideally placed to roll out the coaching programme the company had been pondering for some time. Of course the context was completely wrong. Many of these managers were upset and angry at the prospect of losing their jobs whilst others were so relieved they more or less quit in the spiritual sense there and then. The coaching sessions became downbeat and lethargic and probably did more harm than good.

On the other hand, I also know from conversations that many senior managers worry that external coaches might feel a need

Table 12.1

	Advantages	Disadvantages
Internal Coach	• Understands the organisation • Can utilise established levels of trust • Develops skills that remain within the organisation	• May be too closely involved • May get distracted by demands of the 'day job' • May be unwilling to upset work relationships
External Coach	• Can remain objective • Can bring in a wide range of perspectives • Has highly developed specialist coaching skills	• Cannot afford to be too confrontational • Relies on a continuing relationship • Can be more costly

to protect their livelihood at the expense of recognising that coaching has been successful and that it's time to move on. Having said that the ethical standards in the emerging coaching profession are very robust and have been widely adopted. All the coaches I know recognise that doing the right thing for the client is the best way to cultivate their business in the long term. There has however been a certain amount of jumping on the band wagon in recent years as some have seen coaching as a way of making big money quickly. All of this can be guarded against by devising a clear set of selection criteria and choosing coaches in a professional way.

In the first instance this means that the rationale is right for choosing external over internal coaches. It then means recognising that coaching is forged on a relationship of trust and deciding whether that will be best accomplished by an internal or external provider. You then need to draw up selection criteria and are probably best advised to seek expert help in designing an assessment centre to look for the right skills and personality.

We looked at a list of coaching qualities earlier on, but for an external appointment you'll also need to consider:

- Coaching experience
- Track record
- Work experience prior to coaching
- Fee levels and costs
- Personal style and cultural fit
- Professional body affiliations
- Formal qualifications

I never take on a coaching assignment without first meeting with the prospective coachee and their boss for an informal chat to see if we can get along and work together. Most coaches will be happy to meet with you on an exploratory basis before coming to a formal agreement.

CONTRACTING

So now we're at a point where we have a pool of coaches, be they internal or external, who are trained and capable and ready to be let loose to improve performance or address other worthy aims throughout your organisation. I would suggest that before these people leap in devising aims and exploring reality that we need to deliberately engineer an essential prior step. There is a definite need for a 'contract' to be established before effective coaching can proceed. I'm not talking here about an external provider's contractual relationship with the organisation but rather the contract – formal or informal – that exists between coach, coachee, and the sponsor/commissioner of the coaching – usually, but not always, the coachee's boss.

In my idealistic past I used to contend that a coaching relationship and its content were nothing to do with the boss. I now see this as naïve and realise that a coachee's boss has a massive stake in the successful outcome of a coaching intervention not least because they're often providing the budget for it. I suggest that the first step is for the three parties to meet and discuss:

- What each party believes coaching will achieve
- How each party believes coaching will work
- Each party's expected outcome and critical success factors
- The frequency and timing of each session
- The number of sessions to be booked at a time
- The degree of reporting to the coachee's boss or sponsor
- How matters of confidentiality will be handled

It can be useful to capture the outcome of this discussion in a formal contract document. It is particularly important to make sure that the coachee understands that in order to achieve results they will need to:

- Commit to the schedule of sessions
- Receive feedback in the spirit in which it is offered
- Possibly confront some limiting beliefs and unhelpful behaviours
- Take responsibility for making change happen
- Remember that the coach always has their best interests at heart
- Recognise that the organisation is investing in their development.

This contracting process results in a transparent arrangement with which all parties can feel comfortable and enables the early coaching sessions to become meaningful more quickly.

RUNNING THE SESSIONS

For the purposes of this section I will assume that coaching will take place within a formal framework, but that need not be the case. I am a great believer in Martini coaching – anytime, anyplace, anywhere – as the three key principles of Awareness, Responsibility and Trust can be utilised on any occasion there is a need to learn from an experience or take a forward step. Whilst a coaching conversation around the coffee machine can be highly effective it does require that we consider whether the timing is appropriate. It is always wise to check how much time you and the coachee have available and to agree to schedule some time later on if things begin to get complex.

When coaching happens on a more formal basis it is necessary to get the basics right. First and foremost this means honouring the appointment and turning up on time. Living in the real world I realise that this will be very demanding and that the manager who coaches has a number of other demands on their time, but equally I've seen significant investment wasted where the commitment to coaching falls at the outset. The first one or two sessions are absolutely vital to establishing trust and commitment and these appointments should be seen as written in blood. Thereafter there is perhaps some scope for flexibility particularly if we take time to discuss any conflicting priorities with the coachee.

Similarly, we need to get the environment right. This does not necessarily mean you have to *feng shui* your meeting rooms and have soft lighting and easy chairs, but it does mean a well-lit, comfortable room where people can talk in private. I'm often asked whether it's okay to have coaching session off-site, in the pub or at Starbucks. I think that's fine provided coach and coachee are comfortable, that there's a chance of privacy and that it doesn't diminish what the coaching is designed to achieve.

Finally, the start of a coaching session is an opportunity to establish or reinforce rapport. We looked at rapport in the chapter on sales and it's important in coaching too, particularly if coach and coachee do not know each other well at the outset. Part of establishing rapport especially important in successful coaching is managing the coachee's expectations. We've seen the misconceptions that abound about coaching and if your coachee is coming to a session expecting to be 'repaired' or 'fixed' they may be understandably guarded. You need to reassure them that the coaching is for their benefit and that you intend to let them set the agenda.

You can use the ARROW questioning sequence as a route map through a coaching session and these pointers may be helpful: When discussing Aims you'll need to establish an aim for the session itself and an overall aim for the problem or situation being discussed. At the Reality stage really try to listen and allow the coachee time to think. It's often at the reality stage that the most insightful awareness raising happens. Remember that the Reflection stage can tidy up the coachee's aims and reality and can also serve as an ideal time to end a coaching session where the underlying issue is long term and/or complex. Keep the Options section lively, upbeat and even playful if appropriate and remember that Way Forward is essentially about turning thought into action.

In closing a coaching session be clear about any actions you each intend to take between now and the next meeting and take time to actually schedule a date for the next meeting in your diaries there and then. Good intentions to 'fix a time' tend to unravel when other pressures intervene. A great tip is to end a session by asking the coachee what they have learned that day. Not only does this encourage the coachee to think more deeply around their own issues, it also encourages them to think about the coaching process.

CLOSING

You might think it odd that a book which so revels in the potency of a coaching relationship would devote valuable space to the notion of closing a relationship down, but I consider this to be a vital component of all good coaching. Closing a coaching relationship has little coverage in the literature and is often given only cursory coverage on training events.

I believe that coaching is an exercise in creating independence and that by definition this means that we leave our coachees self-reliant and self-supporting. Coaches, be they internal or external, must be mindful of the need to 'write themselves out of a job' from the outset of a coaching relationship. This is one area in which external coaches face a greater challenge than their internal counterparts given the commercial need to find a replacement client. The benefits to the internal coach of a client or coachee who becomes independent of them are more obvious.

The beauty of a coaching approach founded on awareness, responsibility and trust is that these principles not only require a positive view of people but they also generate one as the results of coaching manifest. In other words it becomes easier to move on from a coachee when you see them doing so well as a result of your coaching and as they become aware for themselves how they can access their new capabilities whenever the need arises. The danger of maintaining a coaching relationship for too long is that the coachee may feel that responsibility has not quite been transferred and trust may suffer as a result. Put simply, the coach can become a source of interference rather than focus.

Nevertheless, it isn't simply a matter of slamming on the brakes and bringing the coaching to a shuddering close. There is both a technical and emotional component to ending a coaching relationship and each needs to be handled sensitively. Firstly we need to consider how we might recognise that coaching has done its job and that it's time to move on. In my experience, the first sign is where the coaching process seems to slow down. By this I mean that it feels more like going through the motions and there doesn't seem to be quite the motivation there was. Sessions get rescheduled and there's a sense that the coachee would rather be pressing on with the actions previous coaching has revealed than spend time in further discussion. You might also pick up signs of disinterest from the coachee or find the coaching conversations seem stuck in old ground. Of course these things may also be signs that the coaching is not working per se and so it's vital that you discuss your observations fully with the coachee before deciding to bring things to a close.

I recommend a series of tapered follow up sessions that become increasingly less frequent and shorter in time. The final session – and you'll each know when the time is right – should be a time to celebrate success and to evaluate the success of the coaching undertaken. More of which later.

SUMMARY

By way of summary let's consider that introducing coaching to your place of work is an exercise in organisational change. As with all change it is necessary to identify the stakeholders and determine what action may be required to secure the support of each stakeholder group. A stakeholder is anyone who is affected by the change in any way whether positively or negatively. Stakeholders can include people who are necessary to implement the change or have responsibility for budgets, sponsorship or information. Stakeholder groups can be further defined by considering who 'wins' and who 'loses' from the change. There may also be those who are neutral, whose circumstances remain unchanged. Those who perceive themselves as winners will be highly committed, will welcome the change and take positive action to see it happen. Losers will oppose the change, refuse to acknowledge any benefits and may take action designed to 'highjack' the change. Neutral groups will simply see the change as an inevitable part of organisational life and be neither for nor against it.

In implementing a coaching programme we can readily see that senior management and coaches are natural winners and that really so are the coachees although they may need the benefits clearly stated and any misconceptions explained. However, nothing happens in a vacuum and you may well get some resistance from unexpected quarters. Managers who coach may feel that an established pecking order is under threat. They might also fear that they are going to lose control and yet still be held accountable for results. Managers who coach will have some new knowledge or skills to acquire and this will take time and they might feel that taking up a coaching approach could create a lot of new work.

Coachees may misunderstand the need for change and see coaching as a remedial activity which they should not subscribe too. They may also see it as the latest 'fad' which will fade into the background along with all the other changes introduced in recent years. There might simply be a high degree of mistrust in senior management or with whoever has been tasked with implementing coaching.

Senior management may also act against introducing coaching if they feel they have been railroaded into adopting the latest management theory rather than seeing a clear set of real benefits.

The good news is that our key coaching principles provide the antidote to this resistance. We need firstly to make all stakeholder groups *aware* of the benefits that coaching will bring. We must not, however, speak in general terms, but talk the language of our stakeholder groups. In simple terms this means talking strategy to senior management but talking day to day benefits to coachees. We also need to encourage our stakeholder groups to take *responsibility* for the change to a coaching approach by involving them as much as possible in every step of the plan. Finally, we must engender *trust* through regular, open and honest and communication, remembering that communication is two-way and that people need a forum in which they can be heard as much as they need information from on high.

CHAPTER 13

EVALUATING THE PROGRAMME

INTRODUCTION

Welcome to the search for the holy grail.

I'm not sure that there's any other part of the world of work so concerned with proving its worth than the training and development function. Can the IT department show that issuing everyone with the latest hand–held electronic gizmo will have a demonstrable effect on the bottom line? Does the marketing department at head office issue evaluation questionnaires to the retail sales staff to see what they thought of the latest campaign? Not in my experience they don't and yet HR and training in particular seems almost constantly being asked to justify its existence.

> Not everything that can be measured is valuable, and not everything that is valuable can be measured
>
> **Albert Einstein**

I think that a concern for evaluating the impact of training and development can turn into an unhealthy obsession so that before we get into the mechanics of evaluation we need to take a step back.

Let's think about what we've discovered about coaching so far. We're talking about a process that is designed to raise awareness, generate responsibility and build trust. The first question we need ask is does this make sense? I often ask my course participants to consider their current high performers and suggest that these people are highly aware, very responsible and both trusting and trust-worthy. No one has so far argued the point. For further reinforcement I might ask the same participants to consider the times in their own careers when they were performing at the peak and suggest that at these times they were at their most aware, responsible and trusting. Once again there is universal agreement. It seems to me that any process that increases awareness, responsibility and trust is so obviously a good thing that any more detailed evaluation is pointless.

However, evaluate we must. The argument I outline above may seem reasonable and is certainly one often taken up within the HR profession but it is not framed in the language of other parts of organisational life that talk in quantitative terms involving percentages and ratios. The most senior roles in both public and private sector organisations are seldom held by former coaches or training managers. Chief Executives and Managing Directors most typically come up the finance route and have often held the post of Finance Director before getting the top job. Certainly if we're to secure senior management support we need to be able to demonstrate the value generated from training and coaching in a robust way. A compelling case should secure strong support and remove the threat of budget cuts the next time trading conditions become difficult.

A sound evaluation approach validates training and coaching as a business tool. Being able to show that training and coaching creates value, positions the training function as a strategic contributor rather than an overhead and encourages line management to properly support training interventions rather than condone non-attendance or cancel courses when things get busy. If you can show a positive return on investment from training and coaching you can illustrate that it makes no sense to ever cut training budgets as there will be a direct impact on revenue. Detailed evaluation can show which aspects of a training programme or matters discussed in coaching are having the biggest organisational impact. Coaching schedules and training programmes can then be revised to focus more on these areas.

This chapter is devoted to a detailed examination of evaluating a coaching programme. Once again we'll assume that the programme consists of initially training managers as coaches and then rolling out a schedule of sessions. We shall examine training evaluation to begin with and then outline an approach to evaluating the coaching programme overall.

WHY EVALUATE?

This is an important question to raise before we get immersed in the detail of how we intend to evaluate. The evaluation of training, coaching or any learning and development initiative is not straightforward and can soak up time that in the end is disproportional to the benefits gained from the exercise. We need to navigate our way through deciding which levels of evaluation to use, which measurement tools will be appropriate, how to isolate the results of the training from other variables and whether a causal relationship can be shown between the training and its outcome. It's clear that we need a strong rationale for the evaluation to justify the effort.

There are four reasons for evaluation, to prove, improve, control or learn. These are not mutually exclusive and most evaluation strategies attend to at least two. However, being clear about what you are using evaluation for, helps to decide later on what questions to pose and which tools may find you the answers. It will also help provide an overall evaluation that satisfies a range of interested parties.

The first reason then is to set out to prove that what was intended is indeed being achieved. This is likely to be of prime concern to training designers and training deliverers who will want to know that the training objectives around knowledge skills and attitude have been achieved. In other words, did the training do what it set out to do? Note though that this does not necessarily mean that the training will have the desired effect in terms of business performance, it's possible to prove a bad design! This underscores the importance of considering evaluation at the training design stage.

We might similarly undertake evaluation in order to improve upon the training design or the way it is subsequently delivered. This is not easy to do if the only evaluation tool is the traditional end of course questionnaire. Course delegates give a personal reaction to how the course made them feel, such a subjective view cannot be relied upon as the basis for making changes.

The third choice is to use evaluation as a means of control. This would be mainly appropriate in large scale programmes that roll out over a longish timescale where there is a need to ensure consistency in achievement and outcome. Organisations pursuing quality standards or subject to external regulation may similarly wish to use training evaluation as a means of showing adherence to these requirements.

Finally, we might wish to evaluate as a way of learning more about our approach to training. Which exercises work best? What is the optimum number of delegates? Is the venue significant? These are all factors that can be included in an overall evaluation approach.

Of course we may be given many reasons not to evaluate training and development, usually from the people who'd have to do the work. You can expect to be told that training evaluation is either impossible or only possible for technical training. Trainers will tell you that evaluation is the responsibility of line management and we can guess what line management will say. In truth, establishing that training and learning is both efficient and effective is the responsibility of all those involved.

DONALD KIRKPATRICK

No chapter on evaluation could be taken seriously without reference to the work of Donald Kirkpatrick [10]. His four-stage model provides the back drop to most research into the efficacy of training and has endured for nearly fifty years.

Kirkpatrick suggests that having lined an employee up to attend some training, there are four outcomes we would like to see and the degree to which these outcomes have been achieved can be measured. Firstly, participants should find the training useful and enjoyable, next they should come away with new knowledge or skills or have their attitudes challenged. The third outcome is that participants apply what they have learnt at work and the fourth is that the organisation performs more effectively as a result. These outcomes – which hold true for all form of training intervention from guided reading to classroom delivery – lend themselves to four levels of evaluation work.

At level 1 we are measuring participants' reaction to the training to see how much they liked it and whether they found it useful. This typically takes the form of the end of course evaluation questionnaire which the trainer hands out at the end; the so-called happy sheet. I would estimate that about 90% of training evaluation in the UK stops at this level which is unfortunate as there is little correlation between training being enjoyable and improved business performance. It can also give rise to the trend for trainers to concern themselves with entertaining at the expense of challenging participants to move outside their comfort zones.

Level 2 is concerned with evaluating how much was actually learnt. The most typical route here is to ask participants to undertake a pre-course questionnaire or test before the training and then to complete another afterwards. The two results can be compared and hopefully reveal that more is known or understood after the training than before. This is a straightforward exercise in technical training but more difficult for training in skills such as coaching.

At level 3 we are determining how much of what has been learnt is being applied and we would typically seek feedback from the participant, their boss, peers, etc.

Finally, level 4 asks whether overall performance has improved at the level of the individual, team or organisation. This is the most powerful form of evaluation since it links directly to the initial expenditure on training. However, it is also the most difficult part of the puzzle to complete and some would argue not worth the time and effort. I would contend that as long as we view evaluation as a means of looking forward to ensure that training is targeted and focused rather than a means of looking backward to contain costs, there are real benefits to be had.

To take these ideas forward to evaluating a programme of coaching skills training we would want a way of ensuring that we provided a memorable learning event that developed participants' knowledge, skills and attitude around coaching. We would then want to see how much coaching is taking place – formally or informally – and to check that this has a positive effect on the performance of the coachees and their teams alike.

EVALUATION TOOLS

There are a number of tools which can be used throughout the whole evaluation process, many of which will yield data at more than one level and I intend to outline the main ones here. I'm working on the assumption that we're talking about a coaching skills training programme, delivered face to face and lasting at least two days. This makes it easier to describe certain tools although most of what I say holds true for other forms of training.

Let's firstly consider a fundamental evaluation resource that is often overlooked, that is the trainee's line manager. A trainee's line manager has a stake in the outcome of any training and is likely to operate in the same area of work as the trainee and thus be a good source of performance feedback when the training is implemented. In the first instance the line manager should be involved in a pre-course (or pre-learning) meeting with the trainee in order to discuss their personal aims and objectives and begin to explore the likely effects on work performance. The main benefit of such a meeting being that the trainee is primed to expect certain outcomes from training and therefore more oriented towards finding opportunities within the material presented to fulfil that need. It also makes the whole evaluation task easier if trainee and line manager are clear about what outcomes the training *should* deliver.

The main evaluation tool at level one is the reaction questionnaire. This will normally invite the trainee to rate aspects of the training such as duration, pitch and the quality of the trainer where one is involved. Ratings can be given against a scale – typically 1–10 – or there may be space for qualitative comments. Most questionnaires are a combination of both. These sheets are useful in that they show a commitment to evaluation and can be the source of some useful instant feedback. However, they give a highly unreliable result. Many trainees will be most influenced by how much they liked the trainer and if the questionnaire is only handed out at the end of the course or piece of training, most trainees will be too tired or anxious to leave to give reasoned, considered responses. They are better than nothing but only just. I would generally recommend that they are supported by a trainer's summary where appropriate as well.

Pre and post course quizzes or tests are a useful measurement tool at level 2 and can be fairly easily constructed. The most practical way is to pick out the main learning points from the training course and to turn them into questions. If you can use multiple choice, true/false or yes/no type question structures so much the better as it becomes easier to compare pre and post test results.

The line manager becomes crucial again at level 3 when we are concerned with establishing whether what has been learnt has been implemented. A good post-course debriefing with a line manager should ensure that the trainee is certain about opportunities to act on what they learnt during training and the line manager will certainly have a view on how well they do so. This can be supplemented by asking the trainee to self-report and by asking some of their coachees to provide feedback.

Level 4 is trickier because when we consider whether training a coach has had an impact on business performance we need really to consider whether their coachees are performing better, and this will always be a judgement call. I might coach a salesperson who goes on to double their results in the following month but how can I be certain that this improvement was a result of my coaching? The improvement could have been caused by a change of circumstances at home or they could have seen something on television that gave them some new ideas, we could never be certain. Nevertheless we should observe the coach in action, collect coachee evaluations and look at coachee performance in order to determine how the business has benefited from the coaching skills training.

ISOLATION

We can now widen the scope of our examination of evaluation to include the coaching sessions as well as any coaching skills training.

Any researcher will tell you that one of the great challenges of showing any causal relationship, i.e. that a given input created a specific, linked outcome, is isolating the variables. In terms of evaluating coaching this means getting to a point that an identified increase in performance or effectiveness can reasonably be attributed to the coaching intervention.

> The best we can ever do is show the proximate link between coaching and improvements in the executive's performance.

Terry Bacon

What holds true for the executive applies to all coachees as far as I'm concerned and the problematic nature of isolation means that we need to have a realistic view of the results of a coaching evaluation. They must be viewed as a strong indicator of success (or otherwise) but not treated as empirical data. Aside from isolation there is also the fact that coaching is a new field with a variety of practices going by that name and that coaching activity is progressing much faster than the research into its effects. This means that you need to be cautious and circumspect in how you use the results – justifying further investment, say – but that any positive correlation between coaching and success can be viewed very optimistically against a background of such conservatism. We will look at this in more detail later on.

If we cannot fully solve the problem of isolation then we need to get to the best position we can. There are three recognised ways of doing this.

Firstly, we can perform a *pre/post coaching analysis*. This involves assessing performance before and after coaching and comparing the two sets of results. This can be quite straightforward in environments with an existing performance measurement culture and well established mechanisms, a contact centre for example. However, any increase in performance can only be reliably attributed to coaching if all other factors are held constant. If there was other training happening during the coaching period, a product or service launch, or any other major change, these could also be fairly cited as the explanation.

Secondly, we could work with *control groups*. This means we would have a coached group and a non-coached group and if the results of the coached group were better we could reasonably assume that this was down to the coaching, assuming, once again, that other factors were held constant.

The third option is known as *expert estimation*. Put simply, this means that we talk to coaches, coachees and their bosses to see how much of any given improvement they would attribute to coaching. This is the most subjective of the three methods but also the most widely used. Organisations and businesses are concerned with servicing their clients' and customers' needs not with social experiments and are understandably unable to isolate groups of people from other initiatives purely to prove the worth of coaching.

CALCULATING RETURN ON INVESTMENT (ROI)

Let's just take stock. We may wish to evaluate our coaching programme to prove its effectiveness and/or to improve the way it operates. This may include evaluating any coach training that we've done. We can evaluate both training and coaching at four levels: Was it useful and enjoyable? Did learning take place? Was that learning implemented? Did performance improve as a result? The more rigorous evaluations seek to consider all four levels and use a variety of tools from reaction questionnaires to expert estimation. The ultimate extension of all of this work is to see if we can establish a return on investment (ROI).

Let's imagine that you've run a coaching programme during the current year and you have every indication and lots of anecdotal evidence to suggest it was useful and successful. Let's also imagine that the Finance Director sits you down and tells you that she has a spare £20,000 in the budget. She goes on to explain that the bank have demonstrated a return of 3% per annum if she deposits it with them but wonders what return you could offer if she gave it to you to run another coaching programme. Now you've really got to be able to talk about coaching in those terms whether you want to or not. We need to be able to calculate ROI.

In *Coaching that Counts* [1], authors Dianna & Merrill Anderson present the following ROI formula:

$$\frac{\text{Adjusted benefit} - \cos t}{\text{Cost}} \times 100 = \text{ROI}$$

The difference between this and more orthodox calculations is in adjusting the benefits to allow for the difficulties in establishing the payback and isolating the results attributable to coaching. We need to estimate the monetary value of tangible business benefits, multiply that by the percentage of those benefits attributable to coaching, and multiply again by the percentage of our confidence in those estimates.

Let's take a worked example and say that for ease of calculation last year's coaching programme had total costs of £20,000. In the twelve months that followed the sales department won a new order for around £60,000 that hadn't seemed likely beforehand and that some coachees in the administration department identified cost savings of about £20,000, making £80,000 of benefits from the coaching programme. However you think that perhaps only 50% can truly be attributable to the coaching programme and you feel about 90% confident in your calculations. We can now calculate the ROI as:

$$\frac{(80,000 \times 50\% \times 90\%) - 20,000}{20,000} \times 100$$

$$\frac{36{,}000 - 20{,}000}{20{,}000} \times 100$$

$$\frac{16{,}000}{20{,}000} \times 100 = 80\%$$

Which seems a pretty decent return and certainly a good deal more than the £600 on offer from the bank. Even if we thought that only 10% of the benefits were attributable to the coaching and were only 10% confident in our calculations we could still show an ROI of 4%.

We must of course, be highly cautious in using formulae of any kind and some people will remain highly sceptical given the subjective nature of the data. In the next two sections we'll look at quantifying benefits and costs as accurately as possible.

QUANTIFYING BENEFITS

The ROI calculation outlined above requires us to establish exactly how the organisation has benefited from introducing a coaching programme. There is always a need to exercise judgement here; hence the inclusion of the confidence estimate in the formula, but you should nevertheless consider the following indicators.

Consider firstly each coachee's personal productivity. This might be measured as units produced or data input or whatever but consider also things like absenteeism and lateness for work, both of which can be positively influenced by coaching. You can extend this thinking to team productivity as well and look at time spent in training and levels of overtime incurred.

In a commercial setting you can expect a coaching approach to produce an increase in both sales and lead generation and these should already be being measured. You should also see a reduction in costs in terms of things like scrap, rejections and returned items.

Aside then from increased productivity, increased revenue and reduced costs, I would suggest that coaching will have a measurable effect on quality which you should be able to measure in terms of customer turnover, accidents, re-work, and customer satisfaction.

I consider these the main 'hard' measurable benefits but there are also a host of 'soft' intangible benefits, the financial return of which you'll need to estimate.

Coaching improves staff retention, for example. A recent survey by Reed Consulting showed that the most important trigger for a member of staff leaving is limited career and personal development. It is in fact three times as influential as salary and benefits and yet this is what most employers focus upon. The report suggests that matters can be improved by providing employees with opportunities to 'evaluate their strengths and focus on new objectives.' If that doesn't sound like a coaching session, I don't know what does. The CIPD estimates the average cost of an employee leaving at £4,625; clearly a cost worth addressing.

A coaching approach demands and generates a more positive view of human nature. It requires us to treat people as aware, responsible and trustworthy folk who can be relied upon to perform if motivated and managed effectively. Small wonder then that in another recent CIPD survey, 77% of respondents reported that the use of coaching in their organisations had increased rapidly in recent years, with a consequent positive effect on working relationships.

Staff who are coached welcome responsibility, do not have to be chased or watched to get things done and free managers to perform their more overarching functions, which there never seems enough time to do. Furthermore, out of respect for individuals, improved relationships and the success that accompanies coaching, the atmosphere at work will change for the better. Where coaching is the norm, staff can expect to be treated with respect, to have their ideas and opinions sought and to be thanked occasionally. Management will then benefit from a group of people who are willing to go the extra mile when the need arises.

Coaching recognises that real business performance happens when staff choose to use their discretionary effort rather than just do the minimum to get by. This benefit is almost impossible to quantify but in these competitive times it is almost priceless.

QUANTIFYING COSTS

We must take a similarly inclusive view on determining the true cost of a coaching programme if the results of our ROI calculation are to be credible. My banking days taught me about conservatism in accountancy and I apply the same principle here. If you are in any doubt about whether to include a cost or not, include it or it's likely that someone will query its omission.

If you're using external coaches the costs ought to be easy to determine. They are most likely to charge a day rate plus expenses for travel and so on and these should all be included.

You may have produced some materials such as workbooks and action plans and the costs of producing and distributing these will need to be factored in.

If using internal coaches you'll need to show a rate for their time in the same way as if you used an external coach. If an internal daily rate is not available, I tend to take annual salary divided by number of working days in the year. You can then take this figure and multiply it by the number of days spent coaching. Remember to also make a similar calculation for anybody involved in administering the programme and include time outside coaching sessions, conducting meetings or planning the evaluation!

For real credibility I recommend also including an element for 'opportunity cost', in other words what was the cost of *not* having the coach and coachee doing their normal work. For example, in a coaching programme we ran at a school we factored in the costs of supply teachers that were hired to cover lessons while coaching sessions took place. In a sales environment we might similarly look at the monetary value of the average leads or sales that could be generated in a day spent on coaching.

The overriding idea is to accurately compare the situation after the coaching programme with the situation if we'd done nothing.

SUMMARY

This chapter has covered the thorny old subject of evaluation, a subject that has seen many a developer of people running for the hills. By way of summary I'd like to cover the four questions on evaluation that I get asked time and again.

Does evaluation add value?

We need to be sensible. You could of course evaluate your evaluation and try to see if your efforts produced a return on investment but I recommend you don't. In broad terms evaluation adds value if it garners support for the coaching programme from the main stakeholders; coaches, coachees and sponsors. Sponsors defined as those in the organisation who give the agreement for the coaching programme to proceed and who provide the budget for it. Beyond this evaluation adds value if it proves that coaching has worked because this can win over the sceptics and also galvanise the self-belief of the already enthusiastic. Finally, evaluation only adds value if the effort is proportional to the benefits and this is something only you can decide.

Who is it for?

Less a question for me and more one for you to pose yourself, I would suggest. Typically the evaluation will be at the behest of a senior manager who is asking you to make the case for coaching. Sadly you can go to a great deal of effort and produce a detailed evaluation in keeping with the ideas explained here, only for it to be dismissed as spurious in any event. Before proceeding down the route of detailed work remember that the drive for proof often disguises the deeply held mistrust of the people development function and that you may be being invited to contribute to your own downfall. What's needed is a healthy discussion beforehand that can scope out the evaluation in terms of the time and work involved, how the results will be used, how the results will be acted upon, etc. The simple answer to the question *who is it for?* is anyone with an interest in seeing coaching *succeed*, not fail.

What's the best way?

In this chapter I've tried to steer clear of magic formulae and specific models because my experience suggests that one size really doesn't fit all when it comes to evaluation. My best advice is to do what suits the size and shape of your organisation. The owner manager who attended a coaching skills training course may simply want to know that it was money well spent. The multi-national with a coaching programme that rolled out to hundreds of leaders and managers will want something highly sophisticated.

The last question is one that normally gets asked when you're deep in the detail and wondering why you ever got involved.

Remind me . . . why are we doing this?

Because we're believers in coaching with an innate conviction that people are resourceful and can make a massive contribution if given the opportunity and setting to do so. However, we operate in a world where we get called naïve and where the desire for proof pervades. We must adapt and talk this language if coaching – or any form of people development – is to flourish in the years to come. It's not easy and it mainly requires diligence, logic and effort, but it works and it's worth it.

But please, please, please never lose sight of the fact that it's about people not numbers.

CHAPTER 14

MAKING THE BUSINESS CASE FOR COACHING

INTRODUCTION

I like to think this whole book has been about making the business case for coaching.

Right at the outset we discovered that most people at work are considered to be performing at somewhere around 30–60% of their potential. That means there is at least 40% more to go at for very little additional cost. I bet there's not a single piece of plant or even office equipment that your organisation would be prepared to use so inefficiently.

Having looked at reducing interference to release some of that potential we looked at sustaining performance by promoting learning and enjoyment. People who enjoy their work perform better. They take less time off, they contribute discretionary effort. They take a pride in their work and in the organisation for which they do it. People who maximise their learning at work spot opportunities for improvement, make fewer mistakes and become an invaluable source of best practice.

What about our key principles of Awareness, Responsibility and Trust? What if I could sell you those qualities? How much would you be prepared to pay? If you're currently being bashed by the competition have a look at their people. Are they not more aware, responsible, trusting and trustworthy?

The case for coaching is highly compelling, but the take up patchy. This may be because of a lack of empirical evidence, but is probably more due to a reluctance to invest the time and money for fear the results will not become apparent quickly enough. Coaching generally pays off in the medium to long-term, but most managers are compelled to produce measurable results in a twelve month time frame.

And yet this hesitancy does not seem to affect other parts of working life so readily. Let's go back a few years to a time when organisations were considering replacing their clunky old type-writers with word processors. They'd have asked themselves the following questions:

- Will it mean we can work more quickly? Yes.
- Will our work look more professional? Yes.
- Will our work be more accurate? Yes
- Will business results improve? Er, not necessarily.

There is no direct relationship between buying a word processor and improving results but we do it because it makes sense. In the same way, I believe that coaching simply makes sense and this chapter is about presenting the evidence for that belief.

We'll start by looking at the numbers.

TSIO ltd – it stands for 'try switching it off' – is a micro business. It is owned and managed by Debbie and offers IT support to small businesses. Debbie employs one other consultant and an office administrator. Trading is okay, but Debbie thinks she could grow the business if she were better able to manage her colleagues and indeed better able to focus herself. Here's a summary of TSIO's accounts:

	£
Sales	200,000
Direct Costs	(100,000)
Gross Profit	**100,000**
Payroll	(60,000)
Overheads	(20,000)
Net Profit	**20,000**

Debbie spends a few hundred pounds on a coaching skills programme and applies enthusiastically what she learns over the next year or so. What would happen if this resulted in sales increasing by 1% and costs reducing by 1%?

	£		£
Sales	200,000	+1%	202,000
Direct Costs	(100,000)	−1%	99,000
Gross Profit	**100,000**		**103,000**
Payroll	(60,000)		60,000
Overheads	(20,000)	−1%	19,800
Net Profit	**20,000**	**+16%**	**23,200**

That's 19% increase in net profit with an almost negligible impact from coaching. What if the coaching resulted in sales increasing by 5% and costs reducing by 5%?

	£		£
Sales	200,000	+5%	210,000
Direct Costs	(100,000)	−5%	95,000
Gross Profit	**100,000**		**115,000**
Payroll	(60,000)		60,000
Overheads	(20,000)	−5%	19,000
Net Profit	**20,000**	**+80%**	**36,000**

These are only modest estimates of the tangible results that coaching can achieve and yet the impact on the bottom line is astonishing.

To be really accurate I would have needed to adjust the figure for overheads to include the cost of the coach training, but in this example such costs would be minimal. It's also fair to say that we've looked at a very simple organisation in very simple terms, but the point is not to scrutinise these figures but rather to illustrate that if coaching has a positive impact on two or three key organisational areas the cumulative effect is real, measurable performance improvement.

Elsewhere in this book I've repeatedly stated that coaching is so much more than just an approach to solving problems, but given that solving problems is what most people look to coaching for in the first instance let's pay that due regard here. What follows are the typical problems our clients cite as reasons for being interested in training their managers and leaders as coaches. I've grouped them under four headings:

- People problems
- Resource problems
- Change problems
- Pressure problems

PEOPLE PROBLEMS

Poor relations

Work places are a collection of people; a micro society and just like any society some people will get along and others will clash. In fact, in certain instances those clashes can be quite useful and be the spark behind creative ideas or the fuel for a cohesive team. However, in the end collaboration and co-operation will outperform competition and conflict. Rather than promote some Utopian ideal, coaching suggests that the key to healthy relations at work is establishing high levels of trust. A manager who coaches will be demonstrating a faith in people that they are likely to feel motivated to repay. In such a climate even difficulties between team members can be more readily resolved given the prevailing atmosphere of openness and honesty. I remember coaching two clients of mine who had each asked for help in resolving a work relationship issue. It turned out the problem they had was with each other. Through coaching they each resolved that they had to stop enduring this situation and take a stand. Whilst their chosen tactics were arguably a little on the aggressive side they started talking to each other and all conflict resolution starts with dialogue. Coaching creates dialogue *between* coach and coachee but also *amongst* coachees who become used to communicating this way.

Boredom

Boredom kicks in when learning and enjoyment have gone. People are exhorted to perform and given substantial external rewards for doing so, but find that this is not enough. Let's put the learning and enjoyment back in. Even the most mundane tasks can become interesting and enjoyable again if through coaching we encourage people to re-focus and notice what they notice. It's almost impossible to be highly aware and bored at the same time. If it's not possible to foster learning and enjoyment by changing the nature of the task or job can you look for other activities to provide a new challenge such as serving on a committee or providing training to more junior colleagues? A coaching approach here will reveal what's right for the individual concerned.

Low morale and motivation

Similarly, low morale and motivation kick in when learning and enjoyment are missing and/or when trust is being abused. The latter can take the guise of inflation busting pay rises for the top team with derisory increments to the staff. It may also manifest as broken promises, unending uncertainty, relentless pressure and mean spirited practices. People do not like to be treated as commodities or things. They do not think of themselves as human resources or – God forbid – human capital. They like to be treated as human beings and with respect. A simple dose of treating others as we would wish to be treated ourselves can work wonders for morale and motivation.

Unconfident staff

A lack of confidence is a big source of internal interference and this is where coaching scores over other ways of trying to solve this problem. Motivational talks and training courses that show videos of confident people address the symptom and not the cause. The raised awareness that coaching brings is once again the answer. To become more confident I need to become of aware of the circumstances in which I am unconfident. What are the triggers? What makes it worse? What makes it better? With the help of a coach I can then contrast this with situations in which I feel confident and begin to access those qualities when I need them. A good coach is a source of confidence when they demonstrate through their words and actions that they have unwavering faith in our ability to learn how to cope in even the most difficult of circumstances.

High staff turnover

Constant re-recruitment is not only a drain on financial resources it is demoralising for those that remain and handle the added workload whilst replacements are found. The simple truth is this: People join organisations but leave managers. I can't remember where I first found this phrase – I think I read it somewhere. I was thinking about it when I heard of a report published by Dimension Data called the *Merchants Global Contact Centre Benchmarking Report 2005*. The report showed that staff turnover rates in contact centres around the world rose to 23% in 2004 from 19% whilst investment in training and development had gone *down*. This has got to be more than coincidence and not limited to the contact centre industry I'm sure. Of course the problem is that organisations are unwilling to invest in training and development if staff are only going to leave. It creates a vicious circle. This cycle can be broken by coaching. Having managers who coach is far more cost effective than endless external training and will improve the organisational climate at the same time.

Modern work attitudes

Without doubt people entering the world of work today have a very different attitude and approach to previous generations. I think discussions around *better* or *worse* are meaningless, they're simply different. People look for work to fulfil different needs in their lives these days and that requires a different management approach. We need to become people centred and recognise each team member's unique contribution. Coaching honours this uniqueness and encourages thought, ownership and responsibility in a way that command and control could never match.

To much time 'in' the team

Here's a familiar tale. A particularly skilled and willing team member gets promoted to team leader or manager in recognition of their technical skills. They find the move quite unsettling especially when it comes to getting results through others. They continue *doing* the work rather than *managing* the work because this is an area in which they are both comfortable and able to generate short term results. It also takes less time than coaching and developing the team. Because team members are not therefore being developed, they are never able to take on higher level work which means the leader has to continue doing it. The team members get bored and move on and so it continues. Let's start promoting the great coaches alongside the great technicians and let's teach the technicians how to coach so that they can quickly maintain and develop the team's performance through understanding the power of awareness, responsibility and trust.

Old fashioned management

Why do some managers persist with a tell style that is patently out-dated, ineffective and probably quite exhausting? There are many reasons but lack of perceived alternative is probably high amongst them.

In fairness, we cannot expect managers schooled in very different ways for very different times to simply take up the coaching approach because it's suddenly become trendy and 'the done thing'. We need to provide training in coaching skills that is simple, clear, effective and above all provides a viable alternative to other approaches. Coaching, when it is understood at the level of principle, is entirely in-keeping with the values of management that have been around for ever. Providing direction and clarity, making the most of resources, and seeing meaningful results are the concern of coaching just as much as any other style.

Lack of promotion opportunities

This depends on what you mean by promotion of course but for most people this means a senior role with the higher salary and other external rewards that come with it. What if we promote learning and enjoyment as well? Will people still feel frustrated at a lack of promotion opportunities if they are learning and developing? Will they be frustrated if they really, really enjoy what they do? In truth, some will of course and it's their prerogative to pursue other opportunities but for others that magic combination of performance, learning and enjoyment can be all that's required to keep people happily focused on the here and now rather than dreaming of what's to come.

RESOURCE PROBLEMS

People in wrong jobs

In my experience people are seldom appointed or promoted to the 'wrong' job. I don't deny that it happens but generally organisations make a considerable effort to build robust recruitment and selection mechanisms. What happens is that we 'take our eye off the ball' and find that something has happened to create a wrong person/wrong job scenario. There are only two variables, so either the person has changed or the job has changed. If the person has changed it is likely due to a new instance of external or internal interference and coaching, as we know, can quickly reveal the source. If the job has changed, or indeed if the jobholder *perceives* it has changed, then again coaching can help the jobholder decide whether they can accept the change or whether they need to move to another role. Some would argue that this could cost a business a lot of money, but I would suggest it costs a lot more to keep people in the wrong jobs.

Lack of skills

There is a war for talent being waged at the moment. In the age of the knowledge worker organisations are competing hard for a share of the skills available in the labour market. Coaching helps because a coaching culture can be an attractive part of the employment offer in the first place. Above and beyond this, a coaching approach will ensure that employees keep up to date and are motivated to constantly hone their skills. Coaching accelerates skills acquisition and develops them to a higher level than skills training alone.

Poor quality

It has to be said that if you have an essentially poor product or service, then you need more major surgery than coaching alone can provide. A more common challenge though is to *motivate* people to see quality as important. I also think we need to take a broad perspective, it's so much more than just applying Japanese manufacturing style intense scrutiny to product and procedures, it's about reacquainting people with a sense of pride in everything that they do. Coaching can undoubtedly help. Firstly by inviting me to think about matters of quality and then developing some ways forward. However, coaching must be presented properly for this to happen. Invite me to work with a coach to *repair* me and I'm likely to resist, but ask me to work with a coach to help me do the very best I can and I'm likely to be more keen.

People with baggage

Okay, it should be clear by now. 'Baggage', be it prior experiences, bad relationships, mistakes or low self confidence are all types of interference. Interference obstructs potential and less of it is turned into performance. Coaching makes me aware of the interference, its source and its consequences. Once aware I can do something about it, until I'm aware I will carry the baggage around and it will weigh me down and similarly affect those I work with.

No budgets

Let's look firstly at the question of there being no budget for coaching or coaching skills training. No budget is not the same as no money. Organisations spend money on things and activities that offer value. To the profit making concern that is probably some sort of monetary return on investment, and to the not for profit organisation it is the wise spending of a scarce resource. Organisations will spend money on coaching and indeed any other form of development if there is a sound case for doing so.

But what about the question of small budgets or limited financial muscle in general. Once again coaching provides an answer in its capacity to get the maximum value from the greatest resource of all – people. If you have managers trained as coaches you have people development managers on site, on-call 365 days a year providing highly focused, learner centred development on a just in time basis. No other form of training can compete in value for money terms.

High cost of training

Training costs can indeed be high, particularly when little thought is given to focusing the training on the needs of the learners. All too often organisations simply reach for the internal or external training directory, line up a few courses and hope that will do. Coaching sessions identify real training needs and offer insight into the best ways those needs can be fulfilled. This is because coaching asks 'What do you need?', not 'Would you like to attend?' Training is expensive and finance for it is precious so let's use coaching to get the right training, at the right time, delivered in the right way.

CHANGE PROBLEMS

Poor at change

I hear a lot about organisations being poor at change, I hear even more about people being poor at change. Both statements confuse me. Human beings are surely the most adaptive creatures imaginable, embracing change of one kind or another from the cradle to the grave.

When I used to get involved in career coaching I was always amazed at the number of people who would explain to me that they'd been offered redundancy from their firm because they didn't seem able or willing to change anymore and then go on to explain how they intended to start a business, travel the world, or work for a charity. All of which require an astonishing ability to cope with change. People are very good at change and organisations are simply collections of people so something else must be happening.

I think that in an organisational setting people are poor at *learning* from change. Such is the pace of change that we lurch from one project or initiative to the next without pausing for breath or taking stock. I propose that every change project includes an opportunity for those most affected to have some coaching on what their learning experience has been like and the lessons that must be taken forward next time.

Stuck in comfort zones

The problem with comfort zones is that we get comfortable *with* them as well as *in* them. By this I mean that we may well realise that we and our colleagues are operating within our comfort zones but we don't choose to do anything about it. Normally what follows is some sort of crisis or major change which has us operating way outside our comfort zones into an arena that I call the panic zone. In the panic zone we experience an adrenalin rush and can probably feel the fight or flight reflex kicking in. This is not the ideal set of conditions from which to learn from the experience and leaves us exposed should a similar set of circumstances arise in the future. Some people of course thrive in this sort of sink or swim situation but I would rather err on the side of caution. Working within a coaching culture, on the other hand, would mean that our comfort zones are always being gently expanded into our learning zones. Whilst it's inevitable that crisis situations will still crop up we should be better able to cope and certainly better able to learn positive lessons from the experience.

Blame culture

Within a coaching culture mistakes and problems are viewed as opportunities to learn and avoid similar things happening again. This is not some soft and fluffy rationale for avoiding account-ability but a sound business-like process. Things go wrong and people need to come forward and take responsibility for what's happened including any consequences, but a blame culture leads to cover ups and finding scapegoats. Mistakes are not learnt from, but resentment builds up and actually increases the chances of things going wrong or problems remaining unidentified.

PRESSURE PROBLEMS

The final set of problems for which coaching offers solutions are to do with the prevailing climate at work these days. I never meet anyone who says they aren't under pressure. Even discounting the modern phenomenon of stress envy and the fact that we all like to appear virtuous and hard working, it seems the modern world of work is characterised by unrelenting pressure to achieve more and more with less and less. If coaching could relieve just some of the stress that accompanies this it must be worth having.

Pressure to improve performance

Everyone understands the need for improved performance. We've all attended the presentations where business leaders talk at length about the march of technology, declining market share, the eco-nomic back drop, the rise of the tiger economies with their miniscule labour costs. The list is endless, it's all completely under-standable but people get tired. Explaining that people *have* to perform at higher and higher levels is not enough, we need coaching to help them discover *how* they can do this and we need coaching to provide an outlet for discussing the stress and fatigue that is the inevitable result. People have the potential for high or increasing performance but awareness, responsibility and trust must link the two.

Pressure to maintain performance

Just because we can reach levels of high performance does not mean we can automatically stay there. There is sadly no valve to stop performance levels dropping off. The key is learning and enjoyment which coaching seems to cultivate better than any other development approach. This is probably due to the fact that coaching is tailor made for the individual performer and thus discovers exactly what learning is required for that individual and how that individual can best enjoy what they do.

There is also the challenge of switching aims. It is arguably more difficult to sustain a level of performance than to get there in the first place as any serial dieter will tell you. The best bet is to switch to time related performance goals, i.e. to forecast how *long* we can maintain a level of performance.

Red tape

I guess it might all sound a bit unreal by now and seem as if I'm suggesting that coaching is some kind of cure all. Coaching isn't a panacea and there are plenty of problems it won't solve. Neither is it a universal approach to managing people and there will be times when we need a more directive approach. Nevertheless coaching is a way of mobilising potential and helping people find a way forward. It can allow people to explore their frustrations with work and that can include devising ways of coping with the creeping bureaucracy and seemingly needless procedures that seem to be on the increase these days. The principle of responsibility is really useful here in that we can invite our coachees to consider other options to the bureaucratic processes that cause frustration. It's surprising how often people realise that rules concerning health and safety, confidentiality, data protection and so on are actually very necessary and also the sort of rules they'd invent themselves if that was their task. This realisation can help generate a feeling of ownership and responsibility.

Low productivity

Low productivity, if it persists, can be quite demoralising for all concerned. It will also result in some alarming consequences if left unchecked. Unfortunately demoralised or frightened people do not produce their best performance and so we need a way of getting things back on track. Through coaching we can understand the reasons for low productivity, we can set some carefully constructed performance goals to bring it back on track and we can enable those whom we coach to share in the responsibility for restoring productivity. In this way we will not only address the low productivity but also learn how better to avoid the same problems recurring.

Busy

At the other end of the scale is the pressure that comes from being too busy. All managers recognise the vicious circle that this can produce: Too busy to coach and develop; unable to delegate work and tasks. Therefore the busyness continues. We can also have the entire organisation seeming too busy to coach and develop the staff. There is no magic wand and ultimately someone has to make the decision to invest in the long term as well as attending to current workloads. The good news though is that coaching is the quickest and most effective way of bringing people on. Then we can delegate and grow people's skills. Then we'll seem less busy and we can take more time out for development and then we're really up and running.

Pressure to achieve quality standards

Achieving quality standards enables organisations to demonstrate that they meet their obligations to external bodies. It also illustrates that our organisation can rise to a challenge and be self-scrutinising. This can be helpful in building a brand image amongst customers and employees alike. We can use coaching to generate a sense of ownership of the work involved in achieving the standard and also to examine the policies and processes that may need to change. The reality stage of the coaching ARROW can be particularly helpful in this regard.

SUMMARY

Summarising the business case for coaching also enables me to make the neatest of summaries for the book as a whole.

In these times of tightening labour markets, scarce skills and the war for talent a big part of the case for coaching is the positive contribution it can make to a reputation as a sound employer. Surely the single biggest influence on an employer brand is the treatment of staff by managers and leaders. Coaching can help reduce staff turnover as ultimately people leave managers not organisations and the reduction in turnover will have as big an impact on stability and retaining skills as it will on the recruitment budget. A stable, capable workforce then provides a pool of talent to provide for succession needs, lessening the need for external appointments and ensuring an emerging leadership with a deep understanding of the organisation and its operations.

Coaching is about learning and so the case for coaching includes recognising that mistakes and errors will be fewer but that learning from them will be greater. With coaching we can ensure that people new to the organisation can be brought to a level of performance quickly and start making a positive contribution.

The case for coaching relative to other training and development is also a strong one. Coaching is the ultimate in 'just in time' learning. It is immediate and entirely focused on the needs of the learner. It is by far the cheapest form of training because nothing is superfluous; everything is relevant. Managers who coach become constant training managers providing support and growth every working day every year. In this way learning, enjoying and performing are combined and in balance and we've seen what this can do.

Coaching is art not science but with an *awareness* of the business case we can take *responsibility* for making it happen and *trust* that results will follow.

EPILOGUE

In times of change the learners will inherit the earth, while the learned find themselves beautifully equipped to deal with a world that no longer exists.

Eric Hoffer

Writing in the preface of *The Inner Game of Work* [5], Peter Block states that 'high performers are people who simply learn faster'.

Can there be a more pressing need in today's world of work than to help people learn faster? This is not the preserve of the HR department though because it is, in fact, line management that is best placed to be the catalyst for learning for the most important employees in any organisation – those closest to the customer.

In fairness line managers have understood this for a long time but have struggled to replace the command and control methods on which they have been raised and which they still see modeled with an up to date and effective alternative. I believe coaching provides the answer.

I run a coaching skills training consultancy called Peak and we involve ourselves in a range of activities designed to turn managers into coaches. This includes training programmes, key note talks and consultancy. If you would like to know more, please do get in touch with me at:

Peak

Alligator House
Wearfield
Sunderland SR5 2TA
United Kingdom

www.mattsomers.com/peak
matt@mattsomers.com

INDEX

accreditation 264
achievements 282
action plans, ARROW model
    109–11
adding value 293
adult learning 262–3
aims
    see also dreams; performance goals
    ARROW model 93–7, 102–3, 110
    career development 230–1
    common mistakes 123
    performance reviews 208–10
    personal organisation 186–7
    presentations 167–8
    sales 145
Amazon UK 2
Anderson, Dianna 289
Anderson, Merrill 289
andragogy (adult learning) 262–3
applications 135–240
appraisals 199–217
aptitude tests 237
arrogance 223
ARROW model 92–113, 120,
    129–31, 154–5, 195, 215–16,
    224, 273–4
    action plans 109–11

aims 93–7, 102–3, 110
assumptions 103
awareness 98–100
career development 224
coaching questions 96–7, 100–7,
    109–11
coaching sessions 129–31
comfort zones 108–9
dreams 93–5
fear of failure 107
honesty 103
ideas 104–6
options 104–8, 195
performance goals 93–5
performance reviews 215–16
pitfalls 108
processes 93–5
reality 97–103, 154–5, 195, 224
reflection 101–4
responsibility 120, 129
running sessions 273–4
SMART goals 95
thinking 104–6
trust 101
way forward 108–11
'ask don't tell' philosophy 85–6
assertiveness 180, 185–6, 188–90

assessment centres, career
   development 236–8
assumptions 103
AT&T 4
attention, paying attention 89, 127
attitudes 1–2, 35, 184–5, 215, 283–4
   see also behaviour
audience profile 164–5, 169, 267
awareness 67–71, 77, 98–100
   ARROW model 98–100
   competence/incompetence model
      69–71
   conscious/unconscious behaviour
      69–71
   definition 67
   Peak Model 67–71, 77, 98–100
   raising awareness 67–71
   'telling' style 69

Back Up North advisory organisation
   247
Bacon, Terry 287
balance, work/life 180
behaviour 12–15, 68–71, 127, 179,
   215, 250–1
   conscious/unconscious behaviour
      68–71
   control systems 250–1
   habits 127, 179
   management 12–15
   performance reviews 215
   Theory X/Theory Y 12–15
beliefs 15, 26–9, 55, 74, 144, 224,
   246
   career development 224
   faith in products 144
   limiting beliefs 26–9, 224
   Peak Model 26–9
   performance 55
   self-belief 15, 74
   stories 246
belonging 39–40
benefits evaluation 290–2
bespoke training 262–3
blame cultures 21–2, 25, 310
   change problems 310

external interference 21–2
   fear of failure 25
   internal interference 25
body language 127, 189
books 2–3
boredom 301–2
budgets 307
business case 297–314
   change problems 308–10
   example 298–300
   people problems 301–5
   pressure problems 310–13
   problems 300–13
   resource problems 305–8
business pitches 167–8
business plans 256
busyness 312–13
buying signals 143–4
   see also sales

career development 219–40
   see also jobs; staff
   aims 230–1, 239
   arrogance 223
   ARROW model 224
   assessment centres 236–8
   critical variables 226–30
   CVs 225, 233–4, 239–40
   desire to work 228
   email 234
   fear of failure 223–4
   feedback 221
   interference 221–4
   interviews 226–8, 230–1, 234–6,
      239–40
   job searches 232–3
   letters 233–4, 239
   limiting beliefs 224
   opportunities 231
   outside influences 222
   PLE triangle 224–6
   processes 231, 239
   professionalism 228–9
   ratio of talk input 227
   recruitment 220
   security 229

REFERENCES

[1] Anderson, D. & Anderson, M. (2005). *Coaching that Counts*. Elsevier Butterworth Heineman.

[2] Clutterbuck, D. & Megginson, D. (2005). *Making Coaching Work: Creating a Coaching Culture*. CIPD.

[3] Covey, S. (1989). *Seven Habits of Highly Successful People*. Simon & Schuster.

[4] Gallwey, T. (1975). *The Inner Game of Tennis*. Jonathan Cape.

[5] Gallwey, T. (2000). *The Inner Game of Work*. Texere.

[6] Handy, C. (2004). *The New Alchemists*. Hutchinson.

[7] Herzberg, F. (1993). *Motivation to Work*. Transaction.

[8] House, R. & Dessler, G. (1974). *The Path Goal Theory of Leadership*. Southern Illinois University Press.

[9] Johnson, G. & Scholes, K. (1997). *Exploring Corporate Strategy*. Prentice Hall.

[10] Kirkpatrick, D. (1998). *Evaluating Training Programmes*. Berrett Koehler.

[11] Kline, N. (1999). *Time to Think*. Ward Lock.

[12] Knowles, M. (1984). *The Adult Learner: A Neglected Species*. 3rd edn. Gulf Publishing.

[13] Kolb, D. (1985). *Experiential Learning*. Prentice Hall.

[14] Lambert, T. (1997). *High Income Consulting*. Nicholas Brealey.

[15] Lapidus, T. (2000). *High Impact Training: Getting Results*. Jossey-Bass.

[16] Maslow, A. (1987). *Motivation and Personality*. 3rd edn. Longman.

[17] McGregor, D. (1987). *The Human Side of Enterprise*. Penguin.

[18] Rosinski, P. (2003). *Coaching Across Cultures*. Nicholas Brealey.

[19] Somers, M. (2002). *Coaching in a Week*. Hodder & Stoughton.

[20] Tammenbaum, R. & Schmidt, W. (1973). *How to Choose a Leadership Pattern*. Harvard Business Review.

selection 231
sense of looking forward 229–30
suggestions 232–8
taking control 238–9
transferable skills 239
value clashes 222
Carrot and Stick motivation 46
change 1–2, 76, 275–6, 308–10
  attitudes 1–2
  blame cultures 310
  coaching programmes 275–6
  comfort zones 309
  organisations 275–6
  poor at change 308–9
  problems 308–10
  trust 76
closed questions 91
closure
  coaching relationships 274–5
  deals 141–2, 151–2
Clutterbuck, David 243
coaches 261–70, 274
  external coaches 268–70, 274
  internal coaches 268–70, 274
  training 261–8
coaching
  see also coaching questions
  analyses 287–8
  applications 135–240
  concepts 1–3, 9–10
  culture 243–57
  definitions 9–10
  implementation 241–314
  importance 1–5
  overview 5
  Peak Model 9–133
  programmes 259–77, 279–95
  qualities 123–5
coaching analyses 287–8
coaching culture 243–57
  business plans 256
  control 250–2
  core culture 255–6
  cultural web 245–56
  definition 243
  egalitarianism 254–5

groups 245
indicators 245–56
language 256
organisation structures 249–50
performance reviews 248
power structures 252–3
routines/rituals 248
senior management 256
stories 246–7
symbols 253–5
coaching programmes 259–77,
    279–95
  change 275–6
  closure 274–5
  contracting 271–2
  evaluation 279–95
  maintaining momentum 260
  running sessions 272–4
  selecting coaches 268–70
  senior management 260, 268–9,
    277
  stakeholders 276–7
  training coaches 261–8
coaching qualities 123–5
coaching questions 85–93, 96–7,
    100–7, 109–11, 122–3, 126–7
  see also questions
  ARROW model 96–7, 100–7,
    109–11
  common mistakes 122–3
  criteria 88–91
  critical variables 88
  enabling tight focus 89–90
  feedback 90–1
  frameworks 91–3
  GROW mnemonic 91–2
  listening 126–7
  open/closed questions 91
  paying attention 89
  Peak model 85–93
  process 91
  thinking 86–7
coaching sessions see sessions
Coaching that Counts (Anderson &
    Anderson) 289
Coaching in a Week (author) 92, 211

comfort zones 108–9, 309
　ARROW model 108–9
　change problems 309
commitment 111, 272–3
common mistakes 122–3, 131–2
communication 57–67, 81–2, 152–3
　developing staff 64–7
　experiences 67
　HR example 64–7
　leadership styles 57–64, 81–2
　Peak Model 57–67
　philosophy 62–4
　sales managers 152–3
　Tammenbaum & Schmidt model
　　58–64
competence 69–71, 203–4
competition 141
confidence 144, 166, 188, 204–5,
　302–3
　assertiveness 188
　performance reviews 204–5
　presentations 166
　sales 144
　staff confidence 302–3
conscious behaviour 69–71
contracting 130, 271–2
control 62–3, 186–9, 238–9, 250–2,
　282
　assertiveness 188–9
　career development 238–9
　coaching culture 250–2
　evaluation 282
　leadership 62–3
　personal organisation 186–7
　self-control 188–9
　systems 250–2
　Theory X 251
control groups, evaluation 288
costs
　coaching 292–3
　opportunity costs 292–3
　training 308, 314
counseling 117–18, 131
covering letters 233–4, 239
covert coaching 76
Covey, Stephen 132, 196

creative thinking 2, 104–6
credibility, external interference
　120–1
culture 179, 244–6, 310
　see also coaching culture;
　　organisations
　blame cultures 310
　cultural web 245–6
　definitions 244–5
　group culture 244–5
　organisation culture 179
curriculum vitae (CV) 225, 233–4,
　239–40
　see also career development
customer objections, sales 143, 150–1
cynicism 34

deal closures 141–2, 151–2
delegation leadership style 58–9, 61,
　63–4
desire 56, 228
　see also needs
desk tidiness 193
Dessler, G. 43–5, 55
detachment 207
direct questions 173
directive coaching 82
discrimination 23
distractions 128, 185
dreams 93–5, 146, 168, 187, 209,
　230–1, 239
　see also aims; performance goals
　ARROW model 93–5
　career development 230–1, 239
　performance reviews 209
　personal organisation 187
　presentations 168
　sales 146

egalitarianism 254–5
eighty/twenty rule, Pareto 182
Einstein, Albert 279
emails 234
emotions 117, 158
employees see staff
employment see jobs

enjoyment 45–7, 49, 51–5, 142,
   163–4, 182, 205–6, 224–6,
   301–2
   see also PLE triangle
   boredom 301–2
   career development 224–6
   learning 53–4
   Peak Model 45–7, 49, 51–5
   performance 53–4, 205–6
   personal organisation 182
   presentations 163–4
   sales 142
environments 119, 160–1, 273
   coaching sessions 273
   poor environment 119
   presentations 160–1
epilogue 315–16
equipment, presentations 160
ethical standards 270
evaluation 279–95
   achievement 282
   benefits 290–2
   coaching costs 292–3
   coaching programmes 279–95
   control groups 288
   expert estimation 288
   improvement 282–4
   isolating variables 286–8
   key questions 293–5
   Kirkpatrick 283–4
   learning 282–4
   line management 285–6
   means of control 282
   multiple choice tests 285–6
   performance 286
   pre/post coaching analyses
      287–8
   productivity 290–1
   quality 291
   quantifying benefits 290–2
   reaction questionnaire 285
   ROI 288–90
   self evaluation 213
   tools 284–6
   value creation 280–1, 293
evidence, limiting beliefs 27–9

expectations 24
experience 24, 67, 162, 264,
   268
   negative experience 24
   presentations 162
   prior experience 162
   staff development 67
   training coaches 264, 268
experts 252–3, 288
Exploring Corporate Strategy (Johnson
   & Scholes) 245
external coaches 75, 130, 268–70,
   274, 292
external interference 19–23, 118–22,
   139–40, 159–61, 179–80,
   201–3, 221–2
   see also interference; internal
      interference
   blame cultures 21–2
   career development 221–2
   credibility 120–1
   discrimination 23
   existing relationships 119
   getting it right 119–20
   ideas not accepted 21–2
   the inner game 118–22
   opportunities 23
   performance reviews 201–3
   personal organisation 179–80
   poor environment 119
   presentations 159–61
   problem solving 120
   restrictive policies 21
   sales 139–40
   too much coaching 121
   work pressures 118–19
Extrinsic motivators 36–8, 40, 46,
   55

failure *see* fear of failure
fake listening 128–9
fear of failure 25–6, 107, 161, 189,
   223–4
   ARROW model 107
   assertiveness 189
   blame cultures 25

career development 223–4
internal interference 25–6
presentations 161
feedback 90–1, 216–17, 221
career development 221
coaching questions 90–1
judgements 221
performance reviews 216–17
feelings 117, 158
filing systems 194
flat structures, organisations 1–2,
249–50
flexibility, training providers 265–6
flip charts 172
focus 78–82, 208
coaching questions 89–90
interest 80–1
Peak Model 78–82
performance reviews 208
single focus 80
trying hard 79–80
forms, performance reviews 212

Galatea effect 15
Gallwey, Timothy 4, 86
goals 43–4, 55, 91–2, 95, 146, 168,
187, 209–12, 231, 239
see also performance goals
career development 231, 239
GROW mnemonic 91–2
Path Goal Theory 43–5, 55
performance reviews 209–12
personal organisation 187
presentations 168
sales performance 146
SMART goals 95, 211
Goethe, J.W. 181
Golem effect 15
group culture 244–5
GROW (Goal, Reality, Options and
Will) mnemonic 91–2

habits 127, 179
see also behaviour
handouts 171
Handy, Charles 15, 125

Hays Travel 154
Hertzberg, Frederick 41–3, 54–5
hierarchical structures, organisations
249
High Impact Training (Lapidus) 261
High Income Consulting (Lambert)
147–8
Hilton International 221
Holden, Robert 220
honesty 103
House, R. 43–5, 55
Human Resources (HR) 64–7, 202
Hygiene Factors, Two Factor Theory
41–3, 54

IBM 4
ideas 21–2, 104–6
'I'm okay' attitude 35
implementing coaching 241–314
important versus urgent tasks 183–4
improvement 214–15, 282–4,
310–11
in-tray exercises 237–8
incompetence 69–71
informality 122
information presentations 167–8
the inner game 4, 118–22, 131
intangible benefits 291
interest 80–1, 128, 170–1
interference 9–31, 118–22, 138–42,
159–63, 178–82, 201–5, 221–4,
307
see also external . . . ; internal . . . ;
potential
career development 221–4
the inner game 118–22
management 20
Peak Model 9–31
performance reviews 201–5
personal organisation 178–82
presentations 159–63
resource problems 307
sales 138–42
internal coaches 268–70, 274, 292
internal interference 23–6, 141–2,
161–3, 180–2, 203–6, 223–4

see also external interference; interference
blame cultures 25
career development 223–4
expectations 24
experience 24
fear of failure 25–6
performance reviews 203–5
personal organisation 180–2
presentations 161–3
sales 141–2
self-talk 25
interruptions 127–8, 191
interviews 226–8, 230–1, 234–6, 239–40
Intrinsic motivators 36–8, 41, 46–8, 55
INTRO presentations mnemonic 170–1

jobs 118–19, 179–80, 210, 211–15, 232–3, 303–6
see also career development; staff
people in wrong jobs 305–6
performance reviews 210, 211–15
personal organisation 179–80
pressures 118–19
roles 210, 211–15
searches 232–3
work attitudes 303–4
work simulation tests 237–8
work systems 179–80
work/life balance 180
Johnson, Gerry 245
judgements 99, 221

King, Martin Luther, Jr 213
Kirkpatrick, Donald 283–4
Kline, Nancy 107
knowledge 1–2, 77–8, 139, 214, 283–4
Kirkpatrick 283–4
Peak Model 77–8
performance reviews 214
product knowledge 139

Knowles, Malcolm 262
Kolb's learning cycle 52

Lambert, Tom 147–8
language 256
Lapidus, Todd 261
laws of coaching 16, 47, 51, 54, 57, 73, 77, 99, 121, 126
leadership 43–5, 57–64, 81–2, 152–3
communication 57–64, 81–2
control 62–3
delegation style 58–9, 61, 63–4
emergency situations 59
Path Goal Theory 43–5
preferences 62
sales managers 152–3
styles 58–64
Tammenbaum & Schmidt model 58–64
team needs 59, 62
'telling' style 58–60, 62–4, 66
learning 45–7, 49, 50–5, 142, 163–4, 182, 205–6, 224–6, 262–3, 282–4, 301–2, 314
see also PLE triangle; training . . .
adults 262–3
boredom 301–2
business case 301–2, 314
career development 224–6
enjoyment 53–4
evaluation 282–4
Kolb's cycle 52
Peak Model 45–7, 49, 50–5
performance 53–4, 205–6
personal organisation 182
presentations 163–4
sales 142
letters, covering letters 233–4, 239
Lexus GB 251
life/work balance 180
limiting beliefs 26–9, 224
career development 224
evidence basis 27–9
Peak Model 26–9
RAS 28–9
reconsideration 27

reinforcement 28–9
'true' statements 26–7
line management 266–7, 285–6
listening 125–9, 132, 208
  attention 127
  body language 127
  coaching questions 126–7
  distractions 128
  faking 128–9
  interest 128
  interruptions 127–8
  openness 126
  Peak Model 125–9
  performance reviews 208
  unhelpful habits 127
looking forward, career development
  229–30
low morale 302

McGregor, Douglas 12
MACSPROUT goals mnemonic 212
mailing lists 192
maintenance tasks 184
management 12–15, 20, 34, 140,
  152–3, 266–7, 285–6, 304–5
  see also senior management
  behaviour 12–15
  external interference 20
  line management 266–7, 285–6
  sales 140, 152–3
  staff cynicism 34
  style 304–5
  Theory X 12–15, 20
  Theory Y 12–15
  training success 266–7
Maslow, A. 38–41, 44, 54
'measles' test 193
meetings, time loss 190
Megginson, David 243
Mehrabian, Albert 236
mentoring 116–17, 131
mistakes 122–3, 131–2
money, motivation 36–7
morale 302
motivation 35–50, 55, 302
  Carrot and Stick 46

Extrinsic motivators 36–8, 40, 46,
  55
Hygiene Factors 41–3
Intrinsic motivators 36–8, 41, 46,
  55
Maslow 38–41, 54
money 36–7
Motivation Factors 41–3
Path Goal Theory 43–5
Peak Model 35–50, 55
people problems 302
PLE triangle 45–7
profit sharing example 42
Two Factor Theory 41–3
multi-media clips 172
multiple choice tests 286

needs 38–41, 44, 54, 59, 62
  leadership 59, 62
  team needs 59, 62
needs theory 38–41, 54
  belonging 39–40
  Maslow 38–41, 44, 54
  Path Goal Theory 44
  physiological needs 39
  safety needs 39
  self-actualisation 40
  self-esteem 40
negative expectations 24
negative experience 24
negative self-talk 25, 162–3
nerves 161, 174
  see also confidence; pressure
    problems
Neuro Linguistic programming
  (NLP) 3
The New Alchemists (Handy) 15, 125
NLP *see* Neuro Linguistic
  programming
notes, presentations 171

open questions 91, 148, 173
openness 126
opportunity 23, 231, 292–3
  career development 231
  costs 292–3

external interference 23
options 91–2, 104–8, 195
   ARROW model 104–8, 195
   creative thinking 104–6
   GROW mnemonic 91–2
   telephone calls 195
organisation *see* personal organisation
organisations 1–2, 179, 202, 249–50,
   256, 275–6
   business plans 256
   change 275–6
   coaching culture 249–50, 256
   organisation culture 179, 202
   structures 1–2, 249–50
orthodox training approaches 1–2
output control systems 250–1
overhead questions 173
ownership, responsibility 73

panic zones 309
paperwork 191–4
   filing systems 194
   mailing lists 192
   'measles' test 193
   personal organisation 191–4
   telephone calls 192
   tidiness 193
   weekly reports 192
Pareto's eighty/twenty rule 182
Path Goal Theory 43–5, 55
paying attention 89
Peak Model 9–133
   ARROW model 92–111
   awareness 67–71, 77
   coaching definitions 9–10
   coaching qualities 123–5
   coaching questions 85–93
   common mistakes 122–3
   communication 57–67
   counseling 117–18, 131
   enjoyment 45–7, 49, 51–5
   external interference 118–22
   focus 78–82
   Herzberg 41–3
   the inner game 118–22, 131
   interference 9–31

knowledge 77–81
learning 45–7, 49, 50–5
limiting beliefs 26–9
listening 125–9, 132
Maslow 38–41, 44, 54
mentoring 116–17, 131
motivation 35–50
   needs theory 38–41, 44, 54
   Path Goal Theory 43–5, 55
   performance 17–19, 30–1, 34–5,
     45–56, 61–2, 75–6
   PLE triangle 45–55
   potential 9–19
   in practice 115–33
   preparing for coaching 33–5
   responsibility 72–3
   running sessions 129–31
   self-fulfilling prophecies 15–16, 30
   skills 77–81
   state of mind 77–81
   Theory X 12–15, 20
   Theory Y 12–15
   training 115–16
   trust 74–7
   Two Factor Theory 41–3, 54–5
people problems 301–5
   see also staff
   boredom 301–2
   business case 301–5
   confidence 302–3
   low morale 302
   management style 304–5
   motivation 302
   poor relationships 301
   promotion 305
   teams 304
   work attitudes 303–4
perfectionism 181–2
performance 1–2, 17–19, 30–1, 34–5,
   45–56, 61–2, 75–6, 142, 163–4,
   182, 199–217, 224–6, 286,
   310–11
   see also performance goals;
     performance reviews; PLE
     triangle
   appraisals 199–217

beliefs 55
career development 224–6
definitions 17
desire 56
enjoyment 53–4
evaluation 286
gaps 18–19
improvement 310–11
learning 53–4
maintenance 311
Peak Model 17–19, 30–1, 34–5,
   45–56, 61–2, 75–6
personal organisation 182
poor performance 34–5, 75–6,
   204
potential 17–19
presentations 163–4
pressure problems 310–11
promoting performance 47–50
reviews 199–217
sales 142
willingness 56
performance goals 93–5, 146, 168,
   187, 209, 231, 239
   see also aims
ARROW model 93–5
career development 231, 239
performance reviews 209
personal organisation 187
presentations 168
sales 146
performance reviews 199–217
aims 208–10
ARROW model 215–16
attitudes 215
behaviour 215
coaching culture 248
competence 203–4
confidence 204–5
consequences 202–3
critical variables 206–8
detachment 207
feedback 216–17
focus 208
frequency 212–13
goals 211–12

improvement 214–15
interference 201–5
job roles 210, 211–15
knowledge 214
listening 208
MACSPROUT goals mnemonic
   212
organisation culture 202
personality 206–7
PLE triangle 205–6
poor performance 204
praise 213
processes 209
progress tasks 201
PUNCHY feedback mnemonic
   216–17
ratio of talk input 206
relationships 203
review forms 212
reviewee reactions 207
self evaluation 213
skills 214
suggestions 210, 211–15
time 201–2
personal organisation 177–97
aims 186–7
assertiveness 180, 185–6, 188–90
attitudes 184–5
control 186–7
critical variables 183–6
distractions 185
importance versus urgency 183–4
interference 178–82
maintenance tasks 184
organisation culture 179
paperwork 191–4
perfectionism 181–2
planning 183, 196–7
PLE triangle 182
processes 187
procrastination 180–1
progress 184
stress 186–7, 196
suggestions 188–95
telephone calls 194–5
time loss 190–1

time management 177–8
urgency versus importance 183–4
work systems 179–80
work/life balance 180
personal power 253
personality 141, 206–7
philosophy 63, 85–6
physiological needs 39
pitfalls, ARROW model 108
planning 169, 183, 196–7
PLE (Performance, Learning and
    Enjoyment) triangle 45–55, 142,
    163–4, 182, 205–6, 224–6
  career development 224–6
  enjoyment 46, 52–4
  learning 46, 50–2
  Peak Model 45–55
  performance 46–50, 205–6
  personal organisation 182
  presentations 163–4
  sales 142
  staff placements 225–6
policies, restrictive policies 21
poor performance 34–5, 75–6, 204
potential 9–19, 40
  see also interference
  Peak Model 9–19
  performance 17–19
  self-actualisation 40
  self-fulfilling prophecies 15–16
  staff 12
  Theory X/Theory Y 12–15
  working percentages 11–12
power structures 252–3
PowerPoint 171–2
practice sessions 267
praise 213
pre/post coaching analyses 287–8
preparation 33–5, 169–70, 174
  coaching 33–5
  presentations 169–70, 174
presentations 157–75, 238
  aims 167–8
  assessment centres 238
  audience profile 164–5, 169
  critical variables 164–7

environments 160–1
equipment 160
fear of failure 161
feelings 158
handling questions 167
handouts 171
interference 159–63
INTRO mnemonic 170–1
negative self-talk 162–3
nerves 161, 174
notes 171
planning 169
PLE triangle 163–4
preparation 169–70, 174
prior experience 162
processes 168
questions 172–3
room layout 165–6, 169
scheduling 165
self-confidence 166
structure 170–1
subject familiarity 166–7
suggestions 169–73
time constraints 159–60
types 167–8
using questions 172–3
visual aids 171–2, 174
pressure problems 161, 174, 186–7,
  196, 310–13
  busyness 312–13
  low productivity 312
  nerves 161, 174
  performance 310–11
  quality standards 313
  red tape 311–12
  stress 186–7, 196
problem solving 120
procrastination 180–1
productivity 290–1, 312
products 139, 144, 150
  benefits 150
  faith in products 144
  knowledge 139
  sales 139, 144, 150
professionalism 228–9
profit sharing example 42

progress tasks 184, 201
promotion 305
psychometric tests 237
public speaking 157–75
PUNCHY feedback mnemonic
  216–17
Pygmalion effect 15, 74

qualifications 132
qualities, coaching 123–5
quality 291, 306–7, 313
  evaluation 291
  resource problems 306–7
  standards 313
questionnaires 285
questions 91, 112, 147–9, 151, 167,
  172–3, 293–5
  see also coaching questions
  closed questions 91
  evaluation 293–5
  open questions 91, 148, 173
  presentations 167, 172–3
  rhetorical questions 173
  sales 147–9, 151
  'why' questions 112

raising awareness 67–71
rapport 143, 145, 147, 273
RAS see Reticular Activating System
reaction questionnaire 285
reality 91–2, 97–103, 154–5, 195,
  224
  ARROW model 97–103, 154–5,
    195, 224
  GROW mnemonic 91–2
  sales 154–5
  telephone calls 195
recall 67
reconsidering beliefs 27
recruitment 220
red tape 311–12
Reed Consulting staff retention
  survey 291
reflection, ARROW model 101–4
reinforcing beliefs 28–9
relationships 119, 203, 274–5, 301

coaching closure 274–5
  existing relationships 119
  performance reviews 203
  poor relationships 301
reports 192
research 12–15
resource problems 305–8
  business case 305–8
  coaching budgets 307–8
  interference 307
  people in wrong jobs 305–6
  quality 306–7
  skills 306
  training costs 308
respect, clients 145
responsibility 72–3, 77, 120, 129,
  312
  ARROW model 120, 129
  choice 73
  coaching sessions 129
  ownership 73
  Peak Model 72–3, 77
  problem solving 120
  red tape 312
  role-playing 72–3
restrictive policies 21
retention, staff 291–2, 313–14
Reticular Activating System (RAS)
  28–9, 96
return on investment (ROI) 288–90
reviews see performance reviews
rewards 257
rhetorical questions 173
Risner, Nigel 180
rituals 248
Ritz–Carlton hotels 255
ROI see return on investment
role play 72–3, 237
room layout 165–6, 169
Rosinski, Philippe 244
routines 248

safety needs 39
sales 137–55
  aims 145
  buying signals 143–4

competition 141
confidence 144
critical variables 142–5
customer objections 143, 150–1
deal closure 141–2, 151–2
dreams 146
faith in products 144
handling objections 143, 150–1
interference 138–42
management 140, 152–3
performance goals 146
personality 141
PLE triangle 142
poor systems 139–40
processes 146
product benefits 150
product knowledge 139
questions 147–9, 151
rapport 143, 145, 147
reality 154–5
respect for clients 145
solution presentations 149–50
suggestions 145–52
targets 140
winning concept 141
scheduling presentations 165
Schmidt, W. 58
Scholes, Kevan 245
security 229
selection
career development 231
coaches 268–70
self-actualisation 40
self-belief 15, 74
see also beliefs
self-confidence *see* confidence
self-control 188–9
see also control
self-esteem 40
self evaluation 213
see also evaluation
self-fulfilling prophecies 15–16, 30
self-talk 25, 162–3
senior management 256, 260, 268–9, 277
see also management

coaching culture 256
coaching programmes 260, 268–9, 277
selecting coaches 268–9
sessions 129–31, 272–4
ARROW model 273–4
coaching programmes 272–4
commitment 272–3
environments 273
rapport 273
running sessions 129–31
The Seven Habits of Highly Successful People (Covey) 132
skills 2, 77–8, 214, 239, 283–4, 306
career development 239
Kirkpatrick 283–4
Peak Model 77–8
performance reviews 214
resource problems 306
SMART goals mnemonic 95, 211
SMOG directive coaching mnemonic 82–3
Socrates 85–6
Specsavers 154
staff 12, 59, 62, 64–7, 84, 153, 167–8, 225–6, 291–2, 301–6, 313–14
see also career development; Human Resources; jobs
confidence 302–3
cynicism 84
development 64–7
placements 225–6
potential 12
presentations 167–8
problems 301–5
retention 291–2, 313–14
teams 59, 62, 153, 304
training 167–8
turnover 303, 313–14
wrong jobs 305–6
stakeholders 276–7
standards 270, 313
state of mind 77–81
status symbols 253–5
stories 246–7
stress 186–7, 196

see also pressure problems
structures 1–2, 170–1, 249–50,
  252–3
  organisations 1–2, 249–50
  power structures 252–3
  presentation 170–1
subject familiarity, presentations
  166–7
success 257, 266–8
suggestions 145–52, 169–73, 188–95,
  210, 211–15, 232–8
  career development 232–8
  performance reviews 210,
    211–15
  personal organisation 188–95
  presentations 169–73
  sales 145–52
surveys 291
survival scenario testing 237
symbols, coaching culture 253–5

TA *see* Transactional Analysis
talk, self-talk 25
Tammenbaum, R. 58
targets, sales 140
teams 59, 62, 153, 304
  see also staff
  leadership 59, 62
  people problems 304
  sales managers 153
technical expertise 124
telephone calls 190–2, 194–5
'telling' style 58–60, 62–4, 66, 69,
  82, 304–5
  awareness 69
  directive coaching 82
  leadership 58–60, 62–4, 66
  management 304–5
  people problems 304–5
tests 237–8, 285–6
theory of andragogy (adult learning)
  262–3
Theory X 12–15, 20, 251
Theory Y 12–15
thinking 86–7, 104–6
tidiness, desks 193

time 159–60, 177–8, 190–1, 201–2
  loss 190–1
  performance reviews 201–2
  personal organisation 190–1
  presentations 159–60
  time management 177–8
'time served' mentality 223
Time to Think (Kline) 107
training
  see also coaching . . . ; learning
  coaches 261–8
  costs 308, 314
  orthodox approaches 1–2
  presentations 167–8
  staff 167–8
  versus coaching 115–16
training coaches 261–8
  accreditation 264
  audience profile 267
  bespoke training 262–3
  coaching programmes 261–8
  customers 261
  inexperienced trainers 264,
    268
  line management 266–7
  participants 261
  practice sessions 267
  pre-designed packages 263–4
  providers 264–6
  success criteria 266–8
Transactional Analysis (TA) 3
transferable skills 239
'true' statements 26–7
trust 74–7, 101, 274–5
  ARROW model 101
  change 76
  coaching closure 274–5
  coaching processes 75–7
  covert coaching 76
  Peak Model 74–7
  self-belief 74
  trust in oneself 74
  trusting the coach 75
trying hard 79–80
turnover, staff 303, 313–14
Two Factor Theory 41–3, 54–5

unconscious behaviour 69–71
urgent versus important tasks 183–4

value clashes, career development
    222
value creation 280–1, 293
visitors 191
visual aids 171–2, 174

Waitley, Denis 96
way forward, ARROW model
    108–11
websites 265
weekly reports 192
white boards 172

'why' questions 112, 148
willingness 56
winning concept, sales 141
Witt, Reni L. 96
work
    see also jobs
    attitudes 303–4
    personal organisation 179–80
    pressures 118–19
    simulation tests 237–8
    systems 179–80
    work/life balance 180

*Index compiled by Indexing Specialists
    (UK) Ltd*